POEMS AND POETS

POEMS AND POETS

Geoffrey Grigson

MACMILLAN

London · Melbourne · Toronto

1969

Published by

MACMILLAN AND CO LTD

Little Essex Street London WC2
and also at Bombay Calcutta and Madras
Macmillan South Africa (Publishers) Pty Ltd Johannesburg
The Macmillan Company of Australia Pty Ltd Melbourne
The Macmillan Company of Canada Ltd Toronto

Printed in Great Britain by
R. & R. CLARK LTD
Edinburgh

Contents

List of Plates

ACKNOWLEDGEMENTS are made to the British Council (for *Christopher Smart* and *A Passionate Science*); the Trident Press, New York (for *Resolution and Independence* and *The Sprig of Lilac*); Routledge and Kegan Paul Ltd. (for *John Clare* and *William Barnes*); the Centaur Press (for *On a Poem by Landor* and *Down a Rushy Glen*); the *New Statesman* (for *Proselytizer of the World*); and the *Times Literary Supplement* (for *Poet of Over-Poetry*). Two pieces on Wordsworth, first written as talks for the Third Programme of the British Broadcasting Corporation, are reprinted here, with alterations, from a miscellany of broadcast talks which has been out of print for many years.

To Ruthven Todd

ONE

A Note on Herrick

HAPPY perhaps in their posthumous situation are the poets who do not attract criticism or the niggling attentions — to everything except their poems — of the academic; who attract, in short, only the affection of their readers. Herrick of the *Hesperides* and *Noble Numbers* is an example. Yet I am never quite sure why he escapes, and why the learned articles occasioned by him — see the *Cambridge Bibliography of English Literature* — are so few. The tempting incidentals are there, the curious life in Devonshire, his bachelor condition, his dubious sexuality, the co-existence in his poems and evidently in himself of the fine and the nasty, of delicate acceptance and disgust (rather than soil the pretty image of this poet, all his unpleasant epigrams were excluded from the standard Herrick published by the Oxford University Press — 'a welcome opportunity of clearing away these weeds', wrote the scholar Percy Simpson, 'from the flower-garden of the Hesperides'). Also outside the bed of flowers Herrick left poems enough about himself and his deity to remind us, however peculiar his own temperament may have been, of the generation he belongs to, which was that of George Herbert, Wither, Bishop King, and Quarles.

It is to the point that this writer was born in London, that he grew up in London without a father, and that the family calling in which he was trained was that of goldsmith. Though he did not take to it, the goldsmith's trade may be thought to have influenced the kinds of poem he wrote, mostly brief and curt, trinkets, brooches, pendants, miniatures, intricate in pattern, rhythm, rhyme and shape, filed and finished with scrupulosity —

> *I must confess, mine eye and heart*
> *Dotes less on Nature, then on Art.*

Instead of completing his apprenticeship, Herrick went to Cambridge, took his degree in 1617, and ten years later, in some respects a most unlikely cleric (or so one would think *ex post facto*), was ordained, receiving in 1629 the remote crown living of Dean Prior below the shoulders of Dartmoor. If Herrick hated and execrated the circumstances of his country life, he admitted retrospectively (*Discontents in Devon*) that he never wrote better than where he 'loathe'd so much'. But then his vicarage would have been less remote culturally in the 1620s and 1630s than now: it was not so far from the city of Exeter, capital of a then rich county in the forefront of expansion, whose wealthy 'frolic mariners' according to another of his contemporaries, William Brown of Tavistock, were to be observed by the sea-nymphs playing their games of pitch and toss on the strand with bars of silver and sledge-hammers of gold. (Exeter, too, had given birth to Nicholas Hillyarde, goldsmith and limner.) At any rate Herrick was able to contrive his fastidious goldsmith's poetry out of a diversity of local elements, out of pastoral high jinks and sentiment regarded with a Londoner's sophistication. An extreme hedo-nistic openness to the sensation of the moment, and a mingled deference to Anacreon (see *The Vision*, and *The Apparition of his Mistresse calling him to Elizium*) and to Horatian grace, measure, and properties, were much, though not all, of him. One suspects Herrick of impotence or disinclination (he never married). This would help to explain that not always very attractive playfulness, which would more frequently have been arch in a less healthy age of poetry, coupled as it was with Herrick's inclination to make poems about 'maids' or 'virgins' (two favourite words), young, unmarried, about to be married or just married girls. But he is saved by that professional self-certainty he derived from the circle of Ben Jonson and from Jonson himself, his master and friend, who was Herrick's senior by nineteen years.

No one must expect from Herrick's 'love' poems more than a love of exterior grace:

> *Fain would I kiss my Julia's dainty leg,*
> *Which is as white and hairless as an egg.*

That is about as far and as deep as his nature wishes to go. Herrick is frank about himself: he is 'sieve-like', the sieve holds neither hot nor cold (as he wrote in one of more than twenty poems which were notes, so entitled, 'Upon himselfe'). He was 'wisely wanton': he could wish, he wrote, that 'all who frie' were 'Colde as Ice, or coole as I'.

The inadequacy nagged him. Another of the notes on himself begins:

> *I co'd never love indeed;*
> *Never see mine own heart bleed;*
> *Never crucifie my life;*
> *Or for Widow, Maid, or Wife,*

and after a while one finds oneself no longer surprised by the unexpected face which stares across to the title-page of *Hesperides*. On a bust, but realistic and everyday, between curly hair and a short neck, this engraved face is neither parsonical (the title-page speaks of the works of Robert Herrick *Esq.*) nor poetical: it belongs to a retired major out of *Mrs Dale's Diary*, pension adequate, unmarried, a little irresolute and diffident, quizzical, fussy, rather on the verge of the maudlin, yet more knowing than one might expect, and ready to listen, and so every young body's safe uncle. Odd to find this retired major on a plinth, cherubs flying in the air behind him, roses falling from their wreaths, and Pegasus rearing on a Devonshire hill from the base of which flows the Pierian spring. Odder still, though the innocent can be involved in scandal, to have found this major, retired, in actual amorous situations with Electra, Julia, or Anthea. The amorous situations in his verse are what might have been, *if*. Not what has been. 'Wantons we are', he wrote in a two-line poem about poets —

> *and though our words be such,*
> *Our Lives do differ from our Lines by much.*

One feels rather the same, in fact, as one reads the modern laureate of Miss Joan Hunter Dunn and large-limbed Myfanwy; or one is reminded at times, setting skills together rather more congruously, of at any rate some of the love protestations of Ronsard, already prematurely deaf, yellow and grey, brilliantly celebrating a tradition rather than experiences of love; and celebrating with more fervour of the real thing the forest of Gastines above his father's house, the products of the Vendômois, the flowing of the Braye and the surrounding meadows and wine caves of the Loir.

Against his taste and distaste for Devonshire (and against the unrealness of some of his pastoral trifles and frills) Herrick set poems of such admirable tone as *A Thanksgiving to God, for his House,* and *His Grange, or private wealth,* such sober yet lightly running pieces as *The White Island* and *His Letanie to the Holy Spirit.* As for his 'unpleasant' epigrams, the weeds which Herrick inserted cheerfully enough and which the Oxford don was so glad to have eradicated from the marigolds and violets, I take them, farts, sweat, arse, decaying teeth and all, as the expression of an incomplete man's disgust at nature unquickened by art (see the distich *Neglect*) or at rough and raw fact contradicting grace:

> *Let poets feed on aire, or what they will;*
> *Let me feed full, till, that I fart, sayes* Jill.

Death also distressed him and haunted him — 'Pass all we must the fatal ferry.' But temperament and consciousness of his art prevented a defeat, and Herrick has not been better summarized than by himself in *A Psalme or Hymne to the Graces*:

> *Honour be to the Graces!*
> *Who doe with sweet embraces,*
> *Shew they are well contented*
> *With what I have invented.*
>
> *Worship be to the Graces!*
> *Who do from sowre faces,*
> *And lungs that wo'd infect me,*
> *For evermore protect me.*

For evermore. Also when Herrick collected and published nearly all his verse in the single volume (in 1648) of the *Hesperides*, what a tribute to himself as artist was the care he took for variation of shape, kind (including unpleasant kind), and movement, for arranging or composing the whole book, poem against poem, after meticulous revision.

TWO

George Crabbe: 'The griefs that seize their subject Man'

A MOST awkward poet, of course; sandbagged again and again, as by Coleridge, Landor, or Hazlitt, misinterpreted, neglected, not fitting into schemes, yet resolutely alive; in every period since his day with readers admirers, accepters; a poet too whose admirers have been found in Moscow and in Paris. I have seldom thought of Crabbe without a thought of Thomas Hardy (another admirer), since neither poet was a middle-class gentleman aspiring upwards, and neither was afraid. Neither Crabbe nor Hardy was afraid (and this became a rare thing in English literature between the two of them) to draw the honest logical conclusion from a set of observations: having intellectual integrity, neither Crabbe nor Hardy was turned from a vision of his truth by public ideas.

Yet Hardy fits more easily: the dull historian can say 'Here is the poet, here is the novelist'; whereas in Crabbe, who told stories in verse, fiction and poetry are mixed. So the historian, and readers who follow him, not liking to have their patterns broken or their categories muddled, are always apt to maintain that fiction must be in prose, and that Crabbe, therefore, is prosy.

As a fact, he is not, and there is at last a book to argue that he is not.[1] I hardly think Mrs Haddakin's exposition of Crabbe is very supple, or graceful, or noticeably human; it is academic, I should guess the academy to be Cambridge, and as near as possible to that school of criticism now engaged on *filling gaps* in *fields* with much high, dry, hectoring circumlocution. Such critics 'take commendable steps', they ascribe to poets 'sensibility' and 'the experiencing mind', they remark that 'the link-story which provides the

---

[1] Lilian Haddakin, *The Poetry of Crabbe* (1955).

5

necessary "associating circumstance" is a work of sober-toned verisimilitude'. Yet a book, almost any book on Crabbe, coming from the opposite side to the late F. L. Lucas, begins to argue a new readiness not to bicker about this poet, or not to fit him into some peculiar niche in a denigrating despair.

I see the griefs that seize their subject Man.

That is Crabbe. Closely, he says, 'let me view the naked human heart'. He sees his mission is

The stronger features of the soul to paint,
And make distinct the latent and the faint.

All that is clear to Mrs Haddakin. It is clear to her that all poetry need not be poetry-essence; that there can be poems — Crabbe's poems — of 'great actuality' in an atmosphere of 'dry light', in which all the selected 'objects and configurations 'stand out very distinctly'; that in his work 'criticism accompanies description or narration':

Then silent groves denote the dying year,
The morning frost, and noon-tide gossamer;
And all be silent in the scene around —
All, save the distant sea's uncertain sound,
Or here and there the gun, whose loud report
Proclaims to man that Death is but his sport.
And then the wintry winds begin to blow;
Then fall the flaky stars of gathering snow;
When on the thorn the ripening sloe, yet blue,
Takes the bright varnish of the morning dew.

In those lines, part of an autumnal landscape received into himself by a total partaker, or in the admirable opening of *Delay has Danger*, in which the tale's first indicative sharps or flats are the ammonites by the road, the shapes of nameless worms

Whose generations lived and died ere man,
A worm of other class, to crawl began,

or in the level scene in the fens which took sadness from the sad weak lover (and appealed so much to Tennyson),

Far to the left, he saw the huts of men
Half-hid in mist, that hung upon the fen;
Before him swallows, gathering for the sea,
Took their short flights, and twitter'd on the lea,
And near the bean-sheaf stood, the harvest done,
And slowly blacken'd in the sickly sun,

— in these and a hundred of such passages Crabbe's critical evaluating senses are urgently at work. But there is in Crabbe more than common report and Mrs Haddakin allow of the wondering senses; more of the glittering eye and the possessed element; Crabbe, in fact, not infrequently saw or sensed with that hallucinated absolute clearness which enabled Coleridge to see both the eyes of nightingales and the tears in his child's eyes glittering in the moonlight; and in that he is altogether of his age, in between Chatterton and Darley, even though such interests were disguised by a loosened, less pliant, less antithetical, less regular eighteenth-century technique. Crabbe's absolute clearness, his dry light revealing the blackening bean-sheaf in the autumnal sun on the black fens, sets up more reverberation, more tremor of the senses, than Mrs Haddakin guesses or any critic known to me has ever admitted.

Crabbe's lines have a sad slope, as though printed downhill on the page, yet again and again underneath them, under the stories, under and pushing through the delineation of the naked heart, is the Crabbe who suffered (and recorded) visions under opium, the Crabbe wonderstruck by a close comet across the black heaths of Suffolk, the Crabbe watching figures against the flames in the Gordon riots, the child who read tales of romance and had joys at least to recall:

Joys I remember, like phosphoric light,
Or squibs and crackers on a gala night.
Joys are like oil; if thrown upon the tide
Of flowing life, they mix not, nor subside:
Griefs are like waters on the river thrown
They mix entirely and become its own.

Joy in Wordsworth's sense or Coleridge's was not given to Crabbe. His joy was not liberated, absolute or directly creative. Yet it glitters in a dark-ness. To my way of reading him, Crabbe's wonder stretches his honesties, his subtleties, his sadnesses, at times to a rare and altogether remarkable ten-sion. Flame goes with his smoke, if the smoke tends to hide it. 'Leather Lads' beat him in his dreams, demons fixed him in the rising tide which turned only when it was salt on his lips: if ever a poet of stern and subtle intelligence had a mind both controlled and phosphorescently haunted, it was Crabbe; and Crabbe is not caught unless that is realized. Mrs Haddakin tries; a very determined reader may be glad that she tries; though he may have to say that neo-academic clichés seldom catch what is poetic in a corpus of poems.

Robert Herrick, like a 'retired major on a plinth', from Hesperides, *1648*

Life mask of William Wordsworth, in 1815

THREE

Rock, Cloud, Air, Water, Wordsworth

YOU may recall a guilty passage in Byron's letters in which he turns upon romanticism.

He complains that poets of the day, including himself and Wordsworth, 'are all in the wrong . . . are upon a wrong revolutionary poetical system, or systems, not worth a damn in itself'. He had much else to say at one time and another — for example about 'two sorts of Naturals; the Lakers, who whine about nature because they live in Cumberland; and their under⁄sect (which someone has maliciously called the 'Cockney School'), who are enthusiastical for the country because they live in London'. In the decay, in the new softness of English poetry, Byron thought that 'the best sign of amendment will be repentance and new and frequent editions of Pope and Dryden'. It is an opinion which has been repeated in different ways since by poets as diverse as Hopkins and T. S. Eliot and Mr Auden. Hopkins found in Keats — Byron's 'tadpole of the Lakes' — an 'unmanly and enervating luxury': he found Dryden 'the most masculine of our poets', one whose 'style and rhythms lay the strongest stress of all our literature on the naked thew and sinew of the English language'.

The masculine poet, such as Dryden — or the masculine painter such as Poussin — deals, above all, in the actions of men; desert man too much for nature — particularly for nature as a benign force — and the masculinity is diluted too much by its opposite. Instead of the thew and resilient hard⁄ness of Dryden, one has what Coleridge called 'the mild and philosophic pathos of Wordsworth'; one has a poetry, in all its simplicity and gravity, which corresponds to the peculiar, palpable femininity of the Lake District — at least in its milder times and aspects. The Lake District is one of the chief clues to understanding our romantic 'revolution' in the arts; and it was not, as we are inclined to believe, discovered by Wordsworth, however much it has been vulgarized and popularized as a consequence of his poetry and his residence among the mountains. The discovery was made long before Wordsworth was born, in the course of that great picturesque exploration of Great Britain through the eighteenth century. On the whole, it is true to say that the picturesque places, the 'beauty spots' which have filled the guidebooks ever since, down to Murray and Ward Lock, were explored, celebrated, and established by painters. Painters tramped the lanes and the tracks; the poets, who saw the engravings after their pictures, came later. Celebrated as a Lakeland pioneer, the poet Thomas Gray did not reach the Lakes, with a landscape mirror in his pocket for picturing the finest scenes, until 1769. Lakeland etchings had been published sixteen years earlier than Gray's visit, and seventeen years before Wordsworth was born.

The spirit in all this picturesque exploration was to find those scenes, reduced to a picture either by the pencil or on the pocket mirror (this landscape mirror is described carefully for tourists in the *Guide to the Lakes*, by Thomas West), which afforded sentimental pleasure — pleasure arising from the feelings rather than from reason. All was a matter of sentiment and taste, a matter of indulging the sensations, through all the degrees of beauty to all the degrees of sublimity. A matter also of discovering — in Wales, in the Lakes, or in Scotland, at home and in nature — what the new taste of the century had discovered already in its favourite Old Masters.

Thus Thomas West, who published his famous guide when Wordsworth was an eightyearold child at Cockermouth, arranged the Lakes in what he called 'an order more agreeable to the eye and grateful to the imagination'. 'The changes of scene', he continued, 'is from what is pleasing to what is surprising; from the delicate touches of *Claude*, verified on Coniston Lake, to the noble scenes of *Poussin*, exhibited on Windermere; and from these, to the stupendous, romantic ideas of *Salvator Rosa*, realized on Derwentlake.'

This was the climate of mind in which Wordsworth grew up — the climate of the longing, yearning soul, which was to be flattered by attention

to the beauties of natural scenery. And nowhere were those instruments
of flattery more concentrated than in the Lakes. Nowhere, as Wordsworth
wrote in his own *Guide to the Lakes*, 'within so narrow a compass, may be
found an equal variety in the influences of light and shadow upon the sublime and beautiful features of the landscape'. I have said elsewhere that if
you wish to understand the common, the commonplace romantic vision,
stand in the porch of the Victorian hotel and look down on Buttermere.
Watch mood diluting reality, watch the romantic soul diffused in the water-
glowing air between lake and mountain and sky, embracing and modifying
everything. Watch a few small bits of cloud, white below the black
mountain level, wisping above the lake. Wordsworth, again in his *Guide*,
said that such clouds were 'pregnant with imagination for the poet'. He
wrote that 'vapours exhaling from the lakes and meadows after sunrise,
in a hot season, or, in moist weather, brooding upon the heights, or
descending towards the valleys with inaudible motion, give visionary
character to everything around them'. Those silvery vapours are celebrated
in *The Prelude*.

One may add to all this an extraordinary sweetness in the Lakes, in
the taste of the air, in the light, in the conjunction of green fertility, reflecting water, and small mountain — that sweetness, that palpable femininity of which I spoke. Stern the Lakes are as well, with a sternness
which appealed to the deliberate and strong in Wordsworth; but to me
it seems rather the tender aspect which is reflected in the structural substance of his verse.

Growing up, as I say, in such a climate of the mind, Wordsworth would
have been certain to find the sweetness, the sublimities, and the visionary
character of the Lake District, even if he had not been born on its western
edge at Cockermouth, even if he had not been educated in among the Lakes
at Hawkshead, with Windermere two miles away. As Byron wrote,
Southey, Wordsworth, and Coleridge 'rambled over half Europe' and
saw 'Nature in most of her varieties'. Wordsworth, like the topographical
artists and the picturesque travellers, was a collector of scenery. But not —
and here is the point — not finally and deeply for sentimental ends, not for
flattering the soul, not to indulge himself in the correspondence of feelings;
not, as with the mere moralists who were a little disturbed by this romantic

self-flattery, for what Wordsworth called in the *Prelude* 'Nature's secondary grace':

> *The charm more superficial that attends*
> *Her works, as they present to Fancy's choice*
> *Apt illustrations of the moral world,*
> *Caught at a glance, or traced with curious pains.*

The difference between Wordsworth — or Wordsworth and Coleridge — and the nature-tipsy poets and painters and aestheticians from whom, inevitably, they took so much, is that they were little and Wordsworth and Coleridge were unusually big, were lofty and speculative minds; they dignified something trivial into an instrument of relation and meaning.

The Prelude — particularly the less cautious *Prelude* of 1805–6 — all the same exhibits Nature nearly as God; not as a mirror for the emotions, not as a sentimental something; but as a Being, a source (localized, as it happens, inevitably among the Lakes) by which the emotions are educed, are trained, are given self-knowledge, dignity, and purpose. Nature, not caught at a glance, but entered into; training one into love which acts and exists only with Imagination. Imagination *The Prelude* defines as

> *. . . but another name for absolute power*
> *And clearest insight, amplitude of mind*
> *And Reason in her most exalted mood.*

So in the Conclusion of *The Prelude*, 'This faculty' — this Imagination — 'hath been the moving soul of our long labour':

> *We have traced the stream*
> *From darkness and the very place of birth*
> *In its blind cavern, whence is faintly heard*
> *The sound of waters; follow'd it to light*
> *And open day, accompanied its course*
> *Among the ways of Nature, afterwards*
> *Lost sight of it bewilder'd and engulphed,*
> *Then given it greeting, as it rose once more*
> *With strength, reflecting in its solemn breast*
> *The works of man and face of human life,*
> *And lastly, from its progress have we drawn*
> *The feeling of life endless, the great thought*
> *By which we live, Infinity and God.*

The loftiness of the result — in *The Prelude*, above all in this concluding book — no one can question; but there is much in the process, in Words‐worth's view of nature, in his nearly admitted pantheism, which is question‐able, and was indeed questioned, for example, by Coleridge; and also by Blake.

In discussing *The Prelude*, Herbert Read quoted Coleridge's suggestion to Wordsworth for the great philosophic poem to be called 'The Recluse'. Man was to be treated of in contact with *external* nature. The poet was to inform the senses from the mind, and not compound a mind out of the senses. *The Prelude* does pay some heed to that injunction. Wordsworth does include that passage on Imagination as 'Reason in her most exalted mood' and on the necessity of Imagination; but, all through, the active presence and personification of Nature — Nature with a capital — gets attended to more than mind, or reason, or imagination.

Coleridge had been bewitched himself by pantheism, had realized, so he wrote, the bitterness of its root, and was clear that nature lives only in our life; clear, as he wrote in *Dejection*, that the passion and the life come from fountains inside us and cannot be won from outward forms. Admiration for his poems, reverence for his poems or no, he understood that Wordsworth was not so clear on this matter. Coleridge admitted 'that this inferred dependency of the human soul on accidents of birth‐place and abode, to‐gether with the vague, misty, rather than mystic, confusion of God with the world, and the accompanying nature‐worship, of which the asserted depen‐dence forms a part, is the trait in Wordsworth's poetic works that I most dislike as unhealthy, and denounce as contagious'.

Blake was equally disturbed by Wordsworth's nature‐worship; seeing in Wordsworth 'the natural man rising up against the spiritual man con‐tinually', and denying Wordsworth's statement that the powers needed for writing poetry are first observation and description, and second, sensibility. 'One Power alone makes a Poet,' Blake wrote against it, 'Imagination, the Divine Vision.'

And the nature‐worshipping trait has been contagious. In his life of Wordsworth, Professor Harper confidently affirmed that no one could say Wordsworth's influence 'has had the effect of blunting the poetical sensibili‐ties of our race'; which is precisely what Wordsworth's influence has done

— partly through his deification of a benign nature, and his dependence upon it, partly through the loose and feminine structure of much of his verse and its approach to the simple speech, which naturally go with that deification, that preference for man represented only in his relations to nature rather too narrowly considered. Like Constable in painting, Wordsworth in poetry begat a softness and a sentimentality, divorced from his cultivated insight, from which we still have not recovered. There it is: Byron's 'revolutionary system', the system 'not worth a damn' — the exaggeration was pardonable — which necessitated re-injections of Dryden and Pope.

Still, Blake and Coleridge, if they clearly apprehended the fault, both knew and said, again and again, that Wordsworth was a supreme poet. Hopkins acknowledged his greatness — above all (like Blake), in the *Intimations* ode. Human nature, he wrote, in a very few men sees something, receives a shock, and 'is in a tremble ever since'. In Wordsworth when he wrote that ode, 'human nature got another of those shocks, and the tremble from it is spread-ing'. But Hopkins was severe on Wordsworth's manner of writing, on his weakness in the 'rhetoric' of literature by which he meant its 'common and teachable element'.

In one of his twelve observations on art, Poussin declared that the light of knowledge 'is never to be found whole or even in a large part in a single man'. Perhaps, in our superstitious attitude to the arts, we do not acknow-ledge that — do not acknowledge the compound of dust inevitable in the clearest spirits. One has to read this major poet with some *caveats* about his view of nature, his thought, and his style.

FOUR

What-like was Wordsworth?

YET what about the Wordsworth of *Resolution and Independence*, less the poem than the resolute and independent poet, the rockiness in this strong creature, who walked over the passes and drove his ungraceful legs through the hard snow? There is warrant and relevance in attempting to recall and describe the actual Wordsworth who was alive between 1797 and 1807, which are the years of his great poetry. Hazlitt described him. De Quincey realized that we should not lose interest in Wordsworth; and using a Westmorland expression he asked 'What-like was Wordsworth?' and gave his answer, which does not square altogether with Hazlitt's description. A Yorkshire man writing about another man of Yorkshire descent, Herbert Read was to begin his much criticized book on Wordsworth with a portrait, because he felt that 'to hold in our minds a clear image of the physical features of the man is a salutary preparation for the interpretation of his work and temperament'. I agree with the reason, though I do not altogether agree with the way in which Herbert Read picked over the visual evidence.

Wordsworth was twenty-eight in the year 1798, when *Lyrical Ballads* was published; and thirty-seven when De Quincey met him at Grasmere after those moments of 'intense expectation' when he would have forgotten 'Charlemagne and all his peerage' if they had been behind him, 'or Caesar and his equipage, or Death on his pale horse'. What-like then was Wordsworth in those years, more or less? What are we told by reminiscences and portraits? He was unimpressive until the face was turned upon you. 'His person', Dorothy Wordsworth had remarked, 'was not in his favour.' He was tallish, to be exact five foot ten. His shoulders were narrow and sloped quickly down. Hazlitt saw him first of all curiously dressed in a brown fustian jacket and striped pantaloons. His legs were unshapely, he walked in a lunging, rolling manner, and was neither slender nor graceful. But the face — how different from the round, illuminated lard which was the face of Coleridge! The colour was bronze. Brown hair straggled down over his forehead and past swollen, ugly ears to the shoulders. A great beak of a nose stuck out, seeming to occupy most of the length of his long countenance. The eyebrows were well marked, furrows came down from the nose around the mouth. Hazlitt noted these furrows of 'strong purpose and feeling' and 'a severe, worn pressure of thought about his temples'. But the two indices were the eyes and the mouth above a strong chin. It is curious how the descriptions of the eyes conflict. They were remarkable — everyone agrees to that. They were heavy-lidded, rather small than large below the arching of the eyebrows and the severity of the temples. According to Hazlitt they had a fire in them 'as if he saw something in objects more than the outward appearance'. According to De Quincey they were 'not under any circumstances bright, lustrous or piercing', unlike his sister's eyes which gleamed wildly and ardently. Their effect was at times 'fine, and suitable to his intellectual character'. 'After a long day's toil in walking', says De Quincey, 'I have seen them assume an appearance the most solemn and spiritual that it is possible for the human eye to wear. The light which resides in them is at no time a superficial light; but under favourable accidents, it is a light which seems to come from unfathomed depths: in fact, it is more truly entitled to be "the light that never was on land and sea", a light radiating from some far spiritual world, than any the most idealizing that ever yet a painter's hand created.' It may indeed have been a fierier light which came from the eyes in the great year of 1798 than in the more composed maturity of 1807. Leigh Hunt said they were eyes which would have suited Ezekiel or Isaiah — 'half burning, half smouldering'. But who says a word about their colour (which was grey, according to the journalist William Jerdan)?

The eyes, at any rate, speak for one element in Wordsworth's character and the character of his poetry, and the mouth for another element every bit as important. He was spiritual and he was sensual. Herbert Read makes much of this combination in his study of Wordsworth. He was spiritual, he was animal. But he goes too far and against the evidence when he reads a 'loose brutality' into the mouth. It was a wide mouth, with the lips firm and ample rather than full; sensual, yes, but also generous and tender. And while we are looking Wordsworth in the face, in the eyes, and in the mouth, we should recall at this point something else which Hazlitt recorded. The common notion is that Wordsworth had a face like a horse, and a cart-horse, strong, ugly, solemn, unrelieved. Hazlitt wrote there was also 'a convulsive inclination to laughter about the mouth, a good deal at variance with the solemn, stately expression of the rest of his face'. That has always seemed to me the clue about Wordsworth's appearance which most of us overlook; and I may mention that Wordsworth's physiognomy obviously repeats itself in more than one of his descendants who are alive now. I have observed in two of them exactly this contrast (they will excuse me for saying it) between solemnity, even heaviness, and a convulsive, hovering inclination to laughter; which is extraordinarily attractive. Dorothy Wordsworth, too, has described her brother's 'extremely thoughtful countenance', adding that 'when he speaks it is often lighted up by a smile which I think very pleasing'. To complete the picture, we must add the voice, from Hazlitt. It was a mixture of 'clear, gushing accents' with a deep 'guttural intonation, and a strong tincture of the northern burr, like the crust on wine'. Speech did not come from him torrentially. Dorothy Wordsworth remarked that 'you must be with him more than once before he will be perfectly easy in con-versation'.

What we may conclude from this portraiture is that in his person (this might be said of poets of our time, for instance Mr Auden or T. S. Eliot) Wordsworth was in many ways admirably 'unpoetical'. He was the in-elegant Northerner controlling strong appetites in big or little. We know how frugally he and his sister could live with little money: for a strong appetite in little we have a description of him sitting down and 'attacking' a cheese. We know that he did not dislike alcohol, and that he took too much of it only once, in drinking a libation to the memory of Milton when he was an undergraduate. We know how passion welled up in him when he was twenty-one or twenty-two and broke his incipient restraints and gave Annette Vallon a daughter, we know also how his power of self-control, if in the run of things it damaged him and led him into those conventional and harsh falsities which are so often condemned with too little point or charity, was also a power of almost unexampled self-culture. There were two or more Wordsworths in the 'gaunt and Don Quixote-like' creature, intermixed and inseparable. Outwardly that inelegant, reserved Northerner, inwardly, the atomic heat. Outwardly, the countryman striding on awk- ward but efficient legs across the hills, the practical man who was able in growing cabbages and carrots or could take the mattock from Simon Lee and sever the tangled tree root; inwardly, the hypochondriac liable always to depression and melancholy, deliberate in his search for the roots of happiness. Wordsworth had plenty of personal warrant for writing retro- spectively and prophetically:

> *We poets in our youth begin in gladness;*
> *But thereof comes in the end despondency and madness.*

He described himself as of a 'stiff, moody, and violent temper' when a child. Coupled with that was the 'violence of affection' described in him as a young man by Dorothy Wordsworth — 'a sort of violence of affection . . . which demonstrates itself every moment of the day, when the objects of his affection are present with him, in a thousand almost imperceptible attentions to their wishes, in a sort of restless watchfulness which I know not how to describe, a tenderness that never sleeps, and at the same time such a delicacy of manners as I have observed in few men'. Wordsworth's hypochondria is no doubt the explanation of those periods after his return from France which are blank in the record of his life. Coleridge wrote of his 'occasional fits of hypo- chondriacal uncomfortableness — from which, more or less, and at longer or shorter intervals, he has never been wholly free from his very childhood'; and he went on (the letter was written in 1804) 'he both deserves to be and is a happy man; and a happy man not from natural temperament, for therein lies his main obstacle . . . but . . . because he is a Philosopher, because he knows the intrinsic value of the different objects of human pur- suit, and regulates his wishes in strict subordination to that knowledge'. That self-culture was one of the reasons which made the great, if then youth- ful, Coleridge feel himself 'a little man by his side', one of the reasons, too, for Coleridge's belief that a good poet was always a good man.

Herbert Read's *Wordsworth*, which so upset the circumspect scholars, is a book not to be overlooked if you are under the fascination of Wordsworth. It is one of the books which broke the platitudinous spell binding the study of the poems and the worship of the poet and made an end of evading the cavernous complexity of Wordsworth's character. I do not agree with it altogether, the evidence is sometimes misused, and Herbert Read assumes where the evidence is lacking or insufficient. The crux of the matter is this self-culture of Wordsworth and the hermetically cultivated sanity of his creative life. There is a passage I must quote. We know how Wordsworth changed from revolution into what we call reaction. Herbert Read gives as the cause Wordsworth's separation from Annette and the death of his passion for her during the nine years' interval of war with France. He writes: 'We grow to hate the object of a dead passion, but we do not acknowledge this to ourselves; we transfer that hatred to things associated with the dead passion. In this manner Wordsworth gradually renounced the cause of France and then the cause of revolution, and finally the cause of humanity.' There are several answers one could make — even that Annette and her brother were Royalists and against the Revolution when Wordsworth and she were in love, and when Wordsworth was a revolutionary; or that we do not know enough about Wordsworth and Annette to draw firm con-clusions; or that Herbert Read forgets the parallel change in the sentiments of Coleridge, who had no French lover and daughter; or even that we have the example of the change of poetic hearts *vis-à-vis* the Communist revolu-tion, uncomplicated by Russian mistresses and daughters. But to press that analysis — here is the true answer — to press it, except perhaps as a contribu-tion, is to deny the nature, value, and force of Wordsworth's cultivation of his own character, to remove the foundation, or so it appears to me, of a heroic greatness and of any clear ability to know 'the intrinsic value of the different objects of human pursuit'. This is the last thing which a devotee of Wordsworth and Wordsworth's poetry wishes to do, or so I should think.

The essence of Wordsworth is the combination of ordinary and extra-ordinary humanity and more than normally human power, of tough and tender; which enabled him to look at the worst and the best, to realize the unity of man and to enter 'into the temple and the temple's heart'. One could get at him by sorting out the complementary differences between himself and Coleridge, even the physical differences between the long-nosed cart-horse and the fat gazelle; or in the record of their different ways of composition. Hazlitt tells us that Coleridge 'liked to compose in walking

over uneven ground, or breaking through the struggling branches of a
copse-wood; whereas Wordsworth always wrote (if he could) walking up
and down a straight gravel-walk, or in some spot where the continuity of
his verse met with no collateral interruption'. De Quincey confirms this
by recording that Wordsworth liked to compose on the highroad. Or we
have records of Coleridge being fascinated by the prison etchings of Piranesi,
Wordsworth by Bewick's wood engravings in little, and by Rembrandt in
great, because Wordsworth could perceive in Rembrandt an analogy 'to
his own mode of investing the minute details of nature with an atmosphere
of sentiment'; also because Rembrandt could 'work something out of
nothing', transforming 'the stump of a tree, a common figure, into an *ideal*
object by the gorgeous light and shade thrown upon it'. Or contrast again
the earnestness of Wordsworth and the bookishness of Southey. 'I have at
all times endeavoured to look steadily at my subject', Wordsworth wrote,
prefacing the *Lyrical Ballads*; and he complained in 1797 that Southey wrote
'*too much at his ease*' — that he seldom

> *feels his burthened breast*
> *Heaving beneath th' incumbent Deity.*

Wordsworth disliked Southey's 'finical' way of using books, Southey disliked having Wordsworth in his neat library. De Quincey described how
Wordsworth 'tore his way into the heart' of a volume of Burke's collected
writings with a knife which had been used for buttering toast. Coleridge's
conversation flew down from the air, Wordsworth's was 'slow in movement,
solemn, majestic'. Coleridge read everything and scribbled a monologue
of criticisms and comment around the margins, Wordsworth ate of fewer
books and did not overflow into marginalia. Good qualities and great
achievements exact their price, characters are mixed, and Wordsworth was
neither deity nor saint. We have no more right to *complain* of Wordsworth's
deficiencies than we have to complain of the great nose on his sallow face.[1]

---

[1] But there is some doubt about that celebrated nose. Mrs Frances Blanshard
in her *Portraits of Wordsworth* (1959) talks of the bold nose — bold & prominent
it certainly was — being lengthened (by painters and sculptors) 'to shorten the
camel-like upper lip; which is certainly confirmed by the craggy life-like mask,
of which there is a cast in the National Portrait Gallery.

The personal details I have given cannot be cancelled. They agree with the poems, they agree with:

> *She sleeps in the calm earth, and peace is here.*
> *I well remember that those very plumes,*
> *These weeds, and the high spear-grass on that wall,*
> *By mist and silent rain-drops silver'd o'er,*
> *As once I passed, did to my heart convey*
> *So still an image of tranquillity.*
> *So calm and still, and looked so beautiful*
> *Amid the uneasy thoughts which filled my mind,*
> *That what we feel of sorrow and despair*
> *From ruin and from change, and all the grief*
> *The passing shows of Being leave behind,*
> *Appeared an idle dream, that could not live*
> *Where meditation was. I turned away*
> *And walked along my road in happiness.*

Indeed such poetry can only come from those poets who are at once tender and tough.

FIVE

Resolution and Independence

As for 'we poets in our youth begin in gladness', recall not only a poem by George Barker, in which he makes Wordsworth reappear and say that the resolution of dependence is 'To keep us alive and kicking with strength or joy', but a midsummer occasion in 1868, eighteen years after the death of Wordsworth, when the young Thomas Hardy, 'in all likelihood' (his own words) 'after a time of mental depression over his work and prospects', wrote down three cures for despair. The first was 'to read Wordsworth's *Resolution and Independence*'.

The poem (though it is hardly to be taken like a Purple Heart) was its author's own cure in a like condition, or more exactly his own recipe against its recurrence. Wordsworth wrote it at Grasmere when he was thirty-two (four years older than Hardy at the time of his note), in early May, in the young vegetative season of the year. As he worked at it, he found a stanza which could hold both exultation and depression, both beginning and end of life, both quickness and lightness and sobriety, both the hare of the opening exultation, which runs in its luminous mist, and the old man bent double, with feet and head coming together, as he neared his end, both unselfaware-ness and the later consolation of knowledge, contriving *Resolution and Independence* out of his experience, his reflection and the power of his own character.

The lines move with quick variation, quickly pivoted on rhymes. Then at the end of lines 4 and 5 in each stanza, the rhyme is repeated; and this doubling makes the stanza pause, and gathers and emphasizes the meaning; a deeper pause coming when the kernel of sound is doubled at the end of the sixth line and the seventh — that closing line which lengthens always and is enabled to carry, when required, the most expressive gravity, 'Solitude, pain of heart, distress, and poverty', or 'The oldest man he seemed that ever

22

wore grey hairs', or 'But thereof come in the end despondency and madness'.

As you read, it is not necessary to know about this poet's thought or cir-cumstances or the circumstances behind this poem: which is complete and self-subsistent, explaining itself. But remembering Coleridge's account of his 'hypochondriacal uncomfortableness' (put down soon after *Resolution and Independence* was written), one realizes that the Wordsworth of Independence was the philosophic regulator of his own desires who made himself happy, and that the Wordsworth of Resolution was the strong-bodied man ruthless and direct in his emotional and intellectual attack, resolute against the difficulties and black dangers inherent in his being.

> *As high as we have mounted in delight*
> *In our dejection do we sink as low.*

The dangers were exceedingly black, and they recurred. So in this poem the most famous lines, too often true, are the rhyme-coupled pair, shorter and longer, which compel a pause of extra solemnity at the close of the seventh stanza:

> *We poets in our youth begin in gladness;*
> *But thereof comes in the end despondency and madness.*

In his end Wordsworth became melancholy, if not mad. The right set of the words also deserted him, and the fineness of response coarsened, the thought became dogma, the poems hardened, like calcium carbonate around a stick, into official verse; and his sister who had been his twin in gladness, became altogether mad. But in May 1802, realizing what might be ahead of him from what was behind him, he was all the same resolved — taking comfort from the grave independence and resolution of the old man by the moorland pool, poor and decrepit, on the bare upland of existence, and from the old man's stately speech. *Thereof*, he admits, of the gladness, come the despondency and the madness: of the gladness in which we begin; which is yet, as in the second stanza, the sunny mist which the hare by her own act raises around herself, and which 'Runs with her all the way, wherever she doth run'.

'By our own spirits are we deified': Wordsworth was firm on the creative role of 'Joy'. The hare raced with joy, which succeeded the roaring night

of floods, and might be succeeded by them again.   He thought of Burns
(stanza VII again),

> *Who walked in glory and in joy*
> *Following his plough, along the mountain-side.*

Joy and our own spirits desert us, let us down, leave us unable to create.
Then we need the firmness of the old man, 'not all alive nor dead', propped
on his 'long grey staff of shaven wood', catching leeches (for which he had
been paid half-a-crown a hundred, Dorothy Wordsworth recorded); who
lost his joy long ago, yet lived, alone, by a hard, humble avocation which
gave health to others, without despair.   Then, whatever firmness we may
have at our own command, we need stimulating or stiffening by such firmness outside ourselves, not being superhuman.

A poem which is self-instruction in this way, and not a release of self-
deifying spirit, needs straight discourse and very simple language — 'And
in this way he gained an honest maintenance'.   Coleridge said, within two
months of reading *Resolution and Independence,* that in Wordsworth's new
poems he found 'here and there a daring humbleness of language and versification, and a strict adherence to matter of fact, even to prolixity', that
startled him.   Yet the straight discourse of the poem is interspersed with its
hymes; with its variations of rhythm against measure; with the action of
the encounter on the moor; with contrasts, the quick hare raising her self-
enveloping mist, the slow old man staring fixedly at muddy water; from
Wordsworth direct matter-of-fact speech, from the old man nothing recorded
directly, only his reported *oratio obliqua* received into the narrator, whose poem
this is; feebleness, and the life in the very old man's pale face, from 'the
sable orbs of his yet vivid eyes'.

And from straight discourse or daring humbleness of language, this poem
lifts or descends without discord into its extra-memorably effective lines: up
into 'All things that love the sun are out of doors', down into 'The sleepless
soul that perished in his pride' (the bright Chatterton who killed himself at
eighteen), or deeper down into that wider line, more inclusive, yet more
naked, 'And mighty Poets in their misery dead'; as this mighty poet was
to be, in a body which continued to work.

Wordsworth — the truest likeness ? — in 1844, aged 74

Walter Savage Landor, appropriately in neo-classic marble, in 1828

SIX

Christopher Smart

I

To be mad or under the influence of opium are strange conditions. The writing of poems is a strange activity, and poets who have written in madness or when opium has in some way altered the activity of their minds, appear doubly, 'romantically', strange or mysterious. So we have our vision of Coleridge interrupted, after his opium sleep, upon the writing of Kubla Khan; of Crabbe pierced, in his opium nightmares, by the keen streamers of the Northern Lights, of De Quincey (a poet in prose) transfixed by minarets; of Hölderlin, mad in his tower above the still Neckar; of Collins howling in Chichester Cathedral; of Blake observing angels or the ghost of a flea; of John Clare lost in a contemplation of the sun, or declaring that the vowels had been picked out through his ears; and of Christopher Smart, praying naked in the rain, or inscribing (a tale, as we shall see, less improbable than some commen-tators have maintained) stanzas of his *Song to David*, with a key, on the wain-scot of his madhouse room. Whether cause and consequence are allied quite in the way we imagine is another matter; but there is no doubt of the frequent intimacy of the strange condition and the strange activity. It is certainly true that in Smart's case the one important activity, the poems, cannot be entirely considered without the other. Either madness, in this case, or the attendant circumstances of confinement, with its release from drunkenness, distraction, responsibility, and other pressures, including the pressure of current intellectual fashion, enabled Smart to concentrate his mind for a while in trance-like statues of pure consciousness. He was able to release, combine, and shape the important elements of his life, intellectual and sensual.

A first fact of Christopher Smart's poetry is confirmed by the prologue of his life, the fact of a contradiction in himself, psychologically and intellec-tually, and between himself — between his own psychological constitution

—and the particular, and rather cautious balance of mind commonly
favoured or approved in his century.   Smart was born in 1722 at Shipbourne
on the edge of the Kentish Weald.   There he lived for his first years, his
father steward to the Vanes (he was perhaps named Christopher after Sir
Christopher Vane, the first Lord Barnard who died at Fairlawn the year
after his birth), himself free of his parents' garden, of the Vanes' estate of
Fairlawn, and of an exceedingly rich and speckled and variegated countryside, full of flowers and fruit, wooded, cultivated, watered, valley-divided,
part wild, part subdued and ordered, the country of the visions to come of
Samuel Palmer.   He was schooled a few miles away at Maidstone, on the
slow silvered stream of the Medway.   He had been premature at birth, and
he remained delicate as a child (and later), an only son among sisters, who
was dosed with cordials, which may have conditioned him, it was believed
in his family, to his later drunkenness.   In addition he was small, below
normal height; as small a creature, in later manhood, as John Clare or De
Quincey.   His father died when this peculiar child was eleven years old,
whereupon the family left Kent for the native Durham of the Smarts.   This
was a deprivation; but in the north Christopher Smart also had — and
greatly enjoyed, one may think — the freedom of a different neighbourhood,
no less remarkable than the one he had left, the florescent limestone country
of the Teesdale estates of Raby Castle, headquarters of the noble family
which had employed his father in Kent.   In his Durham years he appears
to have undergone an experience with its parallel in the lives of De Quincey,
Hölderlin, and John Clare — a second experience of deprivation.   He fell
in love, it seems, with Anne Vane, daughter of his patron Lord Barnard,
and attempted a childish elopement with her.   The suggestion that she was
afterwards the ideal object of his constancy (though he set himself at other
women, married, and had children) would fit in well with Smart's mental
and imaginative history.   He refers to Anne Vane several times at any rate
in the half-mad antiphony of his *Jubilate Agno*.   She was Hope (having
become Lady Anne Hope):

> *For X is hope — consisting of two check G — God be gracious*
> *to Anne Hope,*

she was Constancy, and he had visions of her:

Let Constant, house of Constant rejoice with the Musk-Goat —
I bless God for two visions of Anne Hope's being in charity with me,

and he appears once to remember her with a special liveliness and poignancy:

For the blessing of God upon purity is in the Virgin's blushes.

For the blessing of God in colour is on him that keeps his virgin.

For I saw a blush in Staindrop Church, which was of God's own colouring.

For it was the benevolence of a virgin shewn to me before the whole congregation.

In *Jubilate Agno* Smart was also to remember the delight of living at Shipbourne, calling for a blessing on the Fairlawn estate:

Let Shechem of Manasseh rejoice with the Green Worm[1] whose livery
is of the field.

For I bless God in SHIPBOURNE FAIRLAWN *the meadows the brooks*
and the hills.

It was his schooling, and his university in particular, which overlaid at
first this prologue of his being. He was deeply excited, at times possessed,
by the splendours and sparklings of nature. This excitement could be
justified by a simple *Te Deum laudamus*, a *Benedicite, omnia opera;* but even
then it tended towards a heat of imagination beyond reason, which this
fellow of his college (as he became in 1745), this classical scholar, could not
approve. It invited metaphyscial speculation, on the side of 'enthusiasm',
which he would be chary of accepting. His madness overwhelmed him
first in 1756, in his early thirties. Whether written in his Cambridge or his
London years, as a fellow of Pembroke Hall or as a publisher's hack, his
poems up to that time had been mostly of the kind which critics and readers
looked for. In songs 'sweetly elegant and pretty', in facetious verses, even
in his pieces of solemn rhetoric, and more complex organization, and more
imaginative tone, he was a conformist. He could translate a snowball into
a snowy orb — 'When, wanton fair, the snowy orb you throw', or with a
more solemn triteness he could instruct the reader in an *Ode on Saint Cecilia's
Day* that the saint was a 'matchless Dame'. Yet such conventionalism was

[1] The grass-snake?

now and then breached or contradicted.   Sometimes his later width, depth
and sparkle of a baroque vision flickers into view and disappears:

> *As some vast vista, whose extent*
> *Scarce bounded by the firmament*
>   *From whence it's sweep begun;*
> *Above, beneath, in every place,*
> *Mark'd with some grand distinguish'd grace,*
>   *Ends with the golden sun:*

Sometimes a sparkling item of the vision of earth finds the right crystallization
in a poem otherwise awkward:

> *Their scythes upon the adverse bank*
>   *Glitter 'mongst th' entangled trees,*
> *Where the hazles form a rank,*
>   *And court'sy to the courting breeze.*

Or a spontaneous recognition of the moment overcomes conventional
artifice, Smart, for example, ending a poem which he wrote in 1752 in the
garden of a Quaker friend, in this way:

> *Where Light and Shade in varied Scenes display*
> *A Contrast sweet, like friendly* yea *and* nay.
> *My Hand, the Secretary of my Mind,*
> *Left thee these Lines upon the* poplar's *Rind.*

  Readers excited by the summit of Smart's baroque peculiarity and grandeur of adoration are apt to turn to his earliest sustained poem, *The Hop-
Garden*, published in 1752, but evidently written when he was a boy, and
then to turn away from it disappointed.   It is certainly an exercise — a very
odd one at times, as when beautiful Dorinda starts and frowns with indig-
nation at finding in the dried foreign fruit for the Christmas pudding a negro's
toe-nail — in that eighteenth-century Miltonism which was reserved for
celebrating pastoral pursuits or topographical sublimities:

> *Whether you shiver in the marshy Weald,*
> *Egregious shepherds of unnumbered flocks,*
>   *. . . or in fair Madum's vale*
> *Imparadis'd, blest denizons, ye dwell;*

> *Or Dorovernia's awful tow'rs ye love:*
> *Or plough Tunbridgia's salutiferous hills*
> *Industrious, and with draughts chalybiate heal'd,*
> *Confess divine Hygeia's blissful seat.*

But examine *The Hop-Garden* with a retrospective sympathy, and there will be found in it a number of those first sensory impacts, those metallic illumina-tions, which were to obsess Smart years later in the creative excess of his vision. Silver surfaces (of the Medway) reflect:

> *Now bloom the florid hops, and in the stream*
> *Shine in their floating silver . . .*

Silvery fish, at any rate 'silver bleak, and prickly pearch', glide through the river; Northern Lights sparkle; Chanticleer is the bird which 'explodes the night'; green leaves suggest the music of Orpheus, who is to become the great psalmist of *A Song to David*; and Shipbourne, or the Fairlawn estate in Shipbourne parish, suggests already to Smart that recurrent image, of the interaction of the wild and the composed, of nature and art, of imagination and reason, of the hard gem of an uncultivated flower and the scythe-shaven grass, which was to become a structural integrator of Smart's vision:

> *Next Shipbourne, tho' her precincts are confin'd*
> *To narrow limits, yet can show a train*
> *Of village beauties, pastorally sweet,*
> *And rurally magnificent. Here Fairlawn*
> *Opes her delightful prospects; dear Fairlawn*
> *There, where at once at variance and agreed,*
> *Nature and art hold dalliance. There where rills*
> *Kiss the green drooping herbage, there where trees,*
> *The tall trees tremble at th' approach of heav'n,*
> *And bow their salutation to the sun,*
> *Who fosters all their foliage — These are thine,*
> *Yes, little Shipbourne, boast that these are thine —*
> *And if — but oh! — and if 'tis no disgrace,*
> *The birth of him who now records thy praise.*

II

The Hop-Garden is the adolescent's tribute to the loved place. The university,
a master's degree, a fellowship, wider reading and enquiry supervene; and
against *The Hop-Garden* should be set the five blank verse essays which won
Smart the Seatonian Prize in 1750, 1751, 1752, 1754, and again in 1756.
Smart's ultimate grandiloquence crystallizes in a conjunction of the natural
and the grandly visioned, the curiously observed and the grandly imagined,
a baroque vision, as if a soaring, crowded, sparkling, coloured, active three-
dimensional interior, shall I say, of an eighteenth-century German baroque
church by the brothers Asam or Dominikus Zimmerman, full of flowers,
fruits, figures, emblems, immediacies and infinities, and scraps of reflective
surface, had been condensed and simplified in Protestant terms. This
baroque vision of Smart's was given its trial run in the Seatonian poems.
The prize, established under the will of the Cambridge divine and hymnolo-
gist Thomas Seaton, went each year to the best poem celebrating a perfection
or an attribute of the Supreme Being. It was in 1749 that Smart had left
Cambridge for London, a victim of drink and debt, a man whose clowning
and inconsequential gaiety were at some odds with his inner nature, a
recognized scholar already looked upon as a weakling and an eccentric on
the way either to the debtor's prison or the madhouse. So his prize poems
were all of them written in his new and even less satisfactory life as a London
journalist. Year by year they at least kept him a footing in the university
world from which he was now an exile. They were popular. They were
also a fervent counterbalance to his daily writings of squibs and songs and
occasional pieces, a recurrent reversion to his graver interests, emotionally and
intellectually. In the second of these poems, *On the Immensity of the Supreme
Being* (1751), Smart already looks on himself, publisher's creature or no, as
a psalmist in the succession of David, the poem beginning abruptly:

> *Once more I dare to raise the sounding string,*
> *The poet of my God — Awake my glory,*
> *Awake my lute and harp — my self shall wake,*
> *Soon as the stately night-exploding bird*
> *In lively lay sings welcome to the dawn.*

It is David who opens the poem *On the Power of the Supreme Being* (1754); and, with still more emphasis and effect, this hero of Smart's opens the last of these prize poems, *On the Goodness of the Supreme Being* (1756), in which, classical scholar as well as Christian exegete, Smart adopts an identification of the David of the Hebrews and the Orpheus of the pagans, the two sweetest singers and musicians:

> *Orpheus, for so the Gentiles call'd thy name,*
> *Israel's sweet psalmist, who alone could wake*
> *The' inanimate to motion; who alone*
> *The joyful hillocks, the applauding rocks,*
> *And floods with musical persuasion drew;*
> *Thou, who to hail and snow gav'st voice and sound,*
> *And mad'st the mute melodious! — ...*
> *   ... in this breast*
> *Some portion of thy genuine spirit breathe,*
> *And lift me from myself.*

In these poems, these annual liftings of Smart from the Grub Street of London, he not only combined detail of earth and the choir of heaven, he combined his experience of a limited and a wider nature, observation with reading, his own eye with the eye of travellers, naturalists, and scientists, — the known to him with the imagined by him. The Supreme Being, eternal, immense, omniscient, powerful, and good, his seraphim and his cherubim, are conjunct in the poems with — for example — astronomical phenomena, sun, moon, comets, stars, planets, Saturn and his ring. Meteorological or optical concerns, refraction, colours, rainbow, thunder, hurricane, join heaven to earth; on earth the 'central magnet', and ores, fossils, crystals, gems sparkling in the deep mines of Gani, Roalconda, Peru, Ceylon, the Pyrenees, diamond, jasper, garnet, moss-agate presenting its curious pictures, and ruby —

> *Where the rich ruby ...*
> *   ... sparkles ev'n like Sirius*
> *And blushes into flames*

— all these encounter corals, pearls, and amber observed in sea-depths; and these hard brilliants are in turn associated with other activities, other strange or brilliant items of the created earth: with earthquakes and eruptions and molten fire; with cataracts, caves, lakes, mountains; with beasts: lion, elephant, Leviathan, African camels (carrying ingots of gold); with insects: ant, glow-worm, bee; with birds: woodland warblers, woodlark, red-breast, linnet, ring-dove, jay, nightingale, peacock, raven; with flowers: tulip, auricula, peach blossom, lilies, roses, hawthorn, pansies, deadly night-shade, dock, hemlock; with fruit: pomegranate, pineapple, cherry, plum; and these again with the spices and gums of Arabia; all in a geographical range outwards to the Antarctic. The catalogue is curious, though hardly exceptional — scientifically, in view of Smart's known and probable reading, or poetically in its glitter and variety — if we think of poets from Marvell and Milton and Waller to Pope himself, whom Smart greatly admired. Also images and glittering objects in array are one thing, poetry is another. For the most part these Seatonian poems by Smart indicate, but do not involve, do not create and proffer. They indicate a supposed creation, indicate the God-made, God-declaring, divinely good universe which Smart observes, but they do not condense it and transform it into com-pelling poetry. The rhetoric, like the rhythm, is still conventional (even at times absurd, as, for instance, when Smart writes of 'the domestic animal' — scilicet 'dog' — who 'from th'ematic herbage works his cure'), and is little shaped by that 'impression', verbal, rhythmical and constructive, which was soon to be the mark of Christopher Smart in his poems of mad-ness, or at least of confinement. So the interest is prospective. These Seatonian exercises declare his bent, in the intervals between the writing of facetiae and empty lyrics, or in the intervals of being carried home dead drunk from the London beer-houses. They exhibit a ranging, but not yet a compelled constructive sensuality, a quadripartite openness to sight, sound, touch, scent —

> . . . *sweeter than the breath of May*
> *Caught from the nectarine's blossom*

— yet not much more than a spectator, who faces the wonders of creation, and recites his own Benedicite.

The mix is made, the thermometer has still to rise, the new substance has still to combine and emerge.

In part, the somewhat conventional ardour of the religious spectator in these poems may have been due to Smart's own chariness of 'enthusiasm', a taint of which, or of anything at all intellectually or physico-theologically unusual, it would hardly have been tactful or proper to display on the surface, at any rate, of poems entered in a university religious competition, which might each of them win him a £30 he very much needed. Yet chary or cautious, Smart was not ill-informed in natural philosophy as well as in the mere natural history of his day. There is particular evidence of that in the curious jottings of *Jubilate Agno*. There is a poem, too, which he wrote in 1751 about one of the women he admired, in which Smart seems to make fun of himself or his own more phlegmatically inquisitive moments:

> *Pedants of dull phlegmatic Turns*
> *Whose Pulse not beats, whose Blood not burns,*
>   *Read* Malebranche, Boyle, *and* Marriot;
> *I scorn their Philosophic Strife,*
> *And study Nature from the Life,*
>   *(Where most she shines)* in Harriote.

He had looked into the physico-theologians, into Malebranche, more or less pantheistic and tainted with enthusiasm, into Boyle, and no doubt into the *Essais de physique* of Edmé Marriotte, whose name gave him so convenient a crambo rhyme for the girl; and it has been plausibly argued that he went further (in the London years of his intermittent madness after 1756?) by accepting at last a Berkeleyan attitude, that nature, more than declaring the glory of God to the passive spectator in a direct psalmody, is joined to ourselves in our direct active perception, in which it exists concretely and brilliantly, and as a portion of divine language.[1]

Such an acceptance, still rational, and avoiding 'enthusiasm' or pantheism, would help to explain the difference between the Seatonian poems, and the clipped, concrete, brilliant eloquence of *A Song to David*, which Smart, student of Bishop Berkeley as of King David and the Three Children in the burning fiery furnace, was to achieve at some time within the next seven years of intermittent mental illness.

[1] Compare Gerard Manley Hopkins (page 135) on dull and lively glory.

The seven dubious and anxious years lasted from 1756 to 1763. But neither the exact time-table of these years nor the exact nature of Smart's madness are known.   That he was ill in mind in 1755 or 1756, before being shut away, is certain from the *Hymn to the Supreme Being* (*on recovery from a dangerous fit of illness*), which he published in 1756, a stronger poem more directly, verbally, rhythmically in key with his emotion than any he had yet written.   He suffered from 'horrible despair', reason left him 'and sense was lost in terror or in trance'.   But he recovered:

> *My feeble feet refus'd my body's weight*
>   *Nor would my eyes admit the glorious light,*
> *My nerves convuls'd shook fearful of their fate,*
>   *My mind lay open to the powers of night.*
> *He pitying did a second birth bestow*
> *A birth of joy — not like the first of tears and woe.*

> *Ye strengthen'd feet, forth to his altar move;*
>   *Quicken, ye new-strung nerves, th' enraptured lyre;*
> *Ye heav'n-directed eyes, o'erflow with love;*
>   *Glow, glow, my soul, with pure, seraphic fire;*
> *Deeds, thoughts, and words no more his mandates break,*
> *But to his endless glory work, conceive, and speak.*

What is certain is that the new birth, new joy, was to be subject to ups and downs, or ups and outs.   Twenty years after Smart's death, his nephew wrote that he had suffered from 'temporary alienations of mind; which at last were attended with paroxysms so violent and continued as to render confinement necessary'.   The violence seems to have come upon him before 1756 was out, and the probable time-table was this, that later in 1756 he was first confined, according to the usual custom of the century, in private lodgings; that, not improving, he was transferred in the spring to the London madhouse of St Luke's Hospital, where (it is certain) he lived for a year, from May 1757 to May 1758, when he was discharged as uncured. For a while he may now have been in private lodgings again or with his family.   Evidently he became much worse in 1759.   Garrick the actor gave a benefit performance for him in February, as if to raise money for a new confinement or new lodgings; and his friends wrote poems for the occasion in language suggesting that all was now over with Smart as a poet and a man. On or soon after August 13 he was shut up once more — probably in Bedlam (and possibly after an especially mad-seeming bout of praising God):

> *For I bless the thirteenth of August, in which I had the grace to obey the voice of Christ in my conscience . . .*

> *For I bless the thirteenth of August, in which I was willing to run all hazards for the sake of the name of the Lord . . .*

> *For I bless the thirteenth of August, in which I was willing to be called a fool for the sake of Christ.*

— and so he continued, until he faced the world again in the New Year of 1763.

How mad was he? Not mad enough at any rate to be unable, even if intermittently, to read, meditate, feel, and write. His sanity ebbed and returned. With violence (which lasted for a while) he mixed a religious mania, both praying and praising as a new psalmist, '*The Poet of my God*', and praying desperately, one may think, against the state he was in. He prayed and praised in public, as we know from Dr Johnson's famous recollection which Boswell recorded in 1763 (the year in which Smart was out and about again). 'Madness frequently discovers itself merely by unnecessary deviation from the usual modes of the world', said Johnson or Johnson-Boswell, who may not have known the full facts. 'My poor friend Smart shewed the disturbance of his mind, by falling upon his knees, and saying his prayers in the streets, or in any other unusual place.' And Boswell also recorded that earlier conversation between Johnson and Dr Burney the musician, in which Johnson so memorably said: 'He insisted on people praying with him; and I'd as lief pray with Kit Smart as any one else. Another charge was, that he did not love clean linen; and I have no passion for it.'

A small, plump, dirtily dressed man sonorously praying and praising in public — praying, as we know from his *Jubilate Agno*, in St James's Park and in the Mall, trying to make others pray with him (think of Gains-borough's painting of elegant ladies promenading under the feathery trees of the Mall) and causing offence, and getting into trouble with the officers of the peace, and the night watchmen:

> *Let Ahimaaz rejoice with the Silver-worm*[1] *who is a living mineral.*

> *For there is silver in my mines and I bless God that it is rather there than in my coffers.*

> *Let Shobi rejoice with the Kastrel blessed be the name of* JESUS *in falconry and in the* MALL.

> *For I blessed God in St James's Park till I routed all the company.*

> *Let Elkanah rejoice with Cymindis*[2] *the Lord illuminate us against the powers of darkness.*

> *For the officers of the peace are at variance with me, and the watchman smites me with his staff.*

— praying sometimes naked and in the rain for the sake of an extra purity:

> *For to worship naked in the Rain is the bravest thing for the refreshing and purifying the body.*

— or praying on the flat leads of a neat porticoed common-sensible eighteenth-century house:

> *For a man should put no obstacle between his head and the blessing of Almighty God . . .*

> *For the ceiling of the house is an obstacle and therefore we pray on the house-top.*

He not only prayed on his knees in public, literally following, it has been said, St Paul's injunction to the Thessalonians:

> *Rejoice evermore.*
> *Pray without ceasing.*
> *In everything give thanks . . .*
> *Quench not the Spirit*
> *Despise not prophesyings,*

[1] The glow-worm.   [2] The nightjar.

he also composed particular passages of his poems on his knees, that posture which he held to be 'a way to the terrestrial Paradise':

> *For the method of philosophizing is in a posture of Adoration.*

What were the conditions of his confinement? In the ebb and swell of madness Smart certainly felt humiliated and resentful, at first scrutinizing the visitors who came to the raree-show of the madhouse, for someone to save him,

> *For they pass by me in their tour, and the good Samaritan is not yet come,*

at first objecting to the visitors' comments:

> *For Silly fellow! Silly fellow! is against me and belongeth neither to me nor my family.*

If he was violent at times (as when he instructed Andrew to 'rejoice with the Whale, who is arrayd in beauteous blue & is a combination of bulk and activity', because 'they work me with their harping-irons, which is a barbarous instrument, because I am no more unguarded than the others'), he would have known the chains and straw perhaps in a safety cell or dungeon.

Somewhile after that entry on the harping irons, he wrote down, as though restored from such a cell to daylight:

> *Let Sadoc rejoice with the Bleak, who playeth upon the surface in the Sun.*

> *For I bless God that I am not in a dungeon, but am allowed the light of the Sun*

It is on record that, being both a wit and a scholar, he was 'visited as such while under confinement'. After a time he grew fat as if more contented, and he dug in the garden, according again to Boswell's *Life of Johnson*:

BURNEY: 'How does poor Smart do, Sir; is he likely to recover?' JOHNSON: 'It seems as if his mind had ceased to struggle with the disease; for he grows fat upon it.' BURNEY: 'Perhaps, Sir, that may be from want of exercise.' JOHNSON: 'No, Sir; he has partly as much exercise as he used to have, for he digs in the garden.'

Flowers were the consequence of his asylum gardening, 'the Lord succeed my pink borders' Smart says in the *Jubilate*.

All of these details I have picked out and emphasised for one good reason: all of them seem to relate (though the references to the pink borders, and probably the digging and the fatness, date from 1762) to the months actually in the asylum, during which it is most likely — and I think certain, on the evidence which has been advanced — that Smart wrote some of the *Hymns*, finished his *Psalms*, and wrote or finished, above all, *A Song to David*, the most sharply fused and greatest of all his poems; as well as writing the first three of the surviving fragments of *Jubilate Agno*, that antiphony which is half poem, half a species of journal.

Correspondence of topic and image and word suggest that some of the finest of the *Hymns* and the *Psalms* and *A Song to David* were written more or less concurrently with these early fragments of the *Jubilate*, which can be dated from the summer of 1759 to the summer of 1760. 'For the nightly Visitor' (the owl) 'is at the window of the impenitent, while I sing a psalm of my own composing' wrote Smart before the fateful 13 August 1759. He seems to have been at work on the *Song*; and a little later, still before his last confinement, he adds: 'For I pray the Lord Jesus to translate my MAGNIFICAT into verse and represent it'.[1] Perhaps, Bedlam or no, he had finished at any rate the Adoration stanzas by that time, early in 1760, when he wrote down that by the grace of God he was 'the Reviver of ADORATION amongst ENGLISH⁄MEN'.

IV

It seems to me a fair, indeed inevitable conclusion that the 'matchless deed', which has been 'atchiev'd, DETERMINED, DARED, and DONE', as Smart so victoriously celebrates it in the last two lines of *A Song to David*, is capable of a tripartite explanation. Christ, David's 'son', as he explains himself, has brought salvation down; David, 'the best poet who ever lived', has achieved his psalmody; Christopher Smart, too, has achieved, has deter⁄mined, dared, and finished, his own translation or version of those *Psalms*.

[1] Like Yeats setting out a preliminary in prose which he then worked into a poem, does this mean that Smart first wrote out a prose preliminary to *A Song to David*, in something of the style of the entries in *Jubilate Agno*?

It is true that the brief *Song* was not published until 1763, after Smart's release from the asylum, and that the lengthy *Translation of the Psalms of David* coupled with *Hymns and Spiritual Songs for the Fasts and Festivals of the Church of England* was published later still, in 1765. It is also true that in *Jubilate Agno*, in December and January 1763, towards the time of his release, he first asks, 'The Lord help on with the hymns', and then asks that the Lord should 'forward my translation of the psalms this year'. But this does not mean (I think) that the Lord should encourage a work still in progress, but that he should forward its publication. He also says 'I pray for a musician or musicians to set the new psalms' and 'I pray God bless all my Subscribers' (since the *Psalms and Hymns* were to be published by subscription), clearly speaking of something finished. The supposition that best fits the evidence, including the evidence inside the actual poems, is that he had completed the *Psalms*, at any rate a first draft of them all, by some date in 1759, whereupon he composed his own song of gratitude. In some of the *Psalms* it has been noticed that Smart unquestionably refers to himself as the inmate of an asylum, in Psalm xxxi, for example:

> *My name was nam'd as a reproof,*
> *That neither friend nor foes*
> *Nor neighbours came beneath my roof,*
> *And my companions kept aloof,*
> *As other company they chose.*
>
> *The world have all my deeds forgot,*
> *And I am in the place*
> *Of one, whose memory is not,*
> *Whose body damps sepulchral rot*

(the last line suggests a damp punishment cell); or in Psalm xxxv:

> *'All that we surmise has follow'd,'*
> *Let them not with triumph boast,*
> *'His remains the gulph has swallowed,*
> *He has given up the ghost.'*[1]

[1] He perhaps refers to the rather sepulchral commendations which his friends had written at the time of Garrick's performance on his behalf a few months back in February. William Woty, for one, had described him as an 'unhappy bard'

Make them blush with shame ingenuous,
  Which at my distress rejoice;
Who against the truth are strenuous,
  Give them grace to hear her voice.

Let them say, which like the measure,
  That in charity I deal;
Blessed be the Lord, whose pleasure
  Is his servant's bliss to seal.

As for me in heavenly phrases
  I will harmonize my tongue,
Day by day Jehovah's praises
  Shall in sweeter notes be sung.

Having sung the last of the sweeter notes (whatever revision was to come) somewhere about August or autumn of 1759, having come to the last Hosanna of David's psalms, at any rate in the first draft, what could have been more appropriate than to contrive now the psalm of his own composing, to translate his own Magnificat into verse, in the form and superb shape of that poem which Smart described afterwards as having been 'composed in a Spirit of affection and thankfulness to the great Author of the Book of Gratitude, which is the *Psalms,* of DAVID the King', and which he prefaced on the title-page with David's words (2 Sam. xxiii, 2), 'The SPIRIT OF THE LORD spake by Me, and HIS WORD was in my Tongue'?

In some degree his affection for David was increased by the thought of that 'serene suspence' in which David's singing had held 'The frantic throes of Saul'. As David for Saul, so David for Smart:

---

whose celestial harp was broken, 'affecting emblem of its master's fate'.

Ah me! no more, I fear, its tuneful strings,
  Touch'd by his hand, will praise the King of Kings.

Through his life Smart must have heard much of the kind of talk which prophesied jail or madness for him. Gray the poet, as long back as 1747, had written to the poet Thomas Warton of Smart's vanity and lying and debts, all of which 'must come to a Jayl or Bedlam, and not without any help, almost without pity . . .'

His muse, bright angel of his verse,
Gives balm for all the thorns that pierce,
For all the pangs that rage.

Incidentally, restoring *A Song to David* to 1759, or between 1759 and the early months of 1760, may also restore credibility to the tale of the *Song*, the key and wainscot, which has always seemed to me both too vivid and too early (it occurs in the *Monthly Review* for April 1763, in a review of *A Song to David*) to be an invention. In August 1759, if the interpretation is correct, Smart had already begun the *Song*, a little mentally deranged, it may be, but at home or in private confinement. The thirteenth of August then introduced him into Bedlam or some other madhouse. It was soon after 31 August that he called upon Andrew to 'rejoice with the Whale, who is array'd in beauteous blue & is a combination of bulk & activity', because *they* were working him with their harping-irons, as if he were becoming violent, or was appearing violent or in some quieter way specially obnoxious to his keepers. Some time later, as we have seen, he blesses God for not being in a dungeon, as if he had been released from punishment in a dark or dim room, or cell underground, such as the one in which he suffered those 'damps sepulchral' of his Psalm xxxi. The special confine-ment would have taken place while he was still at work on the precise incandescent architecture of the *Song*, and he may well for part of his time in that cell have been 'denied the use of pen, ink and paper', and have hammered out in his head new stanzas of the *Song*, which he was 'obliged to indent with one end of a key, upon the wainscot'.

V

To return for a moment to Smart's translation or version or adaptation, which is the better way of describing it, of the Psalms, it had been medi-tated no doubt for a long while. It is in line with the praise of David reiterated in his Seatonian poems; and was perhaps begun, — so at any rate the style suggests — after that recovery from the first recorded mental attack in 1755 or 1756, which had occasioned the *Hymn to the Supreme Being*, in that state of recovered reason and consequent exultation of which he wrote

D

Brisk leaps the heart, the mind's at large once more,
To love, to praise, to bless, to wonder and adore.

In the small print of the Muses' Library edition of Smart's poems, the *Psalms*, even without the supplementary *Hymns and Spiritual Songs*, fill more than 400 pages; and it is reasonable to think that Smart wrote such a bulk of verse in the lucid, or lucid enough, intervals of his mad years (the portion of them between 1756 and 1759), when he was relieved, most of the while, from the nag of his debts and his normal responsibilities and employment. There is no reason to think that he must rigorously have followed the biblical order as he made his adaptations.   Psalm xxxi, for instance, in which he refers to his asylum and which also contains the first weak version of the 'bastion's mole' of the seventy-sixth stanza of *A Song to David*, must have been written after many of the Psalms which follow.   The very first of them, one may note, is written in the same stanza as *A Song to David*, and exhibits that alliterative tripartite summing of a final line to a stanza, *His bud, his bloom, and fruit*, which marks the Song, and which had appeared in the Hymn to the Supreme Being.   Now and again the Psalms show a little of the ultimate stamp and virtuosity:

> *Praise him, cherubic flights,*
> *And ye seraphic fires,*
> *Angelical delights*
> *   With voices, lutes and lyres;*
> *And vie who shall extol him most,*
> *Ye blest innumerable host!*
>
> *Praise him, thou source of heat,*
> *   Great ruler of the day,*
> *And thou serenely sweet,*
> *   O moon, his praise display;*
> *Praise him ye glorious lights that are,*
> *The planet and the sparkling star.*

Again and again lines out of the *Psalms* are re-used or adapted to new use in the *Song*.

Yet it must be admitted that the *Psalms* for all the amount of interpolation, for all their occasional force, and their scraps of felicity —

> *The cheerful trumpet sound,*
> *And let the horns be wound,*
> *To yeild thro' twisted brass their tone —*

do roll a little tediously along. By the time the great labour was dared and done Smart was at any rate expert in the stanza of *A Song to David*; he had employed it in some thirty of the Psalms, and the shape and sounds and rhythms of it must have been insistent in his mind. In the *Song*, which was his own *Magnificat*, the psalm of his own composing, the thanksgiving for his completed version of these *Psalms of David*, he was at last free altogether of any original; free to combine and condense the sensory impacts of a lifetime; free to make the most of wonders whose glow had intensified in successive poems. Now and again an image in the *Song* can be traced far back into his mental life:

> *And, by the coasting reader spied,*
> *The silverlings and crusions glide*
> *For* ADORATION *gilt*

Silverlings are presumably roach, the crusion (properly Crucian or Crusian) is a fish of the carp family, yellow (i.e. gilt), introduced from Asia to continental Europe, and so to England, where it was often put into ponds in the eighteenth century. *Jubilate Agno* shows that in autumn 1759, in his madhouse, Smart had been recalling the fishponds and the fish of that Fairlawn where he had spent his childhood:

> *Let Mary rejoice with the Carp — the ponds of Fairlawn and the garden*
> *bless for the master.*

The twenty-fourth stanza in the *Song* repeats his image of metallic fish gliding through the water or breaking a still surface, David the supreme poet having sung of the shells in the wealthy deep and the shoals which leap on the surface,

> *And love the glancing sun.*

In lines from the *Jubilate* already quoted, when he is returned from a punishment cell into the sunlight, he recalls the bleak, those small, quick-gliding, quick-leaping, silver-bodied fish of English rivers, which cruise in shoals.

There are such fish in *Hymn XIII* (which is closely linked to the *Jubilate* entries) —

> *Tansy, calaminth and daisies,*
> > *On the river's margin thrive;*
> *And accompany the mazes*
> > *Of the stream that leaps alive,*

in the *Psalms* (no. CXLVII), in the fable *Munificence and Modesty*; and all of them occur far back, as I have mentioned, in the childhood celebrations of Kent and the silver Medway which form so much of *The Hop-Garden*. The fifty-second stanza of the *Song* offers one of the most fascinating crystal-lizations and intensifications of a thing seen:

> *For* ADORATION *seasons change,*
> *And order, truth, and beauty range,*
> > *Adjust, attract and fill:*
> *The grass the polyanthus cheques;*
> *And polish'd porphyry reflects,*
> > *By the descending rill.*

Anyone who knows, by good luck, the limestone country of Raby, and of Staindrop Moor alongside (recalled by name in the *Jubilate* in 1759), and Teesdale, will at once see the flower and the rock and the waterfall in a characteristic conjunction which Smart must have known in his Co. Durham days, the limestone so finely polished by centuries of the descending rill, protruding from grass chequered with the lilac umbels, by the thousand, of the Birdseye Primrose.[1]

More than a hundred lines in *A Song to David* can be directly referred to sensations from his reading or from nature which Smart had already recorded in other poems or in *Jubilate Agno*. The point is the way in which (for the most part) such sensations are transformed, as if he had been able to alter their molecular structure; indeed the way in which, or the degree to which,

---

[1] Smart's frequently mentioned cowslips, gem-like

> *Cowslips, like topazes that shine,*
> *Muse by the silver serpentine,*

were rooted no doubt in the Kentish portion of his childhood, along with the gilt crucians, the silver bleak and silver roach. See *Epithalamium, Hymn XIII, The Blockhead and the Beehive,* and *Hymns for Children,* no. XXV.

he also transformed his poetry in this climacteric poem. I am sure the suggestion that he came to something of a Berkeleyan view of nature and of
perception is correct, and that it helps to explain the transformation. *Esse
est percipi*: to be is to be perceived; intense perception is intense being.
Certainly there are statements in the relevant fragments of *Jubilate Agno* which
Smart may have derived from Berkeley's *Siris*, his *Essay towards a New
Theory of Vision*, or his *Treatise concerning the Principles of Human Knowledge*;
the statements, for example, that 'nothing is so real as that which is spiritual',
or that 'an IDEA is the mental vision of an object' (New Year, 1760).
Ideas for Berkeley are things, 'the several combinations of sensible qualities
which are called *things*'. Their reality in the mind, the abolition of the
separation of the mind which perceives from the perceived, burnishes and
enhances their existence. 'Ideas imprinted on the senses are real things, or
do really exist' (*Principles* part I, 90). This notion of impression, of imprint,
is a favourite one with Berkeley; and in the *Jubilate* one discovers Smart pro-
ceeding from an idea, as a mental vision of an object, to take up exactly this
printer's image of impression —

> For my talent is to give an impression upon words by punching, that
> when the reader casts his eye upon 'em, he takes up the image from the
> mould wch I have made.

It is as if nature, in all its width, produced its sense impressions on him,
which he in turn impressed upon words, which in their turn transferred those
impressions to the reader; and one may suppose that a study of Berkeley
had been the refining and strengthening agent of his renewed vision, helping
him to avoid 'enthusiasm' (Berkeley expressly rejected the 'enthusiasm' of
Malebranche — see the second of the *Three Dialogues between Hylas and
Philonous*), to maintain his eighteenth-century respect for reason, and yet to
give more freedom to the excited receptivity of his senses. To appreciate the
degree of transformation or even transmutation one has only to compare the
slackness of Psalm civ,

> *And some of huge enormous bulk*
> *The swelling floods surmount,*

with the punch and the grand immediate perception of the final image in
the seventy-sixth stanza of *A Song to David*:

> *Strong against tide, the 'enormous whale*
> *Emerges as he goes.*

Or from *Psalm xxxi* compare

> *Be thou my bulwark to defend*
> *Like some strong bastion's mole*

with the final wonder of the image in the same seventy-sixth stanza of the *Song*:

> *Strong is the lion — like a coal*
> *His eyeball — like a bastion's mole*
> *His chest against the foes.*

'Impression' for Smart was more than impression upon words. Introducing his verse translation of Horace years later, in 1767, he was to write, in much the same way, of 'the beauty, force, and vehemence of *Impression*' as a 'talent or gift of almighty God, by which a Genius is empowered to throw an emphasis on a word or a sentence in such wise, that it cannot escape any reader of sheer good sense, and true critical sagacity'. He then talked of the 'impression' of qualities, melancholy, strength, grandeur, sweetness, dignity, upon poetry; of impression as the general characteristic of a poem: 'the face of Impression is always liveliest upon the eulogies of patriotism, gratitude' (cf. *A Song to David* as a thanksgiving to David, whose own Psalms were 'the Book of Gratitude'), 'honour, and the like'. Impression shapes lines as well as words in *A Song to David*, stanzas as well as lines, stanza-groups as well as stanzas, and the whole as well as any part.

As usually printed, as printed by Smart himself, a cataract of eighty-six stanzas, without intermission, thunders and sparkles along to a great finale, seeming at first haphazard, even confused, without declaring its structure. The reader needs to consult the analysis of the contents which Smart wrote as an introduction, after which the poem can be read into the intended breaks or pauses between each proper group of stanzas. The analysis could be clearer, it is true; but here are the divisions as Smart seems to have meant them and made them:

I-III: Invocation.
IV-XVII: The twelve Points of the excellence and lustre of David's Character.

XVIII-XXVI: The Subjects of his singing.

XXVII-XXIX: His victories won by song.

XXX-XXXVIII: The Pillars of Knowledge.

XXXIX: A linking stanza.

XL-XLVIII: Exercise on the Decalogue.

XLIX: A concluding stanza to the Exercise.

L: A stanza introducing the transcendent virtue of praise.

LI-LXIV: An exercise upon the seasons, and the right use of them (Adoration stanzas).

LXV-LXXI: An exercise upon the senses, and how to subdue them (Adoration stanzas).

LXXII-LXXXVI: An amplification in five degrees, 'which is wrought up to this conclusion, That the best poet who ever lived was thought worthy of the highest honour which can possibly be conceived, *as the Saviour of the world was ascribed to his house, and called his son in the body*' (in five groups of three stanzas, Sweet, Strong, Beauteous, Precious, and Glorious).

It has been recognized that Smart hammered out the stanzas of the *Song* in groups and multiples of three and seven, the mystic numbers, with an occasional one, numbers which he approves in *Jubilate Agno*:

For there is a mystery in numbers
For One is perfect and good being at unity in himself . . .
For every thing infinitely perfect is Three . . .
For Seven is very good consisting of two compleat numbers . . .
For Nine is a number very good and harmonious,

the important thing being less the occult numeration or combination than the way in which the poem is impressed, again, with an intellectual structure, a harmony and proportion of parts which at once are parts and a whole. It is not a series of random images. In appropriate order, baroque detail, distance and immensity, near and far, small and large, still and active are welded, impressed, into a coherent structure, with strong immediacy, strong verbs, strong inversions, strong rhymes, a strong rhythm (changing to tenderness when required); with those qualities, in short, which Gerard Manley Hopkins spoke of when he felt their absence in his own verse, as roll and rise and carol and creation.

But this total 'impression', shaping and sustaining *A Song to David*, is also, like an 'idea' of Berkeley's, part of the language of the governing spirit. It is 'a talent or gift of Almighty God', Smart had said in the wake of Berkeley; and in Berkeley's phrase (from *Siris*) it is the Author of Nature who imprints the ideas upon our senses:

> The phenomena of nature, which strike on the senses and are under-stood by the mind, form not only a magnificent spectacle, but also a most coherent, entertaining and instructive Discourse; and to effect this, they are conducted, and ranged by the greatest wisdom.

So here is the situation . . . A child is born, Christopher Smart, who has (like Traherne or the artist Samuel Palmer, or Gerard Manley Hopkins) the most receptive and open senses, the keenest ability, in his childhood in Kent, the Garden of England, and in Co. Durham, and later in his man-hood, to perceive: perception, delight in perception, overlaid then renewed, finds religious warrant: religious warrant is subtilized and enforced (as with Traherne, Palmer, or Hopkins again) by philosophical speculation, till words, images, poems (or at least one great poem) are at last informed with a wonderful degree of active perception. For the reader who discounts the God, there remains the degree of perception, the load of a wonderful reality, in a wonderful art. If he reflects that wonder of perception can be induced by drugs, he should also admit that there can be differences of value. There is a difference between a God, or a physico-theology, in the mind, and a bottle of tablets on the hall table, or there would be to a theist, in his feeling about the effects of one or the other. *A Song to David* made a mixed im-pression on those who read it in 1763. 'A strange mixture of *dun obscure* and glowing genius at times' wrote Boswell to Samuel Johnson. 'I have seen his "Song to David" and from thence conclude him as mad as ever' wrote the correctly poised minor poet Mason to the correctly poised senti-mental poet Gray (whose studies in natural history remained outside his evening or antiquarian verse). At the time when he had been taken ill again in 1759, Smart's friend and fellow denizen of Grub Street, Arthur

Murphy, came nearer the mark of his distinction: 'To hear thee', he wrote, when the *Song to David* had still to be conceived,

> *Angels from their Golden Beds*
> *Willing bend down their Star-encircled Heads.*

IV

A Song to David makes the strongest, most sustained use of Smart's peculiarity. In the *Hymns and Spiritual Songs*, in which he was again more free to invent than he had been in the *Psalms*, his praising also triumphs ecstatically, though rather in fragments, in a few stanzas in sequence or in single stanzas, than in whole poems. Extraordinary outworks of praise, forceful and immediate in their attack, in rhythm, in imagery and unexpectedness are to be found:

> *They knew him well, and could not err,*
> *To him they all appeal'd;*
> *The beast of sleek or shaggy fur,*
> *And found their natures to recur*
> *To what they were in Eden's field.*

> *For all that dwell in depth or wave,*
> *And ocean — every drop —*
> *Confess'd his mighty pow'r to save,*
> *When to the floods his peace he gave,*
> *And bade careering whirlwinds stop.*

> *And all things meaner from the worm*
> *Probationer to fly;*
> *To him that creeps his little term,*
> *And countless rising from the sperm*
> *Shed by sea-reptiles, where they ply.*

> *These all were bless'd beneath his feet,*
> *Approaching them so near . . .*

But the reader is inclined to pick and choose among the stanzas, and to break off when the immediacy of impression becomes less. These poems lack the structural cohesion of the *Song*, which in one respect they curiously resemble. In the *Song*, passages of less imaginative force, stanzas XL to

XLVIII particularly, are added, as if by afterthoughts of propriety, to the more compulsive grandeurs. This may be justified by effect, by giving the reader a pause, almost a rest, between the grandeurs. In the hymns, more and less compulsive parts are also joined, but unsuccessfully. For instance Hymn XXXII, on *The Nativity of Our Lord and Saviour Jesus Christ*, begins with five stanzas of rather ordinary writing, and suddenly changes to four stanzas of Smart's most compulsive and impressive felicity —

> *Nature's decorations glisten*
> > *Far above their usual trim;*
> *Birds on box and laurels listen,*
> > *As so near the cherubs hymn.*
>
> *Boreas now no longer winters*
> > *On the desolated coast;*
> *Oaks no more are riv'n in splinters*
> > *By the whirlwind and his host.*
>
> *Spinks and ouzles sing sublimely,*
> > *'We too have a Saviour born',*
> *Whiter blossoms burst untimely*
> > *On the blest Mosaic thorn.*
>
> *God all-bounteous, all-creative,*
> > *Whom no ills from good dissuade,*
> *Is incarnate, and a native*
> > *Of the very world he made*

— as if these four stanzas alone were the ones 'given', the ones which compelled Smart and obsessed him in the making, and as if the five others had been a later intellectual contrivance. The poem falls in two. Smart was writing, after all, in confinement and derangement. To each *donnée* he may therefore have been all the more tempted to add stanzas of more ordinary exposition in proof to himself, if not to others, of his own sanity or coherence of mind. I suspect that, like the *Psalms*, the best of the *Hymns*, if not all of them, were written before the *Song to David*: the best ones read to me as if they had been in effect trial pieces, trial arrangements, which led him to the *Song* itself; the best portions of the best of the *Hymns* seem an outcome of that gathering pressure which at last moulded the *Song*.

And what is one to say of the now celebrated *Jubilate Agno*, the manuscript of which survived by accident, and was not printed (and then in a
misleading form) until 1939? That it is not a *poem*?

So much is probably true. Smart can hardly have considered it a poem,
at least when he returned to sanity, and, as I have said, I look on it as half
a poem, half a journal or journal of praise, which he recorded to begin with,
antiphonally, in a Hebrew parallelism. It does more than reveal facts of
biography, facts of thought and reading, or facts about the ebb and resur-
gence in Smart's illness of mind. Entries such as

> *For black blooms and it is* PURPLE

or

> *Let Ahimaaz rejoice with the Silver-Worm*[1] *who is a living mineral.*
> *For there is silver in my mines and I bless God that it is rather there than*
> *in my coffers.*

or

> *Let Hushim rejoice with the King's Fisher who is of royal beauty, tho' plebian size*
> *For in my nature I quested for beauty, but God, God hath sent me to sea for pearls*

(the last a most admirable and accurate description of himself as a poet), have
shape and effect, and there are passages enough of sharp lucidity, for instance
the celebrated description of his cat Jeoffry, written in the summer of 1760,
to counterbalance the many entries of peculiar praise which he maintained
in desperation or by habit, and which his derangement or his despondency
reduced to a formula.

VII

After madness? To a summit, illness or no, one climbs, *A Song to David*
having been no miracle without roots or prologue; from a summit, sanity
or no, one descends. In the asylum, in confinement on and off for seven
years, Smart was out of the world: whatever distress he felt, he had been
free of intellectual interference, he had been able to dive for pearls in his own
way. Fashions or habits of mental (and literary) style were more against

[1] I.e. the glow-worm.

Smart in the 1750s than they had been, shall I say, against the equally well-educated Traherne in the previous century. Habits of correct and abstract elegance were against him, nor was he in tune with those strains of mood and melancholy which kept the effeminate, sentimental, literary and less 'real' poems of Gray, for example, popular for so long. Smart dealt in the immediate, the concrete, the thing sensed here and now, not in suffusions of mood, not in yearning for the past, or for the townsman's country, or anything else which was not there. Nearer the hard pearliness of the seventeenth century than the softer romanticism of the early nineteenth century, he recovered contact with his earlier habits of perception, he was able to recollect them fruitfully and to renew them, in a way which will be familiar to readers of the *Centuries* of Traherne. (For the probable course of Smart's development from perception to its loss, and then to its recovery, compare the first seven sections of Traherne's *Third Century*.) Confinement, I have suggested, helped him in this, much as it was to help John Clare, by isolating or insulating him. When he was restored to freedom in the early months of 1763, Smart was back in the world, and the world was at him again. He had climbed to a height of praise, a height of concrete passion, which could not be maintained; and the world fuddled and troubled him once more. There is a clear, uncommonly revealing glimpse of Smart in October 1764, when he was forty-two, about a year and nine months after his release. He was busy. He had not returned to his wife and children, or his family. On his sister's behalf, the writer Hawkesworth called on him in cheerful rooms above Storey's Gate Coffee House, opening to a terrace which overlooked St James's Park. He told Hawkesworth he was busy translating all of Horace into verse; Hawkesworth suggested he should go and see his sister in Kent. 'To this he replied very quick' (and one can see him standing there and turning away his head), ' "I cannot afford to be idle" '. In fact within three years or so of his release he busily published *A Song to David*, two small collections of verse, an oratorio, *Hannah* (which was sung at the King's Theatre in the Haymarket), a verse translation of Phaedrus, and his *Psalms and Hymns*, for which he had at last rounded up enough subscribers.

The new poems included two odes, written just before his release, one to an admiral, one to a general, each of whom had recently been victorious in action. (Smart — like John Clare — has a small man's admiration for military prowess.) They exhibit his peculiar concrete eloquence, especially the *Ode to General Draper*:

> *What tho' no bonfires be displayed,*
>   *Nor windows light up the nocturnal scene;*
> *What tho' the merry ringer is not paid,*
>   *Nor rockets shoot upon the* STILL SERENE;
> *Tho' no matross upon the rampart runs,*
> *To send out thy report from loud redoubling guns?* . . .

The poems in his miscellaneous collection of 1763 included also a fable, *Reason and Imagination*, which Smart published so soon after his release as if to assert his restored rationality. Imagination, Queen of Imagery, proposes marriage to Reason, that proper 'Attribute of Man' who is 'solid, weighty, deep, and sound', and offers to elevate him from his hole and ditch 'To gay Conception's top-most pitch'. Reason declines, and proposes to be an ally and nothing else:

> *I cannot take thee for a mate;*
> *I'm lost if e'er I change my state.*
> *But whensoe'er your raptures rise,*
> *I'll try to come with my supplies.*
> *But, ere this treaty be agreed*
> *Give me thy wand and winged steed:*
> *Take thou this compass and this rule,*
> *That wit may cease to play the fool;*
> *And that thy vot'ries who are born*
> *For Praise, may never sink to scorn.*

James Boswell thought the fable 'very pretty', and saw in the other poems 'shivers of genius' here and there, though they were 'often ludicrously low'.

Such shivers recur in the poems Smart had still to write. His translations of Horace — all of Horace — which came out in four volumes in 1767, swing from the shivers to the low, and back again, after an introduction, edgy and slightly eccentric, in which he expounds those too brief views about 'impression'. If at times ridiculous, clumsy or careless, his translation can be very direct in style:

> *I hate the mob, and drive them hence,*
> *Lost to all sanctity and sense . . .*

It can be affecting:

> *Ah! Postumus, the years, the years,*
> *Glide swiftly on, nor can our tears*
> *Or piety the wrinkled age forfend,*
> *Or for one hour retard th' inevitable end . . .*

It can be gay and lyrical:

> *Pyrrha, for whom with such an air*
> *Do you bind back your golden hair?*

It can be entirely surprising in its change of rhythm and manner, for instance in Smart's version of Book I, Ode XXXVIII, to Horace's servant:

> *Persian pomps, boy, ever I renounce them:*
> *Scoff o' the plaited coronet's refulgence;*
> *Seek not in fruitless vigilance the rose-trees'*
> > *Tardier offspring.*
>
> *Mere honest myrtle that alone is order'd,*
> *Me the mere myrtle decorates, as also*
> *Thee the prompt waiter to a jolly toper*
> > *Hous'd in an arbour.*

These translations were once unfairly neglected, they have since been extra-vagantly proclaimed; which is better at least. Smart's lifelong forte, though, was praise; it was praise, not translation — even of David's Psalms— which called out his full power of impression; and, as if in defence of shortcomings, he remarks, in his introduction to the Horace, that 'there is a little-ness in the noblest poet among the Heathens when compared to the prodigious grandeur and genuine majesty of a *David* or *Isaiah*'.

   In verse and in life from now on there are only a few more glimpses of Smart. One or two concrete and affecting scraps illuminate the somewhat exhausted simplicity of his last effort of praise, *Hymns for the Amusement of*

Children, who could hardly have found amusement, shall I say, in the twenty-fourth Hymn, *Melancholy*, in which he asks

> *How to begin, and how to depart,*
> *From this sad fav'rite theme,*
> *The man of sorrow in my heart,*
> *I at my own ideas start,*
> *As dread as Daniel's dream.*

Two years earlier he had written pathetically personal and unmannered songs in his second oratorio, *Abimelech* (1768), the one which begins

> *There is no rose to minds in grief;*
> *There is no lily for despair;*
> *Tears and distraction are relief,*
> *And yews and willows we must wear,*

and better still, the three stanzas which look back, once more, to his earliest life at Fairlawn:

> *Ah, memory, my cruel foe,*
> *How much you daily work for woe!*
> *The past upon the present hour,*
> *How I was miss'd you bring to view,*
> *And all my former scenes renew,*
> *My ev'ning walks, my fav'rite bow'r.*
>
> *The friendship I was wont to share,*
> *The flowers I nursed with so much care;*
> *My garden, grotto, and my bees,*
> *And, all those little griefs above,*
> *My mother's and my sister's love,*
> *And father's blessing on my knees.*
>
> *Yet taunter of the past delight,*
> *That urgest grief in such despight,*
> *Some soothing pow'rs to thee belong:*
> *Do not those soothing pow'rs refuse,*
> *But, as the mother of the Muse,*
> *Shape all my sorrows into song.*

He is to be seen a few times through the eye of the young sixteen-year-old and seventeen-year-old Fanny Burney. He comes to call on her father, his old friend the musician, Dr Burney. 'He is extremely grave', she says in 1768, 'and has still great wildness in his manner, looks, and voice.' He comes a year later in flowerless autumn: 'Poor Mr Smart presented me this morning with a rose, blooming and sweet as if we were in the month of June. "It was given me", said he "by a fair lady — though not so fair as *you*."' From his debtor's prison, to which he was committed in 1771, so fulfilling all of Thomas Gray's early prediction, he writes to Burney, asking him to help a prisoner worse off than himself, and saying that he had himself 'already assisted (him) according to my willing poverty'. It was in prison that he died, not long after his forty-ninth birthday, on 21 May 1771. Yet I would say that these last glimpses present Christopher Smart in the wrong character of pathos. His existence is in the hard immediate exultancy of his truest verse, above all in *A Song to David*, in which, in Coleridge's phrase, he is a bridler by delight, a purifier, contriving a firmness out of the chaotic.

SEVEN

Proselytizer of the World

PERHAPS it is a good thing for a poet of my generation to be brought face to face, however reluctantly, with Shelley in his letters,[1] which I propose to write of only in their relation to Shelley as a poet. After all he was a poet, not a very good one, but still a poet, before he was handed over to hagiography or biography. When John Stuart Mill read Shelley's *Ode to Liberty* to the parents of Bertrand Russell and was so overcome that he burst into tears and couldn't continue, Shelley had become established as the Great Poet, for the wrong reasons. He wrote of Liberty, to which he gave the emotional personifying capital letter he could always so easily find for an abstraction, from Life to Light: his daedal earth swam into ideological mists of one kind or another, which now that the idea of expressing ideas of the kind is less charged with emotion, pro or con, reveal themselves more obviously to be the mists of verbiage.

Verbiage rules nearly all the letters in the first of these two volumes; which is not so surprising, because the volume covers Shelley in England, Shelley in his adolescence and early twenties, a period in which few people, poets or otherwise, have discarded their packing of Scotch tape and brown paper and discovered the genuineness of the selves they are so vastly egotistic about, or recognized the claim others have upon them by their separate existence.

Shelley, though, was already obsessed by ideas, and not at all by the first tangible reality within reach of the sense which is the reality of words. The order was a wrong one, and he was never able to reverse it altogether. When he intruded himself, aged nineteen, into the life of Godwin and his daughters, he wrote to Godwin about his days at Oxford and his expulsion

---

[1] *The Letters of Percy Bysshe Shelley*, ed. F. L. Jones (Oxford University Press, 1964).

for atheism: 'I could not descend to common life. The sublime interest of poetry, lofty and exalted achievements, the proselytism of the world, the equalization of its inhabitants were to me' — and so they remained — 'the soul of my soul.' Even Godwin, prosiest of political philosophers, had to write to this precocious, ardent, evidently intelligent, but evidently secondhand-word-spinning boy that he exhibited a 'false taste in poetry', loving 'a perpetual sparkling and glittering, such as are to be found in Darwin, and Southey, and Scott and Campbell'.

In the first volume it is curious to note where an individual Shelley, where an apprehended reality, breaks through an equally false taste in letter writing. It is not, for example, when his friend Hogg tries to sleep with his sixteen-year-old wife — 'Time flies fast, time long has not fled since he beheld thee the passionate adorer of another.' No, it is when his soul-mate Elizabeth Hitchener (recipient of some of his most intolerably inflated com-munications or moralogues) comes, at his persuasion, to live with himself and Harriet at Lynmouth, and turns from 'partner of my thoughts' and 'thunder-riven pinnacle of rock firm amid the rushing tempest and the boiling surge'— into what?   A thin, tall, sallow, twenty-nine-year-old spinster, 'an artificial, superficial, ugly, hermaphroditical beast of a woman', in short, into the Brown Demon.

The truth comes out, in hard knobs of language, making him astonished at his former fatuity, inconsistency, and bad taste. 'What would Hell be, were such a woman in Heaven?'

Deserting Harriet, in that tribal society, experiencing a total genuineness of passion with Mary Godwin — 'I find that I have no personal interest in any human being but you, and you I love with my whole nature' — dented the pose. He was older, it was no good escaping for a while abroad, and walking with Mary and Claire Clairmont and a mule to Switzerland: he had to come back to London, face the excruciating difficulties, hide from creditors, meet Mary only briefly and in secret (they held hands in St Paul's). These things, in volume I, he manages almost in honest language.

With Harriet he play-acted. With Mary, redoubtable, beautiful, viva-ous, intelligent, and satisfying, he *lived* — at any rate, in between whiles. In volume II the letters are from Italy, he is sexually active and satisfied, with a consequent de-inhibition, a consequent opening of the senses (compare the effect upon D. H. Lawrence of Frieda and Italy and Lago di Garda, making him for a while into an honest writer). Verbal falsity drops away, it is possible to believe what he writes, possible to be amused by it, informed by it, enlightened by it, and moved by it.

The change is obvious in the descriptive letters, long celebrated, which he sent home to Peacock. Actual Italy, actual light and shape, and Italy as the wreck of time, broke into him, and out of him: he felt ilex leaves, and azure, and sun on his arms, and the quiet laocoons of the olive tree, he felt the Lago d'Agnano and the Caccia d'Astioni, 'clear lakes over the dead or sleeping fire' of extinguished volcanoes, he felt Rome. He felt a good deal outside himself, the new poetry, for example, of Keats, and the new cantos of *Childe Harold* and of *Don Juan*, and the difficulties of coping with Byron in his relations with Claire, Mary Shelley's step-sister, and with the forlorn child she had by him. He felt the death of his and Mary's own two children by dysentery.

If the change is obvious — up to a point — in his outflow of poems, it cannot be called exactly transforming in that area. The obstacles included a conviction. He continued, above all things, to want to proselytize the world. He kept a conviction he had expressed long ago to the Brown Demon, in a letter written to her in 1811, affirming that, in his opinion, 'all poetical beauty ought to be subordinated to the inculcated moral — that metaphorical language ought to be a pleasing vehicle for useful and momentous instruction'. From Italy, in 1819, he could still assure Peacock that he considered poetry 'very subordinate to moral and political science', and that if he were well, he would certainly 'aspire to the latter'. And three years later — after *Adonais*, *Hellas*, and the *Prometheus* were all written — he could declare that he wished he 'had something better to do than furnish this jingling food for the hunger of oblivion, called *verse*'.

No doubt he recognized the degree in which he maintained in himself the poetical poet. In England he had written 'a strange melange of mad-dened stuff . . . by the midnight moon', or spent 'most of the night pacing a church yard'. In Italy he had still chosen to read Dante in exactly the right place in the cathedral at Milan — 'one solitary spot . . . behind the altar where the light of day is dim and yellow under the storied window', and he had more recently written *Prometheus Unbound* — or some of it —

among the ruins of the Baths of Caracalla. In the flush of his Italian experience he was forced to a recognition about verse, realizing how this applied,
or failed to apply, to himself. Daylight and moonlight were resplendent,
forms were revealed, clarity abounded; and he had just seen the 'radiance
and magnificence' and the 'white freshness' of the tombs at Pompeii: 'I
now understood why the Greeks were such great Poets' — and why he
wasn't such a great Poet — 'and above all I can account, it seems to me,
for the harmony, the unity, the perfection, the uniform excellence of all the
works of art. They lived in a perpetual commerce with external nature and
nourished themselves upon the spirit of its forms.'

He was despondent about the unnourished style of his own poems,
pleased where it seemed to have something of the 'natural' in the broader
sense (as in the closing lines of the *Prometheus*, the Roman passages of
Adonais or the Drydenesque stanzas in *Hellas*), and I suppose abashed by
his easy descent to jingle —

> *Hum! hum! hum!*
> *From the lakes of the Alps, and the cold grey scalps*
> *Of the mountains, I come*

(admittedly what came was a gadfly) — and his easy sky-lirruping ascent
from the dim vast vale of tears above chill glaciers and clouds and rainbows
(how close it all is to paintings by his radical contemporary John Martin,
who could not paint a great toe, it was truly said, from the life) up and up
and up to the grand vapids where abstract Virtues float and Intellectual
Beauty shines.

A pleasing vehicle for useful and momentous instruction: if he could
have preferred and perfected the vehicle, it would have been momentous
verse (the painful statement of this failure is in the sixth stanza of the *Hymn
to Intellectual Beauty*) instead of verse involved, even during these last few
years before he was drowned, so much in the verbiage — or verbal ridicu-
lousness — which had marked the earlier correspondence.

One sees how the acceptance of ideas of equalization, freedom, universal
truth and love, democracy (if not republicanism), detestation of priestly
moralism and tyranny, and the fact that Shelley was no worm, came within
so few years of his death to elevate a meretricious style into a *ne plus ultra* of

poetic 'beauty' (an analogous process now elevates the frequently meretricious and not infrequently ridiculous writing of Lawrence, who was also
no worm). Though many of Shelley's lyrical poems, and some of his
longer pieces no doubt, retain their pedagogical extollers, I would suppose
that English and American poets have long ago lost the taste, no longer
feeling the need or temptation which assailed John Crowe Ransom years
ago to rhyme Percy Shelley with pale-lemon jelly (Ransom rhymed Keats
with blood of pickled beets, and one may have some sympathy for that as
well). More than thirty years ago W. H. Auden rejected Shelley's verse
for its lack of the object. 'Abstractions which are not the latest flowers of a
richly experienced and mature mind are empty and their expression devoid
of poetic value.' Only a few years ago, in 1962, Robert Graves was explaining to undergraduates that Shelley's *Skylark*, tempted as one may be to let
Shelley off, 'ranks among the shoddiest poems ever wished on us as the
product of genius'. He was explaining the obvious — yet how necessary
it is to go on explaining the obvious and to demonstrate the easily demonstr-
able! Anthologists cling to the *Skylark* (Read and Dobrée in their *London
Book of English Verse*, John Hayward in an Oxford verse book of 1964);
and Mr Edward Blunden — *Chambers's Encyclopædia* of 1955 — plumps for
'the exquisite technical accomplishment of *almost everything* he wrote in the
last four years of his life', but among living poets that fossilized and really
foolish view of Shelley's verse must surely be a minority one, or I would
hope so. If they look at the excellent edition of his letters, the reward — so
far as their calling goes — will be mostly a wry experience of self-deception,
and of the historical accidents and etiology of exaltation after death; not,
I am afraid, an enticement to return to the poems and read resolutely
beyond the few spurts and fragments of success.

EIGHT

On a Poem by Landor

I strove with none, for none was worth my strife:
Nature I loved, and, next to Nature, Art:
I warm'd both hands before the fire of Life;
It sinks; and I am ready to depart.

SOMETHING to the point about Walter Savage Landor and his poems may be discovered from the way we understand, or commonly mis-understand, that most famous of his epigrams, which he called the *Dying Speech of an Old Philosopher*; and which he composed on the evening of his seventy-fourth birthday, on 30 January 1849, at Bath, after dining with Charles Dickens and John Forster, who was to write his biography. Landor, we all know, was a hefty egotist with a loud laugh and a quick and at times violent temper; and we laugh ourselves when we recall that first line of his birthday poem, that curt autobiographical account of him-self, in which he looked back over life and accepted death: we think how singular that of all men Landor, Savage Landor, should say that he strove with none, when his existence seems to have been an intermittent strife from childhood, and school, and university, to his extreme old age in Bath and Florence.

But we are wrong, and Landor was right: Landor wrote his epigram not as the subject of a known biography, as he appears to us, but as a poet and as the prose-master of his *Imaginary Conversations*. In that role, though as a man he might be moiled in lawsuits and libel actions, and might end as a King Lear rejected by his children, this striving with no one, or no other writer, as writer himself, was irremovably at the heart of Landor's creed; and it was stated by him again and again. When his friend Southey died, for example, the distinction Landor accorded him, in a prose epitaph, was the distinction he accorded himself in the epigram: 'Rarely hath any author been so exempt from the maladies of emulation.'

To push, to scramble, to emulate, to compete, to lose independence and selfhood, that was the sin of authorship, the betrayal of talent. 'Authors are like cattle going to a fair', he makes a character say in one of the *Imaginary Conversations*, 'those of the same field can never move on without butting one another.' He butted no one, for precedence (to criticize others, to despise others in their role as authors, in their writings, is something else). He wrote neither for acclaim nor money; and he realized that for this and for other reasons his situation in literature was a lonely one, and might continue lonely or ambiguous after his death.

I admit that Landor's explanation of having striven with none — because no one had been worth his strife — may seem to contradict my interpretation: it suggests that he might have striven, had others been worth it. But I would suspect Landor of a certain irony in the line: a poor lot my literary coevals — if shoving had been thinkable, why should I have shoved in such a herd?

For once he might have been plainer in his compression. But free this poet was, not from pride, but from those maladies of emulation; and the contradictions in him are far less real than they seem. Everyone was for ever regretting them at all stages in his career. When he was old and still unpredictable — or all too predictable — in a vigour of conduct outside the norm, his friends, with a long memory, would say, yes, he has literary power, but why must he give way 'to such strange tempers and crochets and waywardness'?

Elderly Wordsworth, who was an acquaintance but not a friend, also spoke of him rather pompously, as 'a man so deplorably tormented by ungovernable passion', whose character, he had the additional gall to remark, 'may be given in two or three words: a madman, a badman, yet a man of genius, as many a madman is'. It is true the remarks were stung out of him by Landor's frequent, just, and witty ridicule of Wordsworth's tamer side —

ARCHDEACON HARE. Wordsworth is guiltless at least of affectation.
WALTER LANDOR. True; but he is often as tame as an abbess's cat, which in kittenhood has undergone the same operation as the Holy Father's choristers.

— since Landor was divided between admiration for the good in Wordsworth's poems and a contempt for the lapses. Watching Wordsworth's
gradual ossification (which it is now a fashion to deny), he made fun of
the lapses — particularly of the foolish and ridiculous *Thanksgiving Ode*
Wordsworth had written after Waterloo, in which he had informed God
that Carnage was God's daughter. But his dismay is impersonal: it is
always about a poet falling short of his power and betraying style. Wordsworth — and others too — would have done better to remark more in-
sistently that the genius of their madman was characterized by its extreme,
unromantic sanity.

Crochets, waywardness, and tempers, or ungovernable passion — these
go back to Landor's childhood in Warwick, where he was born in 1775,
the eldest son of a well-to-do, and as the years passed, still more well-to-do
physician. 'In my boyhood I was a fierce democrat and extolled the
French.' He indeed told his mother (a foolish woman, or a fussy one,
partly to blame for his unbalanced upbringing) that he hoped 'the French
would invade England and assist us in hanging George the Third between
two such thieves as the Archbishops of Canterbury and York'; in return
for which she boxed his ears. His headmaster at Rugby, who admired his
skill as a Latin versifier, found him too rebellious to keep in the school,
and insisted that he must either be removed by his father, or expelled. At
Oxford (where Southey knew of him as a 'mad Jacobin') he fired a gun
at the shuttered windows of a priggish undergraduate, and was sent down.
So it continued. He quarrelled with his father, he bungled his love affairs,
his inheritance, his estates, his marriage to a pretty, twittering, stupid, ill-
educated girl, who developed into a bitch with a nasty mouth. He was
driven into exile, as a young man by debt, as an old one by fear of damages
in a libel action brought against him by a clergyman's wife. In one part
of himself reckless, passionate, and ungovernable, in his creative part he
was the neo-classic champion of depth, bright surface, and composure.
The unifying clue to Landor is that the one supported the other: he was
the intemperate champion of temperance. Ultra-vigorous support of one
cluster of attitudes involved ultra-vigorous disdain of every opposite cluster,
in politics as in poetry. Born on the day — 30 January — on which, as he
well knew, Charles the First had been executed, rejoicing in Waterloo, yet

dreading 'from that moment the reaction under which the continent groans', he hated for life that 'conspiracy of kings, first against all republics, now openly against all constitutions', which had so much influenced him, Landor said, in writing — in the years after Waterloo — the first twenty-three of his *Imaginary Conversations*. The constitutional opposite of absolutism, oppression, and injustice was a state of things akin to Landor's own preferred style, in prose or in poetry, of composure, bright surface, and nourishing depth:

> *Poet! I like not mealy fruit; give me*
> *Freshness and crispness and solidity;*
> *Apples are none the better overripe,*
> *And prime buck-venison I prefer to tripe.*

Reverting to the *Dying Speech of an Old Philosopher*, every other statement Landor makes in the four lines is confirmed explicitly in his life and his writings. It is Landor's true biography, setting him both in and apart from his time, as our one eminent neo-classic. 'Nature I loved' — if he loved nature, that marked him as a man of his time, whether neo-classic or romantic (not that one would divorce neo-classic and romantic too absolutely), and one may recall Landor's delight — for a while — in the red sandstone valley of his Llanthony estates ('I have made a discovery, which is, that there are both nightingales and glowworms in my valley. I would give two or three thousand less for a place that was without them') or — for a while — in his villa garden on the slopes of Fiesole. Or one may point to many passages in which a modicum of nature finds natural language — 'Now yellowing hazels fringe the greener plain', or

> *Is it no dream that I am he*
> *Whom one awake all night*
> *Rose ere the earliest birds to see,*
> *And met by dawn's red light;*
>
> *Who, when the wintry lamps were spent,*
> *And all was drear and dark,*
> *Against the rugged pear-tree leant*
> *While ice crackt off the bark.*

'*Nature I loved, and, next to Nature, Art*': art, composure, moderation —
'What is there lovely in poetry,' asked Landor, through the mouth of
Boccaccio, in the *Pentameron* of 1837, 'unless there be moderation and com⁄
posure?   Are they not better than the hot, uncontrollable harlotry of a
flaunting dishevelled enthusiasm?   Whoever has the power of creating,
has likewise the inferior power of keeping his creation in order.   The best
poets are most impressive because their steps are regular; for without
regularity there is neither strength nor state.'

As for the last two lines of the epigram — that he warmed 'both hands
before the fire of Life', that the fire was sinking and that Landor was ready
to depart, they are a true summary of Landor's acceptance of life and
death; of the fact that he neither evaded, nor substituted, preferring, for
example, Wordsworth to Byron (Gerard Manley Hopkins percipiently
linked Wordsworth and Landor as members of a school, in which the
award for style went to Landor), nature and natural language to seraglio
and seraglio talk, or faeries and faery talk, or mists, or infinity; preferring
objectivity to autotoxication or autoblabbery, *here and now* to *somewhere else
and then* —

> *Some see but sunshine, others see but gloom,*
> *Others confound them strangely, furiously;*
> *Most have an eye for colour, few for form.*
> *Imperfect is the glory to* create,
> *Unless on our creation we can look*
> *And see that all is good; we then may rest.*

It could be argued, of course, that Landor's classicism was as much a
substitution or an ideal evasion of here and now as another writer's liking
for an ideal medievalism or an aery⁄faeryism derived from the worst in
Drayton or from *A Midsummer Night's Dream*, or border ballads; to which
Landor's reply was that his ideal classic ground — Greek rather than
Roman — and classic principles, demanded height, depth, severity, clarity,
and grace.   In long poems his power to construct, and tell, and hold, is
seldom sufficient, and his pressure does fall too low ; in his short poems
he sometimes goes soft, in the manner of other neo⁄classic poets, architects,
and sculptors (such as Flaxman or Thorwaldsen, whom Landor admired).
But Landor, like the Greek⁄style architects of his time, wanted, and

frequently achieved, what he considered a Greek stiffening of neo-classic sentimentality: the clear and determinate world of Greece was not the misty, indeterminate chaos of the Gothic. There were poets, Landor said, whose books in half a century would be enquired after only for 'cutting out an illuminated letter from the title-page' (Gothicizing poets) 'or of transplanting the willow at the end, that hangs so prettily over the tomb of Amaryllis' (neo-classically sentimental poets). 'If they wish to be healthy and vigorous, let them open their bosoms to the breezes of Sunium; for the air of Latium is heavy and overcharged.'

The Attic, temple-crowned, sun-clear promontory of Sunium was the ideal ground for Landor, as it had been for Hölderlin, Landor's elder by five years:

> Noch dünkt die Welt mir schön, und das Aug entflieht,
>> Verlangend nach den Reizen der Erde, mir
>>> Zum goldenen Paktol, zu Smyrnas
>>>> Ufer, zu Ilions Wald. Auch möcht ich
>
> Bei Sunium oft landen, den stummen Pfad,
>> Nach deinen Säulen fragen, Olympion!

> But yet the world delights me. Longing
>> For the charms of earth my eye escapes to Smyrna's
>>> Coast, to Ilion's wood, to golden
>>>> Pactalos. Repeatedly I'd land
>
> At Sunium too, and ask the tongueless path, Olympion,
>> For your colonnades!

Or, as Landor expressed it again in his poem on the Classick and the Romantick, in the grave, slow line of this poet reflecting, this poet consider- ing ultimates:

> The ancients see us under them, and grieve
> That we are parted by a rank morass,
> Wishing its flowers more delicate and fewer.
> Abstemious were the Greeks; they never strove
> To look so fierce: their Muses were sedate,
> Never obstreperous: you heard no breath
> Outside the flute; each sound ran clear within.

The Fauns might dance, might clap their hands, might shout,
Might revel and run riotous; the Nymphs
Furtively glanced, and fear'd, or seem'd to fear:
Descended on the lightest of light wings,
The graceful son of Maia mused apart,
Graceful, but strong; he listen'd; he drew nigh;
And now with his own lyre and now with voice
Temper'd the strain; Apollo calmly smiled.

When Landor writes — and ends a poem — ' Apollo calmly smiled', the three words are fact and metaphor; but fact all through. Listening to Hermes (the son of Maia) playing the instrument Hermes had invented, the god Apollo calmly smiled, the narrow-waisted, almond-eyed god whom we know in marble, and who is beauty, youth, composure, strength, civilization. The clear-edged congruence of word and object in Landor is one of his virtues, more acceptable, since language allows of less mannerism than stone and stucco, than the clear-edged 'Greek' architecture of Landor's time, Doric, Ionic, Corinthian, which we now value in the buildings of London and elsewhere. But it does not exhaust Landor's value as a poet to say that there is more of that clear congruence in his longer poems than we commonly admit, and to emphasize its creativity in his epigrams and shorter pieces. He is master especially of a calm line which often begins with short emphatic accented words, and then lightens; he makes poetry a matter of rhythm and language and objectivity, not of imagery and meta-physics; and he would certainly have rejected ambiguity as an evil. He is various, like his own large personality. He offers occasional perfection; he offers gravity, strength, delicacy, wit, comedy. He is lyrical, elegiacal, critical; but convinced also of pleasure —

The narrow mind is the discontented one.
There is pleasure in wisdom, there is wisdom in pleasure.
If thou findest no honey in thy cake,
Put thy cake into honey with thine own right-hand,
Nor think it defiled thereby.

He can make flickering fun, or knock down a bullock of stupidity. Criticism, perhaps with interference from the history of literature, has in-clined to make less than it should have done of poems which are counter, in so many ways, to the 'romantic' flow of poetry and the other arts during Landor's extremely long, always active career. In the past many critics and readers seemed unsure or sure in the wrong way of the voluminous work of a man at times so boisterous and in some ways so uninhibited, who sur- vived into a mealy age (when he died in 1864 he was in his ninetieth year). What was to be thought in such an age of a *poet* — better to think of the prose-writer of the *Conversations* — whose appetites and moral taste were suspect, who could write as he did about Ianthe's shell or red Priapus rearing his club among the junipers, who could deliver himself of an epigram so indecorous as

> *Exhausted now her sighs, and dry her tears,*
> *For twenty youths these more than twenty years,*
> *Anne, turning nun, swears God alone shall have her. . . .*
> *God ought to bow profoundly for the favour;*

who was able to contrive poems with as much ease in outmoded Latin as in English, taking behind that thin veil Catullan liberties — *O solite incesta pueros pervertere verpa* Landor began a poem on a Fellow of an Oxford college, which made even Byron wittily enquire how moral and sedate Southey could consort with the 'edifying Ithyphallics of Savagius'; and who was evidently less of a Christian than an elderly loud-mouthed pagan, from Fiesole, who might enjoy the pink and white flowers of the oleander beside a clear stream, or the small yellow-green flowers of the box, but had no very certain convictions of a future life?

In the present, criticism and reading have not caught up. 'Poetry was always my amusement, prose my study and business': Must we take Landor's word for it, continue to insist that the poems are mostly oc- casional — (however: 'Regarding the occasional in poetry; is there less merit in taking and treating what is before us, than in seeking and wandering through an open field as we would for mushrooms?') — and use Landor's prose as an excuse for neglecting the poet (and the verse perhaps as an excuse for neglecting the prose)? At any rate, a glance at the third and supplementary volume of the *Cambridge Bibliography of English Literature* (which places Landor unfortunately among the essayists, and not the poets) shows that no English writer — no English poet — of equal size and quality has been less attended to in the last fifty years; which is a loss.

I stand out a rude rock in the middle of a river, with no exotic or
parasitical plant on it, and few others.   Eddies and dimples and froth
and bubbles pass rapidly by, without shaking me.   Here indeed is
little room for pic-nic and polka.

Not a bad account of himself, as a poet; though Walter Landor — we
might well drop the Savage, which fits only his *alter ego* — was less a rock,
and rough, than a finely shaped structure, graceful, but strong, like his
Hermès in the poem, who invented the lyre and was the son of Zeus as
well as of Maia.   Landor himself had some of the attributes of the herm,
he was more of a whole and healthy poet than many of his time; in justified
pride he thought of himself in a high eagle's sunshine, as in his poem which
begins

> *Ye who have toil'd uphill to reach the haunt*
> *Of other men who lived in other days*

and which ends (after he has established that they found nothing but owls
hooting and shaking the ivy berries on their heads, and vipers hissing at
them, as they crawled down)

> *Now, was it worth your while to mount so high*
> *Merely to say ye did it, and to ask*
> *If those about ye ever did the like?*
> *Believe me, O my friends, 'twere better far*
> *To stretch your limbs along the level sand*
> *As they do, where small children scoop the drift,*
> *Thinking it must be gold, where curlews soar*
> *And scales drop glistening from the prey above.*

NINE

John Clare

I

OHN CLARE was born at Helpston, a village in Northamptonshire, on
13 July 1793. Little enough is known of his family. He was a twin,
his twin sister dying not long after birth. He had two other sisters younger
than himself, one also dying as an infant, the other growing up with him
at Helpston. But she was not born until Clare himself was five, so that in
effect he was an only child, 'coddled up', as he said, tenderly and long.
There seems to have been nothing unusual about the mentality or mental
balance of his father, who worked in the fields and was barely literate, or
of his mother, who could neither read nor write. But there seems to have
been some instability within the family. Dr Fenwick Skrimshire, who
must have known or could easily have discovered the circumstances, put
down 'hereditary' on the form for Clare's admission to the Northampton
General Lunatic Asylum, against the question of the 'supposed causes of
insanity'. His father was the illegitimate child of a Scottish schoolmaster,
whom Clare referred to as 'worthless' and a 'run⁄a⁄gate'. But neither the
schoolmaster nor the girl ('her love was not that frenzy which shortens
the days of the victim of seduction') were unbalanced. Clare's grandmother
lived on at Helpston until she was eighty⁄six. If there was madness in the
family it may have been on his mother's side.

The poet was born a weakly infant — 'so much so that my mother told
me she never could have dreamt I should live to make a man' — and he
remained a weakly child. It was only as a man, and only when he lived
within the detested security either of the asylum in Essex or the asylum at
Northampton that Clare became robust. His delicate poise and unusual
sensibility as a child meant that he was open equally to sensations of delight
and sensations of horror. Unlike Charles Lamb, it is doubtful if at any

time of his life Clare had reason to be mortified by the poverty of his dreams. Later experiences in London, and at home, were prefaced by many terrors in his childhood, by his hatred, for example, of journeys in the dark, past haunted spots between Helpston and the next village. On these journeys he rhymed away to himself and so tried to erase the ghosts and hobgoblins 'and not bring them to remembrance; tho' 'twas impossible. For as I pass'd those awful places, tho' I dare not look boldly up, my eye was warily on the watch, glegging under my hat at every stir of a leaf or murmur of the wind, and a quaking thistle was able to make me swoon with terror.' He was equally in dread of taking animals to graze on the heath in the early evening where invisible badgers and foxes would squeal at him out of the gloom; and he was terrified, lastingly, from having seen a man break his neck by falling from a load of hay: 'The ghastly paleness of death struck such a terror on me that I could not forget it for years, and my dreams was constantly wanderings in churchyards, digging graves, seeing spirits in charnel houses, etc., etc.'

The face of death he believed to be responsible for the fainting fits which came over him. He was cured of them; but he wrote later that every spring and autumn since the accident his fears were 'agitated to an extreme degree', and the dread of death involved him 'in a stupor of chilling indisposition as usual'. Here he was describing what certainly foreran his later troubles and his eventual psychosis. But in childhood the delights of sensation outweighed the horrors. Again and again, in poems and in prose, he celebrated the exultations and delight of a childhood spent idling or working among the fields. In his adolescence, after gardening for a time, he found that 'the continued sameness of a garden cloyed' him and he went back to the fields 'where I could look on the wild heath, the wide spreading variety of cultured and fallow fields, green meadows, and crooling brooks, and the dark woods waving to the murmuring winds. There were my delights, and here I could mutter to myself as usual, unheard and unnoticed by the sneering clown, and conceited coxcomb.' Small, not over strong, and suffering intermittently in his 'gloomy village . . . on the brink of the Lincolnshire fens' from malaria, he was an unusual creature, this boy who was now venturing to commit his 'musings readily to paper'. His look was unusual. His eyes were of a light blue, his hair (as one can tell from a lock of it curled up among the Clare manuscripts at Peterborough) was a remarkably light blond, the colour of pale straw. His feet and hands were delicate. His forehead, as one of the asylum doctors was to describe it long after, possessed 'great breadth and altitude . . . such as we are in the habit of associating with men of the highest order of intellect'.

II

His personality, no less than the circumstances of extreme poverty in which he grew up at Helpston, dictated the happiness and the tragedy of his life. His poems, when he first endeavoured to get them published in the country, were sent by a bookseller to London and accepted by the publisher who was also looking after the work of another poet of the era, John Keats. Clare's first volume stirred polite interest into a patronizing enthusiasm. Clare was a new wonder, a new bird in the curious aviary of peasant poets. He came to London. He was made much of. He met the writers of the day, Coleridge, De Quincey, Charles Lamb, George Darley (though he had the misfortune to miss Keats, who took pleasure in his verse). He was helped, but not with enough tact, or energy, or generosity. His second, third, and fourth books failed. Getting a young girl with child, he hurried into a marriage which was unwise, though not altogether unhappy. His celebrity faded, his London friends died or grew indifferent, and he sank again into the gloom and poverty of Northamptonshire, struggling to be a writer and struggling to keep a family which grew longer and longer. He constructed an ideal of loveliness and love and understanding out of the recollections of the girl Mary Joyce, whom he had known as a boy; and when his health of mind broke down at last his publisher procured a place for him in a private asylum in Epping Forest. He escaped, in search of Mary Joyce, whom he had now married in his delusion (though she had been dead for some years). He was at home for a while, feeling nevertheless 'homeless at home', and was then admitted into the General Lunatic Asylum at Northampton, at the age of forty-eight. Dr Fenwick Skrimshire, who filled in the admission form, came to the question of whether his illness had been 'preceded by any severe or long continued mental emotion or exertion?' and wrote in the celebrated words, 'After years addicted to poetical prosing'.

F

It was in the earlier years of his 'captivity among the Babylonians', as he called his detention — a kindly detention in which he was free to do much wandering — that Clare's previous life and delight welled and sparkled into some of his best poems, and that he also achieved, in a few lyrics of a perfected simplicity of style, his heights both of exultancy and tranquillity. He often identified himself in the asylum (the growth of these identifications can be traced back for twenty years in his prose, his poems, and his experiences) with champions of one kind and another who had faced the indifference or contempt of the world. He was absorbed still in his idealization of Mary Joyce, believing in her presence, and yet aware of her absence. She was the subject of many of his poems still, but never (so far as the evidence goes) of his conversation. She inhabited the centre of what remained to him of the privacy of his inner life; though he went beyond her at last into acceptance and victory. With sixty years behind him his mind broke up more quickly and completely; and after twenty-two years in the asylum he died there on 20 May 1864, aged seventy.

III

Clare tended always to be alone, though he was not without particular friends and a constant yearning to be loved. He was given from childhood to aloof wanderings, to his practice of learning nature by heart, in a district to which at first no enclosure act had been destructively and tidily applied. He began as a peasant among peasantry, who were poor and soon to be poorer still, but who enjoyed more than a remnant of a folk culture of songs and tales and beliefs. Both his father and mother sang to him. His father was 'fond of Ballads, and I have heard him make a boast of it over his horn of ale . . . that he could sing or recite above a hundred; he had a tolerable good voice'. Clare learnt songs from an old cow-keeping woman on the common at Helpston, and he 'went weeding wheat in the spring with old women listening to their songs and stories'. He came to collect songs from a shoemaker, a ploughman, his father, and especially 'from my mother's singing'. Acquiring some skill with a violin, and some knowledge of musical notation, he was also able to record the tunes; and since one of his early books was a copy of Percy's *Reliques of Ancient Poetry*, he must have been encouraged to believe that the songs had value as poetry.

Whatever else helped to shape his writing, it was first indebted to folk-songs; to poems, that is, emerging from an innocent and melodic sensibility akin to his own. But it was some time before he worked himself out of the pastoral patterns and modes of the eighteenth century and worked himself back, aided by Wordsworth and Elizabethan and Jacobean lyrics especially, to lyrical simplicities. When he was thirteen, he met with Thomson's *Spring*. 'I can't say the reason, but the following lines made my heart twitter with joy:

> *Come gentle Spring, ethereal mildness come,*
> *And from the bosom of yon dropping cloud,*
> *While music wakes around, veil'd in a shower*
> *Of shadowing roses, on our plains descend.'*

Clare evidently felt that the discovery of his first poet (before long he bought *The Seasons* complete) mattered more to him than the later discovery of any other poet. Thomson dignified experiences, dignified delights thoroughly familiar to Clare, sunrises, sunsets, rainbows, dew, glitter, the finer than Arabian perfume of bean fields, as well as storms and blackness. Into several of the asylum poems of his older years he worked unconscious memories of *Spring* and *Winter*. He found Thomson at the period of those rhymes he had made to erase the terror of his dark journeyings between the villages of Helpston and Maxey. Soon after he came to read Pope and Robert Bloomfield's *Wild Flowers*, and had some acquaintance with the poems of David Mallet and John Cunningham, and he began to write himself in the short three-stressed and four-stressed lines common to many of the eighteenth-century pastoralists. But it was *The Seasons*, beyond doubt, which moved him deeply; and also, though a little later, *Paradise Lost*, which two were 'the only books of poetry that I have regularly read through'. *Paradise Lost* acted on him much as its harmonious condensation of landscape and moonlight came to reveal consciously to a later Romantic adolescent, Samuel Palmer, the shape and tone of the delights which were natural to him. Clare also wrote of the keenness of his early pleasure in *Pilgrim's Progress*, in the prophetical parts of the Bible, in 'the fine Hebrew Poem of Job', in the prayers of the Prayer Book, and in the Psalms, He learnt the third chapter of Job by heart. Later in mental distress, before and in his

two asylums, he would go back to Job, the Psalms, and the Book of Revela-
tions, and consolingly turn them into verse.

   If one were to draw up a syllabus and a recipe for the making of a poet
at this time, Clare's early life would supply them: a freedom akin to Wordsworth's in the country; a knowledge of folk-song and ballad and of the
elegant pastoral poets, strengthened with a knowledge of those Golcondas
of romanticism, *Paradise Lost, Pilgrim's Progress*, and *The Seasons*; a knowledge of the Bible with a leaning towards its deeper and darker portions; and
added to them all the delicate sensibility which toppled into psychosis.
Lack of a formal education was less of a drawback than the lack of the
country, Milton, Thomson, and folk-song would have been.   Clare learnt
to read and write, but gained little else from his schooling, which was diluted
by hard work alongside his father.   He went out threshing, for example,
taking a light flail which was made specially for him.   He drew geometrical
figures and letters in the dust on the sides of the barn.   There were times when
he 'could muster three farthings for a sheet of writing paper', and when in
learning to read he 'devour'd for these purposes every morsel of brown or
blue paper' in which his mother brought back the tea and sugar.   His
education never gave his mind, it is true, enough exercise and skill; his mind
lacked the breadth of co-ordinating knowledge, just as it lacked such stimulus,
later on (since Clare was twenty-seven when his first book was published and
he began to meet other poets), as Wordsworth had derived from Coleridge,
from his sister, his brothers, and his other undergraduate friends. Isolation interfered with him intellectually, retarded and weakened the develop-
ment of his ideas, and made his eventual madness more certain; but it
also meant his sensibility — his vision and his ability to *hear* — were less
contaminated.   It is curious to contrast Clare with Crabbe.   Crabbe was
rather more fortunate in his emancipation from poverty.   It had not been a
peasant's poverty, leading towards parish help and the workhouse.   His
father had had some education.   He had read 'the graver classics' to his
children, and had seen to Crabbe's education.   Like Clare, Crabbe did
not reach London until he was well on in the twenties; but before he met
Burke, Reynolds, and Johnson, he had moved in a wider and more stimulating variety of experience and acquaintance than Clare ever knew between
the fields, the garden, the threshing-floor, and the limekiln; and he had

contrived to get his *Inebriety* printed and published. By contrast, Clare at Helpston, in his parents' small cottage, in the gloom of the fens, was a wingless insect knowing only two inches around himself in a vast desert. He was a yokel, a whopstraw, when he took the coach to London in 1819, not a medical student with something of a classical education who would soon, and reasonably, be directed into Holy Orders and become a ducal chaplain. The nearest his patrons came to conferring a new livelihood upon Clare was his publisher's offer to educate him as a teacher in a National School. He added, knowing Clare's liking for women and for drink, that teaching would demand 'the strictest moral conduct'. The scheme was abandoned. Always, when he could write at all, Clare was able to summon up the existence of a childhood of delight in poems which are either joyful or regrets for joy. Crabbe calls up, on the whole, an autumnal gloom of childhood, contrasts the things which delighted him with the gloom by which the delights were impaired, and was incapable of writing

> *The flowers join lips below, the leaves above;*
> *And every sound that meets the air is Love,*

as Clare, even in his most melancholic depressions, was incapable of conceiving a poem in Crabbe's mournful, stern and downward sloping rhythms. Crabbe's attitude is one of having always been in chains and making by a moral effort, by a masterful effort, the best of their chafing and drag; Clare's is one of celebrating freedom in the chains put upon him by life. One is the attitude of grim realism, lit by sparkles of pure apprehension, sparkles of a scarcely attained delight, the other the attitude of lyricism. A different Crabbe may be visible here and there in these sparkles, but though he matured, he had to fight against an ugly childhood and a mainly sombre personality. Clare's childhood made him, despite his miseries and his madness, almost automatically resilient. And he matured rather more than it has been the custom to allow.

IV

All of Clare's childhood was spent at Helpston. John Taylor, the publisher he shared with Keats, who had sent him up like a rocket from his Northamptonshire obscurity, paid him a visit in 1821. He was surprised by the

contrast between the scenery of Helpston in fact and the vision of the scene
in Clare's poetry. 'A flatter country than the immediate neighbourhood
can scarcely be imagined.' He had just published Clare's second book,
The Village Minstrel, which contained a poem 'The Last of March —
written at Lolham Briggs':

> *Here 'neath the shelving bank's retreat*
>   *The horse-blob swells its golden ball;*
> *Nor fear the lady-smocks to meet*
>   *The snows that round their blossoms fall:*
> *Here by the arch's ancient wall*
> *The antique elder buds anew;*
>   *Again the bulrush sprouting tall*
> *The water wrinkles, rippling through . . .*

Taylor remembered the poem and looked in astonishment at Clare when
the two of them had reached the scene, for 'with your own eyes you see
nothing but a dull line of ponds, or rather one continued marsh, over which
a succession of arches carries the narrow highway: look again, into the poem
in your mind, and the wand of a necromancer seems to have been employed
in conjuring up a host of beautiful accompaniments, making the whole
waste populous with life and shedding all round the rich lustre of a grand
and appropriate sentiment'. In fact, Clare had projected his own sense oι
happiness and love into an unremarkable landscape. Wordsworth and
Coleridge searched for landscape imagery appropriate to their thought, in
Dorset, North Devon, the Quantocks, Wales, and the Lakes. Clare with
his restriction of thought had neither such need nor such opportunities.
There was ample reciprocity — as far as he dealt with landscape and not
nature in details — between himself and the only landscape he knew,
enough in fact for his life as a poet. No one will find it very rewarding to
visit 'John Clare's Country' instead of visiting and revisiting John Clare's
poetry. Here, in a scene mediocre in itself, he accomplished that business
of learning nature by heart, as a child and as a young labourer. Indeed the
bulk of his poems (including many too highly praised in the spirit which
informed much of the appreciation of poetry in England forty years ago)
recite that learning in all its minutiae. No one, so great is the quantity of
his manuscripts, will ever — or should ever ? — publish a complete edition

of Clare. He versified rather than put down in prose what might have filled the notebooks of another poet. Much of it is poetry humdrum and flat, though lit at intervals with precise and pure observation. Observation and description are not poetry, or at least cannot be poetry of the higher order; and no 'nature poet', if such an oddity has ever appeared, can have been more than one of the lesser poets. But we have so long confused nature with art that we speak of Clare and even of Wordsworth as 'nature poets'. All appreciation of Clare, so far, has attended too much to Clare in this sense, to Clare's innocence of perception, that 'faculty of sheer vision', which the acutest of his critics, Middleton Murry, found not only 'far purer than Wordsworth's', but even purer than Shakespeare's. Clare's vision intensi﹑ fies the selected reality of most things it describes:

> *From dark green dumps among the dripping grain*
> *The lark with sudden impulse starts and sings*
> *And mid the smoking rain*
> *Quivers her russet wings.*

The comparison of such vision with Wordsworth's or Shakespeare's may be completely just. But Murry quickly explained that Clare's vision was 'too perfect', that Shakespeare (thinking of Shakespeare and Clare, one should think of Ophelia's songs) had as much vision 'as a man can have if he is to develop into a full maturity'. And then Murry quoted Words﹑ worth on good poetry as 'the spontaneous overflow of powerful feelings', with Wordsworth's rider that 'poems to which any value can be attached were never produced on any variety of subjects but by a man who, being possessed of more than usual organic sensibility, had also thought long and deeply'. The answer to Clare was that he had not thought long and deeply. The difference between Clare and Wordsworth was that Wordsworth could think, while Clare could not. The one produced harmony, the other melody.

Elsewhere Middleton Murry argued that an object would evoke Clare's feelings, and that the feelings could only be passed on by describing the object, which is certainly true of many of Clare's poems, as it would be true of some of the sketches by his exact contemporary, John Constable. But the claims of the limitation of Clare's thought and the restriction of his

poems to the transmission of innocent feeling and of his perpetual childish‚
ness, in a good sense, his perpetual immaturity, are too absolute; and so are
the parallel claims that Clare learnt nothing of aesthetic economy and form.
Clare thought more at length and more deeply than has been allowed. As
Constable thought of painting as an art by which he was able to pass on
his feeling, so Clare, it is true, held that poetry was another name for feeling.
He tells us so again and again. His 'feelings grew into song'. His own
poetry grew from learning and loving the material of nature, from vision,
into meditated vision. From feeling, he came to meditate upon feeling, upon
himself and so upon man; and at last he reached out into a poetry of ideas.
Keats admired Clare's poetry, so far as he knew it, and rightly observed that
the 'description too much prevailed over the sentiment' (Clare had his say
in return about Keats, that he was 'a child of nature warm and wild', but
that *Endymion* was too stuffed with Dryads, Fauns, and Satyrs, that as a
Cockney 'he often described Nature as she had appeared to his fancies, and
not as he would have described her had he witnessed the things he described').
Yet when Keats read him, Clare had scarcely moved from description to idea
and he was incapable of writing with such metaphysical intimations as came
into his work between 1830 and 1844; he was incapable of such lines as

> *When dead and living shall be void and null*
> *And nature's pillow be at last a human skull.*

An increasing series of deprivations threatened Clare's mind, indeed un‚
balanced him from the delicate thread of his life, but increased his self‚
knowledge and made him look more and more for meanings in that nature
in which, like Hölderlin and so many artists of his spiritual type, he found
a consolation he was unable to discover, after the happiness of childhood,
in the society of men. In the end, Clare's deeper perceptions had to race
against his psychosis. With ups and downs the psychosis gained upon him.
But before his mind lost its power completely, his ideas of nature, love,
creative joy, freedom, and eternity had developed and had informed that
small number of poems which raise him so far above the mere 'naturalist'
of his common reputation. Moreover, with this development there came,
as chaotic notions cleared into certain ideas, an increased rhythmical subtlety
combined with an economy of form.

V

The experiences were his own, but the clue for ordering them and harmoniz-
ing them he found in Wordsworth mainly, and in Coleridge. He had much
to find a meaning for. His poetic life, after childhood, is a history of his
deprivations. He is deprived of the happiness of childhood; he is deprived,
by enclosure, of the actual scenery and objects of that happiness, and so of
the freedom of the commons. He is deprived of love and freedom by a
marriage which on the whole he did not desire, and against which he
developed the fantasy of his ideal wife, Mary Joyce. He emerges from the
penury, the thick obscurity, and hopelessness of his life as a labouring whopstraw, into the success and the hope which attended the publication of his
first book in 1820. He comes to know poets and patrons and friends; to
be deprived of them, and the hope and the success, bit by bit, as his later books
successively failed, and as mental illness was increased by the waxing of
his difficulties. Deprived of the scenery of happiness by the enclosures
around Helpston, he was, by his removal across the stream to the village
of Northborough in 1832, deprived of Helpston itself. When the keeper
arrived at Northborough in 1836 and took him to the asylum in Epping
Forest, he was deprived of his home, his family and his freedom. He regained his freedom by escape; but regained it, for what the freedom was
worth in a cold world, only to discover that his 'poetic fancy', Mary Joyce,
was indeed a fancy. She had been dead for three years.

The asylum reached out for him again. The keepers arrived, and Clare
entered the alien world at Northampton, in which he was to die after a
final deprivation of some twenty-two years.

His ideas, out of the interaction of suffering and delight, of life, love, freedom, creative joy, and eternity, ripened on the withering tree of his mind
round about 1844, at Northampton. But they had begun to shape themselves in 1824 after he had visited London for treatment in his distress of
mind and body. Happiness in nature Clare had discovered to be unreliable.
He had wanted love and he had wanted hope, and he began feeling 'a
relish for eternity'. On the one side he endured dismal dreams of hell and
read *Macbeth* for about the twentieth time, and was anguished by thinking

of the 'dark porch of eternity whence none returns to tell the tale of his reception'. On the other, eternity obsessed him as desirable and as the attainment of victory over the world. 'Mind alone', he put down, 'is the sun of the earth — it lives on when the clouds and paraphernalia of pretentions are forgotten', a thought which ripened into that poem of climax, *A Vision*, in which in the asylum in 1844 Clare wrote himself into immortality and freedom, and release from woman and the lost mortal joys, with the appropriate pen, an eternal ray taken from the sun. Indeed if there is one image around which his poetry circled and grew, from the beginning to the end, it is the image of the blinking, coppery immensity of the sun burning through the clouds of confusion or shining through the trees above the flats of the world, or rising above the white frost of the winter fens.

He had known the poems of Wordsworth and Coleridge for a good many years, since 1820 at the least, and he found in them, no doubt in *Resolution and Independence*, and certainly in Coleridge's *Pains of Sleep*, the last two lines of which remained long in his mind, evidence of situations like his own. He may have read Wordsworth to begin with for his vision of nature, impatient at first with what he held to be Wordsworth's affectation of simplicity, and with their depths. He recorded in his diary of the *White Roe of Rylstone* that it contained 'some of the sweetest poetry' he had ever met with though it was 'full of his mysteries'. The mysteries gained on him. The notion of creative joy took hold of him, as he puzzled over Coleridge's *Dejection*, and over the *Intimations* ode. Moved by these two poems as well as by *Tintern Abbey*, he wrote, not long after, that curious extract of Wordsworth, Coleridge and Clare called *Pastoral Poesy*, to celebrate 'the dower of self-creating joy'. Many more of his poems on love, immortality, and the immortality of nature, and hope are obviously affined to the 'mysteries' of Wordsworth and Coleridge.

> *To be beloved is all I need*
> *And whom I love, I love indeed —*

Coleridge's two lines were, so to say, answered by Clare, if there was no one else to love and be loved in that fullness, through the creation of the ideal of Mary Joyce. Twice, with a length of time in between, he worked the lines into poems calling on Mary.

If Wordsworth and Coleridge helped him to meaning, relation, and harmony, it was help received and not plagiarism committed. In many ways the cases of all three poets (and the case of John Constable) were much alike. All three and Constable were contemporaries caught up in the exaltations and the preordination of their peculiar time, only Clare, however much his limits closed him in, was blessed with that resilience by which he never lost the shaping power of his imagination. In *The Progress of Rhyme* in the twenties, Clare defined poetry as hope, love, and joy. He wrote later of tramps who 'dally with the wind and laugh at hell'. He was another such tramp on the long roads, but one driven down them by thoughts desperately acquired; and when he came to *A Vision* in August 1844, for a while at least he was the victor and not the victim. Love and joy, of earth and even of heaven, had been found out by him, or had left him. Hope he had surpassed, and he proclaimed his penetration to eternity:

> I lost the love of heaven above,
>   I spurned the lust of earth below,
> I felt the sweets of fancied love,
>   And hell itself my only foe.
>
> I lost earth's joys, but felt the glow
>   Of heaven's flame abound in me,
> Till loveliness and I did grow
>   The bard of immortality.
>
> I loved but woman fell away,
>   I hid me from her faded fame,
> I snatch'd the sun's eternal ray
>   And wrote till earth was but a name.
>
> In every language upon earth,
>   On every shore, o'er every sea,
> I gave my name immortal birth
>   And kept my spirit with the free.

However much Blake might have visited upon Clare that reproof of allowing the natural man to rise up against the spiritual man which he applied to Wordsworth, he would have applauded *A Vision* as repentance, as an 'immortal moment' reached for and attained.

VI

Sensibility is the denominator, in literature, in painting, in music, of the period in which Clare lived, a sensibility directed towards nature, from which, Schiller maintained, civilized men were already feeling divorced. 'Nature is for us nothing but existence in all its freedom', and therefore sensibility was directed with emphasis and exaggeration towards nature, so that all but the most intellectually endowed artists plunged into nature, floated for a while in nature, and tended to drown themselves in nature. The personality of artists such as Clare drive them anyway to this refuge; and the individual drive was made more compelling by the general situation of men. Civilized men were in, so to say, a divided and deranged phase of being, from which we as their successors have not yet emerged and which seems to have brought us now to an advanced stage alternating between melancholy and violence. The marvel is that Clare developed so far, and acquired such insight into the sweet and bitter harvest of his senses. The sad thing, perhaps, is that the harvest was, so much of it, left as sensation and nothing else. A superabundance of sensation, that pouring into loose poems of the notebook material of poems, becomes unbearable, just as it would be hard to bear with an endless journal of Dorothy Wordsworth. When Clare could publish no more, when he was both exiled and safe-guarded in the protective arrest of the asylum, his genuine compulsion to write, to spill himself out into poems, was not at first weakened or destroyed. 'I became', he said, 'an author by accident', which is the proper beginning. 'I wrote because it pleased me in sorrow, and when happy, it makes me happier.' The making of poems was part of him, like laughing, feeling sad or feeling elated, like waking or sleeping, Indeed it was most of him. And this is worth saying, obvious as it may be, because so much poetry is always so diseased by being, not a willed product, but a willed product out-side the nature of the poet.

If there is too little of will, too much of flow about Clare's writing, will can only be applied to refine what is given, and to create the circumstances by which more is given. Clare did labour, nevertheless, upon what he received, only the flow from him was enormously incessant through his life like the flow of a river breaking up through flowers out of limestone. It might have defied the labour of a poet far better equipped by the formalities of education. But he was rather more than the lyric poet writing in answer to an intermittency of impulse.

There are 'classic' poets who contrive something at least of shape either because they avoid, or because they are not forced by the exigency of their nature very far into, the bubbling of life. And there are classics forced into that bubbling and greater in themselves than the confusion, which they are able to subdue. Such a romantic as Clare is stationed between them. He goes further than the one class and as far as the other, but his power to cut and shape what is solid out of what is chaotic is certainly limited and was reached expensively and late; yet he makes and endures the right exploration. One may remember T. S. Eliot's remark, the more forcible as it came from a romantic who attempted to become classic by self-mutilation, that the business of romantic is to prepare for the classic. And beyond the delight that comes of reading Clare selectively, even so romantic and fluent a writer has something to teach. Not only is he an exemplar of the pure life of the artist, a purity founded upon an unevasive appetite, but he is a poet who employs a language unsoiled in his strongest work, which he is able to shape into the most emotive of melodic rhythms. He was unique. His uniqueness and stature cannot be diminished by talk of his origins or his shortcomings, or by talk of the peculiarity of the romantic decadence in human affairs. There is a universal element even in the extreme romantic posture. The relationship between man and nature varies, but since man is conscious, it can never be an equilibrium. Clare is a poet who became homeless at home, naturally and tragically conscious of exclusion. Wriggle as we may, that, many times worse, is still our own position. Clare's asylum foretells our need for an asylum, his deprivations foretell our deprivation. Our modern selves have to eat (if we admit to any) our own sins, Clare, as he exclaimed in *I Am*, was the self-consumer of his woes. We could be pardoned, then, for seeing our own case in Clare's. Yet not quite our case, for in Clare there was no failure of nerve, no concealment of such failure under the rhetoric of a false heroism.

What then we have in Clare is a poet in defeat entirely undefeated.

TEN

Clare in Madness

I

LITTLE by little in this century John Clare has been emerging from the bewildering muddle of his papers which are stored in the two Midland towns nearest his home respectively and his asylum. And little by little we begin to discover Clare's nature as a poet. It was not only in-complete knowledge which interfered: our appreciation of his poems, our realization of his stature have always been hindered by a lurking snobbery. Clare was a farm labourer's child, he was 'the Northamptonshire Peasant Poet' (as Hogg was the Ettrick Shepherd). If he had a noble forehead and a blue eye, he walked with a farm labourer's gait. His spelling, his punctua-tion, his grammar were uncertain. He would use singular verbs and plural subjects. Yet we must realize that Clare educated himself remarkably in the usages and traditions of English poetry; and we begin — still only begin — to see in him, at last, one of the most natural, pure, and authentic of English poets with an impulse to lyricism which recurred through life, into madness and into old age. The quality of his work in relation to its bulk raises him altogether above the minor poets of his time whose work we know so much better, above his friend Darley, above the overrated Beddoes and the under-rated Hood; raises him altogether above patronage, and the condescension of those who can spell and insert semi-colons. However handicapped, Clare was keen in intellect as in observation. His occasional criticism of other writers, living and dead, was independent; and shows that he had a certainty of his own power, a confidence in his own discernment. Though not free of it, he was less inclined than his fellows to that poetry of too simple simpli-city, or drawing-room elves and fays and diminutives. He had learned nature too accurately for such middle-class filagree, and so had in him the basis on which alone poetry can rise into exultation. By the time of his middle-aged isolation in the Northampton Asylum he had completed the discovery of his true feeling, he had pushed his exploration to its horizon metaphysically, to that edge beyond which he saw only the eternal.

One should not imagine either that Clare was an even poet, or that his eventual madness was only a delusion of those sane men who put him away or looked after him. The balance between himself and the other world was delicately held years before he became certifiable. On the application form for his admission to the asylum at Northampton it was stated to be fourteen years since symptoms of insanity were first detected. This would mean 1827, when Clare was thirty-four. It was one of his bad times after the failure of his third book, *The Shepherd's Calendar*; but earlier still, in 1819, Edward Drury, the country bookseller who introduced Clare to London and to his fame, wrote to Clare's publisher, 'It is greatly to be feared that the man will be inflicted with insanity if his talent continues to be forced as it has been these four months past; he has no other mode of easing the fever that oppresses him after a tremendous fit of rhyming except by getting tipsy. A single pint of ale very often does this . . . He has rhymed and written for three days and three nights, without hardly eating or sleeping.'

In the winter of 1821, or early in 1822, Clare, in the anxiety and disappointment of his struggles, exhausted himself in composing *The Dream*. He wrote after it 'I musn't do no more terrible things yet they stir me up to such a pitch that leaves a disrelish for my old accustomed wanderings after nature'; and he called his Muse a 'fickle Hussey' who 'sometimes stilts me up to madness and then leaves me as a beggar by the wayside with no more life than what's mortal and that nearly extinguished by melancholy forebodings'. A few weeks later he complained of a 'confounded lethargy of low spirit that presses on me to such a degree that at times makes me feel as if my senses had a mind to leave me. Spring and Fall such feelings it seems are doomed to be my companions, but it shall not overpower me as formerly with such weak and terrible dread and fears of dropping off.' As the years pass, there is plenty of evidence, published and unpublished, of the wave and trough of Clare's mental distress.

There were many causes, or rather aggravations — the grip upon this man, balancing himself along the silk thread of his life, the grip of isolation and of poverty at Helpston, in a society to which he belonged and did not belong, delays and difficulties with his publishers, Taylor and Hessey, and a palpable waning of affection towards his wife. Severely ill, he went to London in 1824 to be treated by the artists' and writers' physician, Dr Darling (who also attended Haydon and Keats). Creatures appeared to him out of the midsummer night — between the houses — 'Thin, death-like shadows and goblins with saucer eyes were continually shaping on the darkness from my haunted imagination'. He felt passers-by in the night to be supernatural agents, 'whose errands might be to carry me away at the first dark alley we came to'. He would not go down Chancery Lane (still such a dismal canyon) for fear of meeting death or the devil. His mental state was too bad for him to write home, his friend Mrs Emmerson, and Taylor, writing the news guardedly to his wife.

During the distress of this visit to London, Clare watched Lord Byron's funeral procession crawling down Oxford Street, and was much possessed by Byron's fame and death, and by a dark and beautiful girl in the crowd sighing and uttering 'Poor Lord Byron'.

Somewhat recovered, he went home; but at Helpston was soon ill and anxious again. He dreamt three times of being in hell, he dreamt before it arrived that he held one of the proofs of his new book, and 'after looking at it awhile it shrank through my hands like sand, and crumbled into dust'. He read *Macbeth* again and recorded in his journal how 'the thrilling feelings created by the description of Lady Macbeth's terror haunted walkings in her sleep sink deeper than a thousand ghosts — at least in my vision of the terrible'. The letters to Clare in the British Museum refer again and again to his difficulties, worries, and illness. His devoted, sentimental friend Mrs Emmerson wrote to him in December 1825, 'be cautious I beseech you, not to indulge . . . in anything that may affect your *Head* — for it is on *its strength alone* you can rely — your poor heart is alas! too yielding', since Clare, as one discovers from her next letter, had been having trouble with his wife, had suffered from her 'temper or injudicious conduct', had been in love with another woman, and had been wandering away from his home — wandering 'from home, from *yourself* and alas! from happiness'. Soon after Mrs Emmerson writes of his mind being 'unsettled by various and pain-ful causes' — 'not the least of those causes arising in the listlessness of Mr Taylor's conduct in your concerns'. Two years later he believed himself —

without reason — to have caught venereal disease from this affair of 1826. Anxiety plunged him into a wild sea of religious repentance.

Meanwhile the delays in publishing *The Shepherd's Calendar* were capped at last by its gray reception, by more delays, more distresses and disappoint/ ments in the settlement of the accounts between himself and Taylor, by severer feelings of neglect, by despondency, and the sense that he had failed in his ambitions.   More children were born — the number of Clare's children mounted to seven, more debts encircled him.   Moving away in 1832 from his small, overcrowded cottage at Helpston (which, after all, was where he had been born, where he had known Mary Joyce, where he had enjoyed the most absolute happiness of being in unison with nature) — moving away from Helpston affected him for the worse.   It was only three miles to Northborough, it was a roomier house he now had, with a small holding attached to it;   but the move tilted his balance still more, destroyed an influence which had so often ameliorated his anxieties, and also increased his expenses and his need of money. Clare's mind plunged in and out of the salt waters of trouble.   Black/ ness, light, and blackness succeeded each other.   So in the autumn after moving to Northborough, into which he had now settled so uneasily, and with such a contradictory blend of feelings, Clare recorded a new dream vital in his imaginative history.   Mary Joyce had appeared to him as his 'Guardian spirit', 'in the shape of a soul/stirring beauty . . . with the very same countenance in which she appeared many years ago and in which she has since appeared at intervals and moved my ideas into ecstasy.   I cannot doubt her existence.'   Two years later Clare's fourth book, *The Rural Muse*, was published; and it failed as *The Shepherd's Calendar* had failed.   Ill and highly, morbidly anxious, he drafted a letter to Dr Darling, describing his symptoms: 'sounds affect me very much and things evil as well (as) good thoughts are continually rising in my mind I cannot sleep for I am asleep as it were with my eyes open and I feel chills come over me and a sort of night/ mare awake . . . I cannot keep my mind right as it were for I wish to read and cannot — there is a numbing through my private parts which I cannot describe and when I was so indisposed last winter I felt as if I had [?heard] circulation in the blood, at times as if it went round me and other times such a sinking as if I were going to sink through the bed. . . .   I fear I shall be

G

worse and worse ere you write to me for I have been out for a walk and can
scarcely bear up against my fancys or feelings.'

The fancies or feelings encroached upon his mind, until when Taylor
went to see him in December 1836, accompanied by a doctor, he was suffering from paraphrenic delusions, having fits of irritation, or sitting listlessly
in his chimney corner saying quickly and repeatedly to himself such things
as 'doctors, doctors, doctors, doctors', or 'God bless them all, God bless
them all, God bless them all'. Within six months or so, Taylor had made
arrangements for Clare. Exiling himself from home, he accompanied the
stranger who had arrived at his door, and found himself in his first asylum
— in Dr Matthew Allen's private establishment at High Beech, within the
trees of Epping Forest.

II

Clare's illness had been both mental and physical. Anguish worked on
his digestion, his mind and his body worked against him together. With
Dr Allen he stayed just over four years, and his bodily troubles cleared up
quickly enough. But his delusions developed. He arrived, according to
Allen, 'exceedingly miserable, every instant bemoaning his poverty, and his
mind did not appear so much lost and deranged as suspended in its move-
ments by the oppressive and permanent state of anxiety, and fear, and vexa-
tion, produced by the excitement of excessive flattery at one time, and neglect
at another, his extreme poverty and over exertion of body and mind'. Allen
was certain that if a small pension could have been obtained then for Clare
'he would have recovered instantly and most probably remained well for
life'. At the end of his first six months, he wrote a letter home — curious
for its pattern. First of all, he makes four statements, that he is getting better,
that he cannot write at length, that he wishes to know how everyone is, and
that the place is beautiful. Then comes a central statement that he was
treated 'with great kindness', after which the first four statements, not all
in the same words, are repeated in the reverse order.

There is little to report of him for the next two and a half years. Allen
recorded that 'ever since he came, and even now at almost all times, the
moment he gets pen or pencil in hand he begins to write most beautiful

poetic effusions. Yet he has never been able to maintain in conversation, nor even in writing prose, the appearance of sanity for two minutes or two lines together, and yet there is no indication whatever of insanity in any of his poetry.'

From time to time Allen sent John Taylor certificates that Clare was still insane and still under his charge. One for 23 December 1839, came to John Taylor's partner with a note, '... I am happy in having it in my power to say, that our friend is improved and improving — in appearance wonder-fully — stout and rosy — and in spirits the very reverse — all life and fun — He now works ...' In July of the next year he told John Taylor that 'our invalid friend' was 'at present, in his best state. He is looking well, and his mind is not worse.' To this month and year belong the two earliest of the Epping Forest poems which are known. Neither one is remarkable, or of Clare's best. 'The Forest Maid' was sent to the *London Saturday Journal* by one of the physicians who visited the asylum, and printed in July. The other, the song, *By a Cottage near a Wood*, Allen sent to a Worcestershire clergyman at the end of the month, saying that it was 'the last little piece of Clare about our sweet cottage, and a sweet nurse he used to admire'.

The stimulus for both poems, it is relevant to say, came from experiences in his life in Epping Forest: they are not merely the memory of old emotions. That applies also to a batch of poems brought away from High Beech twelve months later, in May 1841, by a London journalist, Cyrus Redding. In one of them Clare concentrates much of his life up-to-date and his judge-ment of nature and freedom in a few direct lines and images from the Forest. The soft bracken comes up and uncurls. He can see across to Kent, he can look down to London, where he was once welcomed and lionized. But the Forest is high and real, London is small and nothing.

> *Nature is lofty in her better mood,*
> *She leaves the world and greatness all behind;*
> *Thus London, like a shrub among the hills,*
> *Lies hid and lower than the bushes here.*
> *I could not bear to see the tearing plough*
> *Root up and steal the Forest from the poor,*
> *But leave to Freedom all she loves, untamed,*
> *The Forest walk enjoyed and loved by all.*

Redding, and the friend or acquaintance of Clare's he brought with him, had found Clare, a pipe in his mouth, cutting down thistles with a hoe. With Clare leaning on the hoe, they talked about Byron and *Childe Harold*, Clare suddenly slipping away to that delusion which was to grow in him of being a prize-fighter, and slipping back after a minute to Byron's poetry. Putting together Redding's various accounts, one finds he was delighted with Clare's 'unembarassed manner', his 'correct and fluent language', his appearance of 'great candour and openness of mind', the 'perfect good taste' of his remarks on Byron. Clare was pleased at the visit and leant there on the hoe, 'a continued smile playing on his lips'. Redding describes him as 'a little man, of muscular frame and firmly set, his complexion fresh and forehead high, a nose somewhat aquiline, and long full chin'. 'I found the man agreeable and attaching — one fit for the shepherd's cast of Virgil or Theocritus. I never before saw so characterized personally the Poeta Nascitur, etc. I mean that indescribable something which lifts men of genius above the common herd.' Clare remarked also on the soil he was working, on the Forest scenery compared with the Northborough fens, on his solace in tobacco; saying also, 'I want to be with my wife and family; there is none of woman here.' He was in need of books — 'he wanted works of imagination', and at his request Redding promised to send him poems by Byron. Redding's account, the poems he took away and published, no less than the history of the next few months, show that Clare's mind was not as yet very deeply injured. The spring, the summer, and the autumn of 1841, Clare's escape from High Beech, the month or two he spent at home (until the keepers came to fetch him to the new asylum at Northampton) — all are well illuminated by Clare himself. At the beginning of one small notebook he wrote, 'John Clare's Poems Feby. 1841'. The pages mix lucidity with delusion. The marked delusions are himself as a prize-fighter, himself as Lord Byron, and the delusion that he had two wives — Martha, or Patty, his real wife and the mother of his children at Northborough, and Mary Joyce, to whom also he ascribed a family. Early in the notebook comes the draft of a letter — dated 17 March, to 'my dear wife Patty' — coherent on the whole, though once more the words all begin with capitals; Clare is well, he writes much about his children, he complains of his captivity (though as Cyrus Redding explained, it was a loose captivity, which enabled

him to work or to garden, to move about in the forest, to read and to write).
He cannot understand why they keep him: 'For what reason they keep me
here I cannot tell for I have been no other ways than well a couple of years
at the least and never was very ill only harassed by perpetual bother — and it
would seem by keeping me here one year after another that I was destined
for the same fate again and I would sooner be packed in a slave ship for
Africa than belong to the destiny of mock friends and real enemies.'

Notes made on Easter Sunday and Easter Monday on seeing a boy like
his son Bill and on seeing a young woman in the forest are both clearly
expressed, but capital letters again begin most of the words . . . 'At the
Easter Hunt I Saw a Stout Tall Young Woman Dressed In A Darkish
Flowered Cotton Gown As A Milkmaid or Farm Servant and Stood
Agen Her For Some Minutes Near A Small Clump Of Furze — I Did
Not Speak To Her But I Now Wish I Had And Cannot Forget Her —
Then I Saw Another Get Out of a Gig With A Large Scotch Shawl On
And A Pretty Face.' But the writing clears up, as when he records moneys
earned in the fields during April and May, or notes that he had 'Received
from C. Redding while in Prison on Leopards Hill' nine books on loan
and two as a gift. The Byron which Redding had sent seems from Clare's
note to have been *Don Juan*, incomplete. Reading Byron once more coalesced
with his delusion that he *was* Byron, into the writing of the long poems he
called *Don Juan a Poem* and *Child Harold*. *Don Juan*, an energetic mixture
of madness and sanity, he completed before his escape. *Child Harold*, which
contains some of his most exquisite and certainly some of his most moving
verse, he continued at Northborough in the autumn, and still had not finished
when he was taken off to Northampton. Two letter-drafts, one to an old
love, Eliza Phillips, one to 'My dear wife Mary', talk about the writing of
both poems. 'My dear wife Mary', the one letter begins, 'I might have said
my first wife and first love and first everything — but I shall never forget my
second wife and second love for I loved her once as dearly as yourself — and
almost do so now so I determined to keep you both for ever — and when I
write to you I am writing to her at the same time and in the same letter'.
Later he comes to the poems: 'I have been rather poorly I might say ill for
8 or 9 days before haymaking and to get myself better I went a few evenings
on Fern Hill and wrote a new Canto of "Child Harold" and now I am

better I sat under the Elm trees in old Matthews Homestead Leppits Hill where I now am — 2 or 3 evenings and wrote a new canto of Don Juan — merely to pass the time away but nothing seems to shorten it in the least and I fear I shall not be able to wear it away.' Then a flash of desolation — 'nature to me seems dead and her very pulse seems frozen to an icicle in the summer sun — what is the use of shutting up four women in a petty paltry place as this merely because I am a married man and I daresay though I have two wives if I get away I should soon have a third and I think I should serve you both right in the bargain for doing so for I dont care a damn about coming home now.'

To Eliza Phillips he writes:

My dear Eliza Phillips

Having been cooped up in this Hell of a Madhouse till I seem to be disowned by my friends and even forgot by my enemies for there is none to accept my challenges which I have from time to time given to the public I am almost mad in waiting for a better place and better company and all to no purpose. It is well known that I am a prize fighter by profession and a man that never feared any body in my life either in the ring or out of it — I do not much like to write love letters but this which I am now writing to you is a true one — you know that we have met before and the first opportunity that offers we will meet again. I am now writing a New Canto of Don Juan which I have taken the liberty to dedicate to you in remembrance of Days gone bye and when I have finished it I would send you the vol if I knew how in which is a new Canto of Child Harold also —

> I am my dear Elize
> yours sincerely
> John Clare.

The madness of the letters tunes one more readily to the delusions of *Don Juan* than to the pathetic vigours and beauties and confessional insights of *Child Harold*:

> *Life is to me a dream that never wakes:*
> *Night finds me on this lengthening road alone.*
> *Love is to me a thought that ever aches,*
> *A frostbound thought that freezes life to stone.*

Mary, in truth and nature still my own,
That warms the winter of my aching breast,
Thy name is joy, nor will I life bemoan.
Midnight, when sleep takes charge of nature's rest,
Finds me awake and friendless — not distrest.

Tie all my cares up in thy arms, O Sleep,
And give my weary spirits peace and rest.
I'm not an outlaw in this midnight deep,
If prayers are offered from sweet woman's breast.
One and one only made my being blest,
And fancy shapes her form in every dell.
On that sweet bosom I've had hours of rest,
Though now, through years of absence doomed to dwell,
Day seems my night and night seems blackest hell.

Don Juan is a different matter:

Lord bless me, now the day is in the gloaming
And every evil thought is out of sight.
How I should like to purchase some sweet woman
Or else creep in with my two wives to-night —
Surely that wedding day is on the coming,
Absence, like physic, poisons all delight.
Mary and Martha, both an evil omen,
Though still my own — they still belong to no man . . .

There's Doctor Bottle imp who deals in urine,
A keeper of state prisons for the Queen,
As great a man as is the Doge of Turin,
And save in London is but seldom seen —
Yclep'd old A-ll-n — mad-brained ladies curing,
Some p-x-d like Flora and but seldom clean.
The new road o'er the forest is the right one
To see red hell, and further on the white one . . .

Lord Byron, poh — the man wot rites the werses,
  And is just what he is and nothing more;
Who with his pen lies like the mist disperses
  And makes all nothing as it was before;

> *Who wed two wives, and oft the truth rehearses,*
> *   And might have had some twenty thousand more;*
> *Who has been dead, so fools their lies are giving,*
> *And is still in Allen's madhouse caged and living.*

He was writing *Don Juan* on either side of 11 July. On 15 July in an
Epping Forest thunderstorm he wrote down in his notebook the poem —
precursor of several of the best things he was to write at Northampton —
which ends

> *I live in love, sun of undying light,*
> *And fathom my own heart for ways of good;*
> *In its pure atmosphere day without night*
> *Smiles on the plains, the forest, and the flood.*
>
> *Smile on, ye elements of earth and sky,*
> *Or frown in thunders as ye frown on me.*
> *Bid earth and its delusions pass away,*
> *But leave the mind as its creator, free.*

And about now he must have written the song to Mary in which he
quoted also from the desolation and isolation of Coleridge, the song beginning

> *O Mary sing thy songs to me*
> *Of love and beauty's melody,*
> *My sorrows sink beneath distress,*
> *My deepest griefs are sorrowless,*
>
> *So used to gloom and cares am I,*
> *My tearless troubles seemeth joy:*
> *O Mary sing thy songs to me*
> *Of love and beauty's melody.*
>
> *' To be beloved is all I need*
> *And them I love I love indeed,'*
> *The soul of woman is my shrine,*
> *And Mary made my songs divine.*

In the week before 18 July, he meditated his escape, talked with a gipsy
in the forest who offered to hide him in his camp, came upon an old wide-
awake hat which he thought might be useful; and on 20 July, eluding the
keepers or attendants whose duty it was to watch the patients unobtrusively

on their forest walks, and taking his notebook with him (and five of his books), he began his four days' walk of eighty miles home to Northborough — that walk to freedom and to Mary Joyce, which he described afterwards with such an agony of directness.[1] The poems of these last months, like the purest of the poems he was to write in the madhouse at Northampton, do not depend on the minutiae of description and belie Edmund Blunden's claim that Clare's finest poetry was 'that which grew from the incident and secrecy of wild life' — unless that wild life was Clare's own, was the life of Clare's heart.

III

On the first night of the long, limping, agonizing walk Clare dreamed that Mary Joyce slept beside him in his shed on the trusses of clover. 'I thought my first wife lay on my left arm and somebody took her away from my side which made me wake up rather unhappy I thought as I woke somebody said, "Mary" but nobody was near.' At the end a cart met him with a man, a woman, and a boy in it.

When nearing me the woman jumped out and caught fast hold of my hands and wished me to get into the cart but I refused and thought her either drunk or mad but when I was told it was my second wife Patty I got in and was soon at Northborough but Mary was not there, neither could I get any information about her further than the old story of her being dead six years ago which might be taken from a brand new old newspaper, printed a dozen years ago but I took no notice of the blarney having seen her myself about a twelvemonth ago, alive and well and as young as ever — so here I am homeless at home and half gratified to feel that I can be happy anywhere

> *May none of these marks of my sad fate efface*
> *For they appeal from tyranny to God,*
> > — *Byron.*

In fact, Mary Joyce existed no more. Unmarried, at the age of forty-one she had died and been buried at Glinton, in July 1838, in the first summer

---

[1] Clare's description will be found, rather inaccurately transcribed, in *The Prose of John Clare*, 1951.

of Clare's exile at High Beech. But Clare did not accept her death, or else transmuted it into absence; and it was Mary Joyce now, and Mary's absence, by which he was obsessed. He idealized Mary Joyce, married her and was merged into her in his mind, though the merger was inconstant. Clare had understood the process of symbolization. 'Happiness', he noted down (? in 1834), 'only disseminates happiness while she is present when she is gone we retain no impression of her enjoyments unless we are determined to shape our conduct to her approval and then she is ever with us not her picture but her perfection not in shadow but reality — read this over again and profit.' So at times, Mary Joyce, as herself and as love, became a unity with nature and with Clare, until as the Northampton poems show, love and nature were left without embodiment, love was left without nature, and then love itself was lost in Clare's vision of eternity. In a literal way, a parallel to Clare and Mary Joyce is Gérard de Nerval and that Adrienne whom de Nerval saw and kissed when he was sixteen, whom he heard sing and whom he crowned, at a children's party, with laurel leaves — saw once and once only, after which she became for him a symbol and a presence. In fact, the better parallel is Hölderlin and his Diotima, Susette Gontard. Clare was less fortunate than Hölderlin, since Hölderlin and Diotima loved each other, as mature man and woman; more fortunate than Gérard de Nerval, since his association with Mary Joyce had not endured only the passing of an afternoon. Yet Diotima was the instrument of Hölderlin's realization, Mary Joyce the instrument of John Clare's. And the poignancy and perfection of many of Clare's best poems come out of that incomplete merger, that almost simultaneous feeling that Mary was with him mixed with his understanding that she was absent. When Clare returned to Northborough his emotions worked around that phrase, 'homeless at home', which came at the end of the long description of his escape. He felt as Hölderlin felt in *Menons Klage*:

> *Aber das Haus ist öde mir nun, und sie haben mein Auge*
> *Mir genommen, auch mich hab' ich verloren mit ihr.*
> *Darum irr' ich umher, und wohl, wie die Schatten, so muss ich*
> *Leben, und sinnlos dünkt lange das übrige mir.*
>
> *But the house is empty for me now, and they have taken*
> *My eyes away, myself too I have lost with her.*

So I wander about, and like Shades it seems I too
Must live, and meaningless has long seemed all that's left . . .

Directly after his return to Northborough, he wrote a poem which began

I've wandered many a weary mile,
— Love in my heart was burning —
To seek a home in Mary's smile,
But cold is love's returning.

The cold ground was a feather-bed,
Truth never acts contrary,
I had no home above my head,
My home was love and Mary.

Then a few days later he repeated the tolling of the words 'homeless at home'
in a letter he drafted to Mary — he called her Mary Clare, as if they were
married, addressing it 'to Mary Clare — Glinton': 'Not being able to
see you or to hear where you was I soon began to feel homeless at home
and shall bye and bye feel nearly hopeless but not so lonely as I did in Essex
for here I can see Glinton church and feeling that Mary is safe if not happy
I am gratified.' After a month he wrote to Dr Allen explaining why he
had left Allen's asylum in Epping Forest, and describing his walk from the
Forest to Northborough. He knows, though she lives in him, that Mary
Joyce or Mary Clare is dead:

'One of my fancys I found here with her family and all well — they met
me on this side Werrington with a horse and cart and found me all but
knocked up . . . where my poetical fancy is I cannot say for the people in the
neighbourhood tells me that the one called "Mary" has been dead these 3
years but I can be miserably happy in any situation and any place and could
have staid in yours on the forest if any of my friends had noticed me or come
to see me — but the greatest annoyance in such places as yours are those
servants styled keepers who often assumed as much authority over me as
if I had been their prisoner and not liking to quarrel I put up with it till
I was weary of the place altogether so I heard the voice of freedom and
started.'

He asked for the return of the books which he had left behind and ended
by declaring that he 'cared nothing about the women now for they are

faithless and deceitful. . . . The worst is the road to ruin and the best is nothing like a good Cow — man I never did like much and woman has long
sickened me I should (like) to be to myself for a few years and lead the life
of a hermit — but even there I should wish for one whom I am always
thinking of and almost every song I write has some signs and wishes in Ink
about Mary.'

Most of the poems he wrote in this interlude of homelessness at home are
either poems, in fact, about Mary, or versification from the Scriptures of
wrath, distress and consolation —

> *Lord, hear my prayer when trouble glooms,*
> *Let sorrow find a way,*
> *And when the day of trouble comes,*
> *Turn not thy face away.*
> *My bones like hearthstones burn away,*
> *My life like vapoury smoke decays.*

The winter comes, and

> *The wind sighs through the naked bough*
> *Sad as my heart within.*

Yet the lucidity of his notebooks and their more normal handwriting show
certainly that his mental grasp was now stronger than it had been, however
much despondency stared at him out of the brown fens.   There are many
entries to be marked — quotations (all grouped together) from Lord Bryon:

> *O! would it were my lot*
> *To be forgetful as I am forgot . . .*
>
> *Imputed madness, prison'd solitude*
> *And the mind's canker in its savage mood . . .*

— from Dryden:

> *I've now turned wild, a commoner of nature,*
> *Of all forsaken and forsaking all . . .*

— and from Job: 'They shall dig for death as for hid treasures and shall not
find it.'   There are notes on 'insects in the Chinese rose leaves', and on
clouds; and there are two pieces of coherent prose (his asylum doctor had

written, it will be recalled, of the incoherency of his prose at High Beech).
One, on the difference in their effect on himself of rough grass eaten down
by cattle after harvest time and 'pieces of greensward where the hay has been
cleared off smooth and green as a bowling green', is the old Clare still able
to answer to the day's experience. The other piece, on self-identity, on
whether Clare *was* or *was not*, dealt with a torment which was still to haunt
him and harass him in his second asylum:

> A very good commonplace counsel is *Self-Identity* to bid our own
> hearts not to forget our own selves and always to keep self in the first
> place lest all the world who always keeps us behind it should forget
> us alltogether — forget not thyself and the world will not forget thee —
> forget thyself and the world willingly forget thee till thou art nothing
> but a living-dead man dwelling among shadows and falsehood . . .

It is a seed of the famous *I am: yet what I am none cares or knows.*

Whether Clare could have continued more or less sane, if melancholy,
could have improved, could now have recovered, there is scarcely evidence
to show. Matthew Allen had sent an admirable reply to the letter in which
Clare had written about his escape: he hoped he would be more comfortable at home and told him he would be welcome to come back for a change
at any time to High Beech, where bed and board would be free, and he
would be at liberty to come and go as he pleased — 'you might', he wrote,
picking up Clare's remark about wishing to be a hermit, 'lead the life of a
Hermit as much as you choose and I would contrive to give you some places
for the purpose'.

When Allen had sent for Clare, his wife had replied he was so much
better that she wished to try him for a while; and Dr Darling in London,
whom Clare had consulted on the disturbance of his mind seventeen years
before, gave it as his view that Clare might as well stay at home in Northborough. Enough money to live on, a certainty that the money would
continue coupled with his wife's patience and care, might have reintegrated
him, or kept him from extreme disturbance. But the close, difficult hand
in the last of his Northborough notebooks indicates a dip in his condition.
He wrote a prose fragment in the book about the woods in autumn (including this : The autumn tempest or wind sweeps through the vollying trees
like the long mutterings of continued thunder'); he noted the finding of

unseasonable cowslips in flower, and the thunderous roll with which November starlings rose from an ash tree.

In the summer after his return he had written

> *In this cold world without a home*
> *Disconsolate I go,*
> *The summer looks as cold to me*
> *As winter's frost and snow,*

absent Mary having left his heart without a home.

In the autumn he had written that in spite of 'The pleachy fields and yellowing tree', there was no autumnal change in himself: for himself Mary was still in flower.

In the early winter he now wrote

> *Brown are the flags and fading sedge*
> *And tanned the meadow plains,*
> *Bright yellow is the osier hedge*
> *Beside the brimming drains;*
> *The crows sit on the willow tree,*
> *The lake is full below,*
> *But still the dullest thing I see*
> *Is self that wanders slow.*

One must assume that though his wife had so wished 'to try him', the difficulty of the trial became too great. The Reverend Charles Mossop, who as Vicar of Helpston, where Clare was born, had known him since his early days as a poet, and whom Clare had named in 1824 as one of the executors of his will, came over to see Clare, reported that 'his wife and family appear strange to him' and recommended, 'if any asylum, the new one at Northampton'. So Clare was examined and certified by Dr Fenwick Skrimshire and Dr William Page, and admitted to the Northampton General Lunatic Asylum on 29 December 1841. The application form, filled in by Skrimshire, says that he was forty-nine, that his usual employment was gardening, that he had been married for twenty-two years, had seven children, that he had had several attacks of insanity; and that indications of the existing attack had first been noticed four years ago. The information that he had 'escaped' form High Beech, was twice underlined, and the answers to the questions whether 'he had ever attempted or threatened violence to self or others', and whether he was 'idiotic, mischievous, or dirty' were both 'no'.

That famous answer 'after years of Poetical prosing', to the question whether his insanity had been 'preceded by any severe or long-continued mental emotion or exertion', must be held less against Dr Skrimshire than against the whole race of *les hommes moyen sensuels*. Frederick Martin, Clare's first biographer, whose novelized chapters often had behind them facts and documents now lost, maintained — and well one can believe it — that Clare 'struggled hard when the keepers came to fetch him, imploring them, with tears in his eyes, to leave him at his little cottage, and seeing all resistance useless, declaring his intention to die rather than to go to such another prison as that from which he had escaped'.

His last interlude of freedom had lasted just over five months.

IV

Clare had rather more than twenty-two years to live at Northampton. Gradually in that time his delusions waxed and possessed him. Gradually, yes — but that is not to say Clare could have been called 'sane' during any of the time. The state of his broken mind varied, as it had varied in the preceding four years, and at times he had grasp enough of himself to develop his particular insight and to make poems of the most uncontaminated lyricism, the most unimpeded consciousness of his feeling, a feeling which worked around those notions of joy which he owed to Wordsworth and Coleridge, of love, eternity, and freedom. Clare had fought, and still fought for some years more, to hold on to the central portion of his own spiritual identity (hence the lucidity of his verse, the disorder of his prose and his conversation). He was aware of his madness. As his fellow patient William Jerom described it, 'Clare had "a song in the night"; and if he did not draw his consolation from a divine source, [he] had at least a very happy art in charming the woe-begone moments away.'

His biographers have suggested that, at times, he was actually sane. 'To be sane, even for short periods, while confined within a madhouse, is perhaps one of the most exquisite horrors which can be imagined for any man; and

Clare, in the years to come, must have endured this often.' That is a dangerous attitude. It belongs more perhaps to the romanticism of the 1830s
than to a justifiable estimate of Clare's case. One must guard oneself against
such a romantic view; equally against the attitude that madness itself makes
a man's art; or makes it more rich and original. The mad artist or poet is
the artist or poet who goes mad: the sensibility was there before the disease.
The preliminaries of the confirmed psychosis, the preliminary anxieties and
experiences may provide both material and tincture, which a mind not as
yet too impaired may at first censor or scale down. The disease extends, the
censorship lessens, and peculiarities may show like flowers in a night. The
disease extends still further, the night deepens, the experiences are overwhelming, and the delicacies of the poet's rhythms, or the finenesses of the
drawing by the artist become coarse, and his form loosens towards the incoherent and fragmentary. So it certainly was with Hölderlin in his madness. Clare never had Hölderlin's good chance to develop and refine his
powers of mind, never associated enough with minds of his own rank; but
their two histories are not unlike, beyond the parallelism of Clare's Mary
Joyce and Hölderlin's Diotima. Like Hölderlin, Clare feels threatened in
his personality, threatened by cosmical disaster; he fears catastrophic im-
mensities, immense waterfalls, horrible mysteries, extinction:

> *The cataract, whirling to the precipice*
> *Elbows down rocks and shouldering thunders through.*
> *Roars, howls, and stifled murmurs never cease;*
> *Hell and its agonies seem hid below.*
> *Thick rolls the mist that smokes and falls in dew;*
> *The trees and greensward wear the deepest green,*
> *Horrible mysteries in the gulph stares through,*
> *Darkness and foam are indistinctly seen:*
> *Roars of a million tongues, and none knows what they mean.*

Like Hölderlin, feeling threatened, separate, and alone, Clare looks for love,
comfort, and delight in idealizations, whether of women or nature:

> *There is a charm in solitude that cheers,*
> *A feeling that the world knows nothing of;*
> *A green delight the wounded mind endears*
> *After the hustling world is broken off,*

Whose whole delight was crime — at good to scoff.
Green solitude, his prison, pleasure yields.
The bitch fox heeds him not; birds seem to laugh.
He lives the Crusoe of his lonely field
Whose dark green oaks his noon-tide leisure shield.

Nature is often lit up for him extravagantly, flowers becoming flames; and when woman falls away, he feels himself married to nature, as he was to write in lines for a portrait of himself which was drawn or painted at Northampton — lines like an epitaph:

Bard of the mossy cot,
Known through all ages,
Leaving no line to blot
All through thy pages —
Bard of the fallow-field,
And the green meadow,
Where the sweet birds build,
Nature thy widow.

Like Hölderlin, Clare is forced by his predicament to look beyond nature and love into universality, renewal, and ultimate forgiveness or benediction. The metaphysical connections are made. He regards the Evening Star, and writes

Hesperus! thy twinkling ray
Beams in the blue of heaven,
And tells the traveller on his way
That Earth shall be forgiven.

Who is to forgive? Yet if one rejects, in this age, metaphysical explanations or solutions, there remain the puzzle of consciousness and its trials; and it would be as barbarian, as impoverishing, to reject the art which metaphysical solutions have informed, as to reject the history of man.

v

We must be thankful for the fact that Clare was well used in his asylum, indeed that, as many people testified, he was treated with the most exemplary kindness and consideration. To begin with, Clare was a desirable and

H

interesting patient.   He had been famous as a poet, if for the wrong reasons
largely — far more so in his day, in fact, than Keats.   Within two years
their common publisher had sold more than 3000 copies of Clare's first book.
Of Keats's *Lamia* volume, also published in 1820, less than 500 had been
sold by March 1822.   By the time Clare was admitted to the asylum his
celebrity had faded; but still he was known, and was a welcome subject of
attention and curiosity to the doctors who had charge of him.   And mad or
no, Clare was not so mad that his personality had lost its charm and its
candour.

He had freedom — for many years — to come and go, into Northampton
itself, or out into the country.   He was encouraged to go on writing, especially by the asylum house steward, W. F. Knight.   By the time Knight left
Northampton in February 1850, it is almost certain that all of Clare's major
poems had been written, that he was sinking into that final disintegrated
state in which his psychosis mastered him.   To the fact that Knight encouraged Clare and copied out Clare's poems as he pencilled them down, we
owe nearly all the asylum poetry which has survived.

This is what Knight put at the beginning of the two manuscript
volumes:

> Copied from the Manuscripts as presented to me by Clare — and
> favoured with others by some Ladies and Gentlemen, that Clare had
> presented them to — the whole of them faithfully transcribed to the
> best of my knowledge from the pencil originals many of which were so
> obliterated that without referring to the Author I could not decipher.
> Some pieces will be found unfinished, for Clare will seldom turn his
> attention to pieces he has been interrupted in while writing — and in no
> instance has he ever rewritten a single line — whenever I have wished
> him to correct a single line he has ever shown the greatest disinclination
> to take in hand what to him seems a great task.

Knight's transcripts are probably more reliable than has generally been
allowed; and may well have been read over by Clare himself, who filled
in a line or two of one poem in his own hand.   Roughly the order must have
been chronological (Knight dated many of them), the ones out of order being
presumably those which Knight recovered from other people, many of them
written before Knight was appointed to his asylum stewardship on 30 April

1845. From Clare's own notebooks and letters, from accounts by visitors, letters from Knight and others, including R. S. Prichard, the superintendent of the asylum, one can picture the parallel course of Clare's disease.

To the parson at Northborough, Clare's village, Dr Prichard wrote on 10 November 1843, nearly two years after he had been admitted, 'Poor Clare is in good health but the state of his mind has not improved. It rather appears to become more and more impaired, he used at one time to write many and very good pieces tho' he scarcely ever finished them. He now writes but little and in a coarse style very unlike his former compositions. I much fear the disease will gradually terminate in dementia.' One cannot tell whether any of the surviving poems belong to those early 'many and good pieces'. But there is one poem in the transcripts of the same month and year as Dr Prichard's letter:

> *A sea boy on the giddy mast*
> *Sees nought but ocean waves*
> *And hears the wild inconstant blast*
> *Where loud the tempest raves.*
>
> *My life is like the ocean wave,*
> *And like the inconstant sea:*
> *In every hope appears a grave*
> *And leaves no hope for me.*

S. T. Hall, the mesmerist, had seen Clare earlier in 1843, in May, and wrote years later that he had been 'altogether as clean and neat as if he had just been fresh brushed up for market or fair'. In one of their conversations, Clare had complained that they would not let him go home 'for, you see, they're feeding me up for a fight; but they can get nobody able to strip me'. When Hall mentioned his fame as a poet 'Oh, poetry, ah, I know', said Clare, 'I once had something to do with poetry, a long while ago: but it was no good. I wish, though they could get a man with courage enough to fight me.' Hall added, 'This was just after he had been writing a beautiful and logical poem for my friend, Mr Joseph Stenson, the iron-master.' He also identified himself with the poet James Montgomery, and asked Hall to remember him in London to Tom Spring the boxer. 'Another time on my seeing him, after he had just returned from a long and favourite ramble, he described it all, up to a certain point, with great accuracy and apparent pleasure, in beautiful language, and then broke off into talk it would be wrong to repeat.'

The next year, 1844, visitors who saw him, one of them in July, report much of his delusions, boxing delusions again, delusions of having witnessed the execution of Charles I and the Battle of the Nile, and Nelson's death at Trafalgar. Nelson had become one of his fixed and three most prominent alter egos, along with Byron and the prize-fighter. This delusion went back to seeds in 1824, his year of London sickness and hallucinations, in which he wrote several sea-fighting songs and an unpublished poem beginning 'Great Nelson's glory near the Nile'. Then, too, he had seen Byron's funeral. Yet 1844 seems to have been the year of his major productivity and insight, perhaps under some stimulus from the world outside of which we are ignorant. The poems with a date are mostly unremarkable, it is true. But that finest of all his poems, *A Vision*, the poem free of all mental darkness and anxiety, the regenerative poem, one would say, of Clare's final insight, is dated 2 August 1844; and for various reasons, including correspondences of expression, music, and idea, a playing on freedom, eternity, love, and nature, which tie them together, I believe that a number of undated poems belong to the summer months of 1844, including three more of Clare's greatest pieces, the song which begins

> *Love lives beyond*
> *The tomb, the earth, which fades like dew —*
> *I love the fond,*
> *The faithful, and the true*

(of which there exists a manuscript in Clare's hand); the intolerably moving and crystalline poem to Mary Joyce, in which he talks of walking with her by the water which reflects the horned moon:

> *Spirit of her I love,*
> *Whispering to me*
> *Stories of sweet visions, as I rove,*
> *Here stop, and crop with me*
> *Sweet flowers that in the still hour grew,*
> *We'll take them home, nor shake off the bright dew . . .*

and that poem of infinite sadness, *I Am*, in which Clare complains that, self-consumer of his woes, he is forsaken 'like a memory lost', and living in 'the vast shipwreck' of his life's esteems. The position of these three poems in the transcripts made by the house steward, in that order, suggests also that they preceded, and led to, the writing of *A Vision*.

Few dated poems, and those inferior, belong to 1845 and 1846. In July 1845 the superintendent wrote to the Northborough parson again:

Sir,

John Clare is in excellent health but his mind is becoming more and more obscured by his distressing malady — He enjoys perfect liberty here, and passes all his time out of doors in the fields or the Town returning only for his meals and bed.

A notebook, inscribed inside the cover by Clare, 'John Clare Northborough Northamptonshire Nov. 1845', is filled rather with a mixture of glumness and light singing to girls than with the consequences of derangement. The songs are of a kind he wrote more and more as interest in ideas and in himself powdered away and as his mind deteriorated; but such songs contain many felicities, as the one in this notebook to Mary Ann Abbott:

> *Lay bare those twin roses*
> *That hide in thy hair,*
> *Thy eye's light discloses*
> *The sweetness hid there,*
>
> *For thy dark curls lie on them*
> *Like night in the air. . . .*

On one page he entered a chiefly glum list of books, including Young's *Night Thoughts* and *The Christian's Defence against the Fears of Death*, by Charles Drelincourt (a bestseller for more than a century). There are gloomy fragments of verse:

> *The very shore of shore I see*
> *All shrivels like a scroll*
> *The heavens rend away from me,*
> *And thunder's sulphurs roll.*
>
> *The present is the funeral of the past*
> *And man the living sepulchre of life. . . .*

Also a fragment called *Sorrow is my Joy*, in which snowdrops glow in beautiful Sorrow's raven hair. Among everything else occur drafts of a letter to his wife and a letter to his children. Writing to his wife he sees one of his boys, leading him by the hand in his childhood: 'I see him now in his little pink frock — seal skin cap — and gold band — with his little face as round as an apple and as red as a rose.' He goes on: 'I am in Prison because I wont leave my family and tell a falsehood — this is the English Bastile a government prison where harmless people are trapped and tortured till they die — English priestcraft and English bondage more severe than the slavery of Egypt and Africa.' Writing to his children he asks them to be kind to their poor mother 'for I myself am rendered incapable of assisting or behaving well to anyone even of my nearest relations — I am in a Prison on all hands that even numbs commonsense — I can be civil to none but enemies here as friends' — this was a delusion — 'are not allowed to see me at all'.

An odder entry is:

> '*Eye on weed*⎱
> *Iron weed* ⎰ *weeding pun*'

Clare was evidently down in 1845 and 1846, as the superintendent had indicated in July of the earlier year. The transcripts coincide with a run of mediocre verses (though one poem begins

> *The Sun like the last look of love*
> *Has smiled farewell on tower and tree*),

which suddenly end with that calm *Hesperus*,[1] written probably at the beginning of 1847 (it was published at the end of the year). Poem followed poem in February. On 11 February he wrote the poem on the death and funeral of a young girl, which opens as gravely and exquisitely as anything he ever composed:

> *Flowers shall hang upon the palls,*
> *Brighter than patterns upon shawls,*
> *And blossoms shall be in the coffin lids,*
> *Sadder than tears on grief's eyelids,*

---

[1] Quoted above, on page 105.

Garlands shall hide pale corpses' faces
When beauty shall rot in charnel places,
Spring flowers shall come in dews of sorrow
For the maiden goes down to her grave to-morrow.

The stimulus was perhaps the renewal of contact with an old friend from the sane and free world, an elderly minor poet named Thomas Inskip, who had befriended another 'peasant poet', Robert Bloomfield. He had begun writing to Clare in the previous October. Clare replied. Clare sent him poems, and Knight the house steward sent him some of his transcripts. Inskip promised a visit, came at last early in July, stayed three days, pre-vailed on the superintendent's wife to send him a portrait of Clare (the portrait for which Clare described Nature as his widow), inspired Clare to a sonnet in which he excellently remarked that Inskip was one whose 'musing mind loveth the green recess'; and took Clare to the house of a Northampton journalist, G. J. de Wilde — a meeting which drew a sonnet[1] from another guest:

Let me reveal him when kind Inskip led
The unconscious Poet to your home, De Wilde,
And we sat listening, as to some fond child,
The wayward unconnected words he said, —
Prattle, by confused recollections fed,
Of famous times gone by, — Lord Byron piled
Praise on him in the Quarterly, *and styled*
Him of all Poets as the very head!

Clare told them Byron had reviewed his poetry in no less than twenty-five pages, remembering confusedly the *Quarterly*'s review of his first book in 1820 (which was eight pages long and written by Octavius Gilchrist). Another of Clare's delusions of 1847 one gathers from a letter Inskip had written at the end of July, answering Clare's complaint that his eyes had no pupils. Four weeks before Inskip's visit, Clare, firmly and cursively, had penned a letter to his son Charles; lucid it was — though he warned his sons Frederic (who had died in 1843) and John against coming to the 'bad Place', 'the Bastile': 'I have fear that they may get trapped as prisoners as

[1] In J. W. Dalby's *Tales, Songs and Sonnets* (1866).

I hear some have been and I may not see them nor even hear they have been here.' Knight carefully added a note to say that on the contrary Clare 'is allowed to see any one he wishes — and he is at liberty' — still — 'to walk out for his pleasure — when he thinks propper. He has just left my room to walk in the garden — and if any of you think well to come and see him I am sure he will be pleased to see you.'

Inskip and Clare continued to correspond through 1848 into 1849 (when Inskip died), and both were years out of which good poems or fragments remain. *Solitude* quoted on page 104 ('The bitch fox heeds him not'), is likely to have been written in 1848. So also *First Love*:

> *Are flowers the winter's choice ?*
> *Is love's bed always snow ?*

And in 1849 he probably wrote the song beginning 'I would not feign a single sigh':

> *I would not kiss thy face again*
> *Nor round thy shining slippers crawl.*

But for the most part he composed repetitive and monotonous songs deriving from earlier experience of life or bad poetry. A long letter to his son Charles, in February, is spotted with a little madness about Charles's brothers and sisters and their red heads, gives advice about books, and recalls Sabbath breaking, when he was a boy — recalls fishing instead of church. He wrote more poems than he caught fish — 'in my boyhood Solitude was the most talkative vision I met with Birds bees trees flowers all talked to me louder than the busy hum of men'. In May Inskip wrote to Knight mentioning Clare's delusions of being Ben Caunt the boxer, and late in the month he told Knight that Clare's 'letter to me was written under a paroxysm of in-sanity; his mind smarting under an imaginary infliction, and his Pen guided by the Demon of Madness'. Later Inskip had 'a good and lengthy letter' from Clare — 'he tells me therein that he gets tired of writing poetry'. In July, sitting out in the fields away from the asylum, he wrote his wife one of his most affecting letters: 'I have not written to you a long while, but here I am in the land of Sodom where all the peoples brains are turned the wrong way. . . .' His son John had apparently been to see him — Knight had

several times urged some of the family to come to Northampton, offering to
put them up when they arrived: 'I was glad to see John yesterday and should
like to have gone back with him for I am very weary of being here. You
might come and fetch me away for I think I have been here long enough. I
write this in a green meadow the side of the river agen Stokes Mill and I see
three of your daughters and a Son now and then. The confusion and roar
of Mill-dams and locks is sounding very pleasant while I write it, and its a
very beautiful evening; the meadows are greener than usual after the shower
and the rivers are brimful. I think it was about two years' (it was nearly
seven) 'since I was first sent up in this hell' — and then a *non-sequitur*, seeing
that he *was* outside — 'and not allowed to go out of the gates'. Clare's
letter of 17 October to Charles told the family 'I am quite well and never
was better in my Life thank God for it'. In fact, his physical health was
good nearly to the end of his days in the asylum. He read, Inskip reveals,
Mrs Hemans and Eliza Cook (who was among the list of visitors to Clare
in these asylum years), he complained in a letter to Inskip of being 'fire
logged' (to which Inskip, who did not quarrel with Clare's moods, replied
that he was 'poverty logged'), and before 1848 was finished Inskip thanked
Clare for sending him *To Jenny Lind*:

> *I cannot touch the harp again*
> *And sing another idle lay,*
> *To cool a maddening burning brain*
> *And drive the midnight fiend away . . .*

Inskip remarked that 'Clare's last letter was excellent, only a little mad with
alliteration'. Clare told Inskip he had written *Jenny Lind* on purpose to
please him.

Looking back over the poems, in spite of Clare's ups after being down,
a slight steady deterioration is discernible. Just as Clare was disinclined to
finish poems when the making of them had been interrupted, and never, or
seldom, revised them once they were written, so for the most part the poems
are short — they are the quick records of an impulse. So far as one knows
he wrote only one long poem, *A Rhapsody*, while he was at the asylum:
and this cannot de dated, beyond saying that it must have been after 1850.
A Rhapsody flashes now and then with pure and surprising apprehensions;

but it contains extravagant rhyme which reminds one of Clare's weeding pun, 'Eye on weed, Iron weed', of 1845 or 1846:

> *Tis May and yet the March flower dandelion*
> *Is still in bloom among the emerald grass,*
> *Shining like guineas with the sun's warm eye on . . .*

The lines try, and fail, to keep within a rhythmical plan. Compare *A Rhapsody* with the *Child Harold* of High Beech and Northborough (not to say the long sadly serene poems at the beginning of his book *The Rural Muse*), and one sees how far the mind which produced them all had disintegrated. More and more Clare's personality of music drained out of the songs, even if the substance and imagery were preserved. More and more Clare employs, ready made, the hurdy-gurdy music of Byron in his *Occasional Pieces*, or the trotty movement of the Scottish song-writers, more and more he wrote songs in a pseudo-Scottish dialect; or else, now and again, he would use the three-stressed artifice of Shenstone's *Pastoral Ballad*. And Clare was ageing. In 1849 — the year we have now reached — he was fifty-six. Perhaps the surprising thing is not the mental decline, but the drawn-out slowness of the decline. After all, it is remarkable enough when an impulse to lyricism stays so long with poets who are more normal than Clare was by this time.

One cannot pick much out of Clare's letters home in 1849. In the first of them, with a consciousness of his state, he tells his son that he is happy to hear from him, 'particularly now as I am quite lost in reveries and false ——' (the word is illegible). 'I am now in the ninth year of my Captivity among the Babylonians and any News from Home is a Godsend or blessing.' He told Charles to attend — odd list — to his Latin, Greek, Hebrew, mathematics, and astronomy — 'when I was a day Labourer at Bridge Casterton and courted your Mother I knew Nine Languages and could talk of them to Parsons and Gentlemen and Foreigners but never opened my Mouth about them to the Vulgar — for I always lived to myself' (28 April). A badly, and madly, written letter in June snakes away into a long list of old friends he is to be remembered to. In October, he yearns, in a more fluent hand, 'to get out o' thought and out o' sight in the Fens as usual', 'to get back and see after the garden and hunt in the woods' for flowers — and curious flowers for a wood — 'yellow hyacinths, Polyanthuses and blue primroses'.

In November he wants to know 'have you four boys got each an hebrew Bible?' Also, 'in your next say when Johnny is coming to fetch me away from this Bastile'. The Inskip letters reveal that he had been reading American poets, at Inskip's suggestion, beg him also for 'a little stave to put under your portrait' (Clare had written one such set of verses, presumably the one in the transcripts by Knight, but Inskip had mislaid it), and commiserate on his severe moodiness, a spring moodiness such as he had suffered in the previous May (though earlier Inskip had written to Knight 'some of his letters are very beautiful, all are amusing' — all of them have, alas, disappeared). Some time before 9 August Knight had posted Inskip *The Invitation* — 'I have read it several times with much pleasure', Inskip wrote to Clare, 'and that pleasure has been increased by observing you have bestowed some pains upon it in the finish'.

By November, Inskip, sick, and old, had died on holiday at Brighton. As if by premonition Clare had written down *A Thought* a few months before:

> *A night without a morning,*
> *A trouble without end,*
> *A life of bitter scorning,*
> *A world without a friend.*

— which follows in the transcripts on a maddish song, with this last stanza:

> *Sweet Phoebe my dearest, my beautiful Phoebe*
> *With a face full o' roses and bosom o' snow —*
> *A bosom of snow, love, where Cupid goes beeby*
> *And beautiful veins on the lily banks flow.*
> *Then, Phoebe, my darling, round the strings o' thy apron*
> *I'd uggle my arms like the wings of a Capon*
> *To kiss the milk white of thy bosom so fair*
> *And rose on thy cheek hid in leaves o' black hair.*

VI

Inskip's death was a loss to Clare. It was not only that he was a friend and a correspondent: he had stimulated Knight's concern for Clare and his poems (he wrote once to Knight 'Hear this and take heed, Collect every scrap of Clare's Muse, keep them carefully and never squander one piece on the senseless — the tasteless or the worthless') and he had made Knight arouse Clare from apathy into mental action.   Clare's loneliness was sharp. He saw little indeed of his family — there is no record, though Knight prompted such a visit, of his wife ever coming from Northborough to Northampton.   He was cut away from the stimulus or comfort of the few old friends of his Helpston days who had been in communion with him. The friends and correspondents of his London celebrity — they were all lost.   Mostly they had been of an older generation, and were dead — George Darley, H. F. Carey the translator of Dante, Allan Cunningham, Mrs Emmerson.   Clare and George Darley were nearly of an age; but Darley, himself a sick, lonely, melancholy man had died in London in 1846.   Had he written at all to Clare in the asylum ?   There is no record of it; but it was such tender and warm letters as those Darley used to write that, mad or no, Clare was in need of.   Emotional and spiritual starvation again makes Clare's perseverant hold on himself the more remarkable.   It is a wonder that he continued to write, continued to keep his intermittent buoyancy; and no wonder at all that he fell back for subject on the exper⁄ iences of childhood and adolescence, no wonder that the ideal wedded presence of Mary Joyce, with her black hair and blue eyes, her identity with flower and love, had thinned away into a shade of a shade in his Mary poems. Kindness in the asylum, kindness among the people in Northampton, kind⁄ ness among the third⁄rate authors who came curiously to see him, S. T. Hall, N. P. Willis the American, Eliza Cook, Mary Howitt, and the others — kindness and curiosity were not communion.   John Taylor, his publisher, many years older than Clare, seems to have kept more faithfully in touch with his wife and children, as trustee of the fund moneys which now went towards their maintenance, than with Clare in the asylum.   He appears to have visited Clare at least once, but the date and particulars are lacking.   No wonder, writing home in April 1850, Clare said 'I have got nothing to write about at all for I see nobody and hear nothing'.   But he included one piece of news of import, and bad import, to himself, 'Mr Knight is gone to Birginham' (i.e. Birmingham).

Knight had resigned as house steward months before, on 30 January, and his successor was appointed on 27 February. His removal to another job must have snapped one of Clare's anchoring cables; and there may be some link between his departure, or the threat of it, and Clare's state in January, when delusions in more than usual flurry were concocted by his mind. A notebook exists which he kept late in 1849 and early in 1850, inscribed again, like the notebook of 1845, 'John Clare Northborough, near M. Deeping Decr.26th.1849' — as though he were at home, not at Northampton at all. To start with there are letter-drafts, one to his son Frederic, who had long been dead. Then, once more, he was boxer, Byron, Nelson, the champion outfacing and outfighting neglect or scorn:

> The Humbug called the Ring or the Fancy owes me as Forfeits £1,800
> and I have been 9 years without a Shilling and in this Prison still
> Ben Caunt.

Under 10 January he reveals, as Byron, that he wrote the fourth canto of the real *Childe Harold* when he was courting his wife Patty — 'He began it one Sunday afternoon and finished it in three or four hours under an Ash Tree in Her Fathers Home Close'. He breaks off a song to scribble down

> *Wellington*
> *Albert*
> *Nelson and Bronte*
> *Prince of Wales,*

and a page later Nelson-Clare emerges again from the dark: 'on Board 'L'Orient' Flagship receiving the swords of the Enemy — Blown up by the Spanish Admiral's son — Lord Nelson'. Girls' names grow up like mental weeds round the pages; and he ends the notebook 'Jan 23rd 1850 saw my wife Patty in a Dream she looked well — with little Billy and an Infant carried by someone else all looked healthy and happy — John Clare.'

The only poems are a song, *My old Love left me, I knew not for why*, and a fragment on sunset.

Many people described Clare's delusions. G. J. de Wilde recalled walk-ing with Clare — de Wilde was ignorant of his identity at the time, though a 'towering forehead' and remarks about the scenery suggested he was 'not an ordinary commonplace man'; — and he was startled when Clare claimed quotations from *Childe Harold* and Shakespeare as his own

— '"Yours", I exclaimed, "Who are you? These are Byron's and Shakespeare's verses, not yours!" "It's all the same", he answered, changing a
quid from one cheek to the other, "I'm John Clare now. I was Byron and
Shakespeare formerly. At different times you know I'm different persons
— that is the same person with different names." And then he went on to
identify himself with a most miscellaneous and unselect lot of celebrities —
great warriors, prize fighters and some eminent blackguards.' William
Jerom knew him not from outside, not from casual conversation, not from
seeing him in his smooth stone niche under the portico of All Saints church
in Northampton, where for so many years Clare had gone day after day, with
a quid of tobacco pushing out one cheek; but from inside, from the patients'
side of the wall. Jerom recalled him more as Ben Caunt or Tom Spring
and as Lord Nelson than as Byron. As Nelson, Jerom thought, he used
to sing:

> *Fight on, my boys, he said*
> *Till I die, till I die.*
> *Fight on, my boys, he said*
> *Till I die.*

'He always sang with a repeat: and the words "Till I die" were sung
with a degree of emphasis that seemed to be rather elevating and somewhat
touching.'

Jerom describes his respectable clothing, his better Sunday suit, mentions
his 'very handsome feet and hands', his light flaxen hair, which turned to
silvery white and hung venerably from a bald crown to his shoulders. He
made 'witticisms and crank sayings' on the spur of the moment. 'He possessed a considerable amount of moral courage: his bearing and manner
were indomitable and bold even to a proverb: he was like the King of the
Forest, there was a prowess in his limbs and a majesty in his fiery eye' —
his blue eye — 'that showed the vigour and energy of a mind whose greatness even in ruins reminded one forcibly of what is said in Scripture of the
Leviathan: "None dare stir him up, nor make him afraid".' After
Knight's departure, Clare did pick up again. 'Your father writes to me —
and is seemingly in good health and spirits', Knight remarked in a letter to
Charles Clare in May 1850, still hoping to publish a select volume of the
asylum poems, and still hoping — against, it looks, Charles Clare's resistance

— to get some earlier (possibly Epping Forest) manuscripts which Clare had said he could use. Again, in July to Charles Clare, 'I had a very rational letter from your Father the other day in which he informs me he is quite well.' But the existing letters from John Clare himself to his son are indicative, within a year, of a decline. July 25, 1851, in pencil, the writing elongated, and childish: 'I thought it a long while since I heard from any of U'. The letter goes off into a string of names.

More than a year later, in October 1852, to his daughter, Clare wrote significantly by an amanuensis. He says his health is good: she must not suppose him 'to be at all ailing' — 'it is only that I do not write so fluent and quick as he does that I have asked him to write for me'. An undated note-book, which may belong to this steep fall of 1851 or 1852, contains letter drafts again, but mostly in a mad shorthand. All are to girls, and Clare also scribbled down a list of girls' names. To some were addressed late songs among the asylum transcripts. 'M drst Hlln Mr hw lng t pt m rm rnd r btfl nck nd r chk nd lps — 'Thn drst Hlln ll lv m mr' — My dearest Hellen Maria how [I] long to put my arm round your beautiful neck and your cheek and lips — 'Then dearest Helln will love me more'.

'Whn ppl mk sch mstks s t cll m Gds bstard & whrsp m b shttng m p frm Gds ppls . . .' — 'when people make such mistakes as to call me God's bastard and worship me by shutting me up from God's peoples.' Or '. . . dnt cm hr. gn fr' ts mtrs bd ple wrs nd wrs nd w r ll trnd Frnchmn' — 'don't come here again for 'tis monstrous bad place worse and worse and we are all turned Frenchmen'.

William Jerom's reminiscences were probably compiled for John Godfrey, the secretary of the asylum, who tenderly admired Clare, and probably they were written soon after Clare's death in 1864. Jerom thinks it was twelve years since anyone had seen Clare on his stone seat at All Saints church in Northampton; which would mean that he had not been noticed there since 1852, this year in which Clare for a while was too feeble to write home to his daughter. Yet even if they divided now into smaller pieces, some of the fragments of his mind were still able, if more weakly and only for a time, to reunite. He contrived many more poems. And still intent upon publica-tion and upon preserving each scrap of Clare's Muse, Knight must have left behind him his second volume of transcripts for others to continue in the asylum.   The last poem written out in Knight's hand which has a date, is the *Little Trotty Wagtail* of 9 August 1849, that piece of trotty rhythm for which anthologists have an unfortunate liking.   Knight entered six other poems, then several hundred more poems appear in different hands — unfortunately without dates, and it seems less accurately interpreted and copied.

Many, many of the poems are repetitive in form and sound and content. Yet again what most typifies Clare as a poet recurs snatch by snatch, if not in whole unified poems:

> *The fly I envy settling in the sun*
> *On the green leaf, and wish my goal was won*
> (Written in Prison)

> *A silent man in life's affairs,*
>   *A thinker from a boy,*
> *A peasant in his daily cares,*
>   *A poet in his joy.*
> (The Peasant Poet)

Now and again a line of the *mens divinior* assails one tenderly by vision and sound: 'The moon looks over fields of love, among the ivy sleeps the dove', or 'My love is as sweet as a bean-field in blossom'.   Now and then one finds a curious piece of profundity, like the distich

> *Language has not the power to speak what love indites.*
> *The Soul lies buried in the Ink that writes.*

But more and more one knocks against jagged bits of raw apprehension and cross-reference, strange, coloured solids often in the bombed structure of a poem and of Clare's mind.   A girl is as 'smooth as the freestone in the wall', 'Sweet chestnuts brown like soling leather turn', a girl's neck is 'white as ring doves eggs'.

Other examples are stranger, if within reason:

> *Where the pheasant's red eye for a moment was caught*
> *Then vanished away like a spinning bee's song.*
> (Where the Deer with their Shadows)

> *I looked upon her pink gown that fitted her so well*
> *As felons look on heaven through the burning chinks o' hell.*
> (Mary Featherstone)

John Clare at the age of 27 : 'Peasant Poet' and London prodigy

John Clare in 1844, the asylum year of some of his greatest poems

The black bird sings loud as a lady's piano
With a yellow gold ring round his violet eye.

(Rachel Cooks)

Sheep ointment seems to daub the dead-hued sky
And night shuts up the lightsomeness of day
All dank and absent like a corpse's eye.

(A Rhapsody)

VII

These grotesque crystallizations in the flux of Clare's mind, and Clare's art, acceptable as they are, foretell the end. Yet that still slow, still intermittent process of fragmentation and dissolution dragged on from his sixtieth year, in 1853, for another nine years and a half. Clare helped Anne Baker with words and interpretations for her glossary of the Northamptonshire dialect, which she published in 1854. Dr Prichard, the superintendent, left the asylum, and Clare came into new hands. It was Dr Nesbitt, superintendent with Dr Wing till 1858, who described Clare in a letter as 'essentially a kind-hearted good-feeling man with an unusually large cerebral develop-ment, possessing great breadth and altitude of forehead, such as we are in the habit of associating with men of the highest order of intellect', and he added a bit to the tally of Clare's delusions — that he had been Wellington, had won and fought the Battle of Waterloo, 'that he had had his head shot off at this battle, while he was totally unable to explain the process by which it had been again affixed to his body' — that he would declare he had kicked his poetry out of the clods. Exceptionally, Clare would ejaculate and swear with 'no ordinary violence', when his anger was excited. He went on read-ing poems, and went on writing them; but not for much longer. John Godfrey, who described his last days in a newspaper notice about his death, declared that 'For several years previous to 1860, poor Clare did not write a single line; he would say "I have forgotten how to write"'. The asylum case-books are missing, unfortunately, until 1859. Then, for February, Dr Wing reports that Clare's bodily health was good for his advanced age, that it was still good in January 1860, though mentally he was incoherent. In the spring his mind settled and gathered a bit. He was persuaded to write,

I

and produced two, and then, two more poems, *The Daisy*, in March, and the *Address to John Clare*, and *Early Spring* and *The Green Lane*, all of them childishly, if sweetly simple.   Agnes Strickland, the historian, went to see Clare in August.   He gave her a manuscript of *The Daisy*, of which there were two versions; and told her he could not write because 'they have cut off my head, and picked out all the letters of the alphabet — all the vowels and consonants — and brought them out through my ears; and then they want me to write poetry! I can't do it.'   He finished the conversation by putting his hand on his head and saying vehemently that literature had destroyed it and had brought him to the asylum.   'His remark and action gave one the heartache', Miss Strickland added.

Wing entered up his condition in the case-books for February 1861 — when his health of body was still 'very good', of intellect 'very feeble'. His memory was bad, and 'he occasionally becomes excited, noisy and abusive using both profane and filthy language'. In 1862 he had 'probably . . . a slight apoplectic seizure', slipped and cut his head against the sharp edge of the table. The wound healed up slowly, but still his mind was the same — if not worse. In February 1863 they put him to bed after giddiness, and inability to use his legs. Wing noted again his occasional bad language, his delusions 'as strong as ever, sometimes fancying himself Lord Byron, at others a Sea Captain, etc.' In April his habits were becoming dirty; in July a trifle stronger, 'he is occasionally taken out amongst the flowers to view the beauties of that nature of which he was wont to be so fond, but without apparently awaking any pleasurable emotions.' In October his health had improved, but he was haunted still by phantoms, usually located on his left side, at whom he would 'often swear most coarsely'. But somewhere, it seems, in the winter, he collected himself again, for the very last time of so many times, to write with difficulty and in a childish hand his last poem of all, *Birds Nests*. ''Tis spring', it began, but the stimulus in this winter of 1863 was a spring out of the past, and he wrote of the nest-building chaffinch in the fens, where the wind was bleak, and the sun warm in a wooded corner. He was persuaded to the poem; and above it he set first a misremembered quotation from Burns,

> *The very child might understand*
> *The Deil had business on his hand,*

— as if he had had to start himself off by a recollection of poetry.

Various people visited him, besides Agnes Strickland, in the last year or two, and down to the last months; but in their accounts they add only pathos to the pathetic. Dr Wing is the best witness to the close of John Clare's extraordinary life. In January 1864 he was 'very helpless and quite childish'. In April his health was worse, his side slightly paralysed. His language was bad 'and he sometimes becomes so excited when swearing, that, always having a quid in his mouth, the piece finds its way into his larynx, which brings on a dreadful fit of coughing, and his face and head often become perfectly scarlet and give strong fears of a sudden apoplexy'. But he was still not in bed. A visitor talks of him being wheeled round the garden for the last time, in a chair. On 16 May they put him to bed, because of an awkward boil. The weather was unseasonable:

> May 20. He has appeared to feel the present excessively hot weather extremely and the perspiration would roll off him in streams as he lay in bed — This morning on being visited he was found to be completely comatose and never rallied, but died quietly late in the afternoon.

Statement of the cause of death

John Clare aged 72 years — (he was still two months short of his 71st birthday) died on May 20th 1864 at 4.55 p.m. in the presence of myself and others, the cause of his death being apoplexy.

EDWIN WING, M.D.,

May 21st. 1864   Medical Superintendent.

He arrived home in his coffin at Helpston (having taken his first journey by train) unexpectedly, it was said; and had to lie on trestles in the public house, while someone went off to find the sexton to dig him a grave.

ELEVEN

A Passionate Science

THE poetry of Gerard Manley Hopkins might be called a 'passionate science'. Like other poets and like painters of his era, this poet delighted in the observation and grasping of nature. With the greatest delicacy, strength, and intelligence he possessed his environment, making it the intimate vehicle for the passionate praises of his belief.

Hopkins is 'strange'; and for a long while his poems, which were first published in 1918, twenty-nine years after his death, had to be excused or grudged or argued about. Yet the strangeness of Hopkins is only concentrated in the excess and force of his qualities; there was nothing peculiar about his turn to a strong naturalism, to a passionate science, at his particular time in the nineteenth century; he was born five years after Cézanne, four years after Thomas Hardy, a year after Henry James. The scientific mind had slowly formed, slowly extroverted itself on to nature, and at an even slower rate the concerns of the artist had moved in the same direction, at least outwardly. The process had already known its phases and varieties. A being and a personality had been ascribed to nature; some artists had been pantheists, some nature-drunkards. Passionate emotions declined to an easy, popular sentiment about nature; poets and painters then corrected themselves by looking carefully at its select details.

In the 1860s, at home and at school in London, at the university in Oxford, Hopkins was familiar with the poems of Tennyson, Browning, Coventry Patmore, with the prose of Ruskin, and with the careful painting of the Pre-Raphaelites. Nature, he could well detect, had become something to employ: the selected details were presented almost for themselves, or else as ornaments of a moral tale. Tennyson in the sixties was talking about Irish landscape: 'I saw wonderful things there: twenty different showers at once in a great expanse — a vast yellow cloud with a little bit of rainbow stuck on one corner.' William Allingham, who put this on record, says that Tennyson swept his arm round for the cloud and gave a nick in the air with his thumb for the bit of rainbow; and then added, 'I wish I could bring these things in'. Or again, Allingham and Tenny-son talked of the kinship between white lilies and white peacocks; Alling-ham quoted Browning on a passage in Tennyson's *Princess*: 'Tennyson', said Browning, 'has taken to white peacocks. I always intended to use them. The Pope has a number of white peacocks.'

Browning intended to *use* white peacocks; Tennyson has *taken* to them, Tennyson wanted to *bring in* those things which he noticed so delicately. Hopkins, coming after them, more intelligent, more passionate, did not select details and add them up. He did not make rhetorical gestures to-wards nature; no wave of an arm for the yellow cloud, no nick of a thumb for the rainbow. A central fact of his poems is their birth in a science of empathy, carried so far that it distinguishes him from other English poets.

The journals he kept from 1868 to 1875 help to an understanding of Hopkins and nature. They are not very long, and occasionally they are difficult to read because Hopkins observes so closely and has to find peculiar language for the peculiar. Although he is personal and though he selects, one notices not so much his immediate passion, as a certain more or less scientific neutrality; this observer is free from most of our common associ-ative poetic preferences.

In 1871 Hopkins put down an observation on the leaves of wood-sorrel, a common enough European and English plant. 'The half-opened wood-sorrel leaves,' he wrote, 'the centre or spring of the leaflets rising foremost and the leaflets dropping back like ears, leaving straight-chipped clefts between them, look like some green lettering.' That is easy for the reader to take. Though wood-sorrel is not a species like rose or columbine or iris or lily in the tradition of aesthetic preference, a poet of the mid- or later nineteenth century may be expected to like an organism so crisp and delicate; and the accuracy of the description is quite obvious, the analogue is not immediately too peculiar. This comparison of the tiny, crisp leaves to green lettering by itself delimits the leaves and gives their colour its correct sharpness.

In 1872, on a Holy Saturday warm with thunder, Hopkins observed 'odd tufts of thin-textured very plump round clouds something like' —

and the convincing analogue is less expected — 'something like the eggs
in an opened ant-hill'. Clouds, as well, are poetic properties of the century
for other English poets, Patmore or Tennyson, or Barnes, or Bridges; yet
now the explicative object is more peculiar, the clouds are like ants' eggs in
the opened nest, they are different altogether from Tennyson's clouds in
water-colour; and the nature of the Hopkins science is more revealed. The
more excessive peculiarity begins to demand extra knowledge and attention;
although in his poems Hopkins does check too much eccentricity of observation, too much intrusion of peculiar things which are outside the likely experience of readers. The journal was for himself alone.

In 1870, concerned with the beauties and severities of the winter and
neutrally alive to things as much in one place as another, Hopkins observed
that 'the slate slabs of the urinals even are frosted with graceful sprays'. Or
in Lancashire in 1873 he watched a dying sheep under a stone hedge, making
of it an entirely matter-of-fact record without sentiment: 'There ran slowly
from his nostrils a thick flesh-coloured ooze, scarlet in places, coiling and
roping its way down, so thick that it looked like fat.'

Here, with letter-leaves, ant's egg clouds, roping ooze, and frost-sprayed
urinals, we are divorced from the averagely fine poetic detection of the nineteenth century. Here — and almost everywhere in Hopkins — we knock
our sensibilities against exactitudes and starknesses which may still repel or
dismay either those who live aesthetically in older, gentler modes or those
who do not require to live outwardly at all. The peculiarity goes further,
in one respect. In these notes out of the journal Hopkins uses 'like' —*like*
fat, *like* ants' eggs in the opened nest, *like* green lettering. In his greater
intensities 'like' disappears: adjectives, compound adjectives, compound
nouns, active and embracing and characterizing verbs, take its place; words
have been as starkly and freshly scrutinized and possessed as any other
relevant part or property of the poet's environment, until the selected words
are as close an equivalent as they can be to the things and the actions and
the states which they convey. Thus pigeons go 'strutting and *jod-jodding*
with their heads'. 'Jod' is a rare verb, yet its revival and adaptation are not
frigid or eccentric. One acknowledges quickly, after surprise, that pigeons
do behave exactly so.

In the acceptance of his poems, in the critical unravelling of their verbal knots, in the general consideration of Hopkins as a poet of his time who was yet absolutely distinct, this peculiar science of his does not receive enough attention. To know this poet one does not need dictionaries alone, or a fine recognition of ambiguities alone, or only a knowledge of the Ignatian Exercises or of Duns Scotus, 'Of realty the rarest-veined unraveller': one must also have or must also cultivate some equivalence of pure sensation, some of Hopkins's own accurate empathic cognition of the plants, trees, fruit, metals, skies, clouds, sunsets, birds, waters, surfaces, grains, activities, perfumes, of all the phenomena at which he stared or to which he opened his senses, precisely of

> *Landscape plotted and pieced — fold, fallow and plough;*
> *And áll trádes, their gear and tackle and trim.*

> *All things counter, original, spare, strange;*
> *Whatever is fickle, freckled (who knows how?)*
> *With swift, slow; sweet, sour; adazzle, dim.*

A story is told of one of the Jesuit fathers at Stonyhurst pointing out the young Hopkins to the gardener and telling him that Hopkins was a very fine scholar. The gardener replied that he had seen him hanging round and staring at a piece of glass on one of the paths: he had taken him for a 'natural'. But staring at glass among the gravel may involve the meanings, causes and principles of things.[1]

II

Hopkins was received by John Henry Newman into the Roman Catholic Church in 1866, while he was still an undergraduate. Nearly two years later, in 1868, he joined the Society of Jesus, and destroyed much of his poetry. He was then twenty-four. A long preparation now followed for

---

[1] The story was first recorded by André Bremond ('Je l'ai pris pour un innocent, *a natural*'). See *The Note-books & Papers of Gerard Manley Hopkins* (1937), p. 375. The edition of 1959, p. 408, adds another version from an old lay brother, who said that one of Hopkins's special delights was a path between the Seminary and the College at Stonyhurst. After a shower he would run and crouch down to stare at quartz glittering in the sun. 'Ay, a strange yoong man, crouching down that gate to stare at some wet sand. A fair natural 'e seemed to us, that Mr. 'opkins.'

his service and self-dedication as a priest, during which the making of more poems was abandoned as (his own word in later circumstances) a luxury. A total personality, though, cannot be changed, and the run of the journal which Hopkins kept from 1868 to 1875 proves the continuation, develop-ment, and enrichment of his particularizing science. In the last days of 1875 he returned to poetry with the grandeur and grimness of his memorial poem to the nuns drowned in the wreck of the *Deutschland*:

> *Thou mastering me*
> *God! giver of breath and bread;*
> *World's strand, sway of the sea;*
> *Lord of living and dead;*
> *Thou has bound bones and veins in me, fastened me flesh,*
> *And after it almost unmade, what with dread,*
> *Thy doing: and dost thou touch me afresh?*
> *Over again I feel thy finger and find thee.*

He was thirty-one; and it is the voice now of the man who has been active, dismayed, and exultant in a spiritual contest. In 1877 Hopkins was moving to the end of his preparation and was coming to a May-like crest in his life. His senses were exultantly and ecstatically open to his environment around the hill-perched St. Beuno's College above the Vale of Clwyd, in his purple and pastoral Wales. For a while he allowed himself the hours required for composition, and poem followed on poem. His world now was 'charged with the grandeur of God', stars sat like fire-folk in the air, weeds were shooting 'long and lovely and lush', pied beauty was fathered-forth by that deity he served, the kestrel stood to the gale with pride and valour and act and fire. Summer ended, but stooks of harvest rose around, 'barbarous in beauty', and the hills of Wales also rose around, 'azurous hung', the 'world-wielding shoulder' of his saviour,

> *Majestic — as a stallion stalwart, very-violet-sweet! —*

all in a poem which he made as 'the outcome of half an hour of extreme enthusiasm', on 1 September of that year. On 23 September Hopkins was ordained priest.

Alternating between gladness and dejection, Hopkins now made poems on and off until he died of enteric fever in 1889, the three richest seasons being this year of his ordination, the year 1879, in which he returned for a while to Oxford, where he wrote *Duns Scotus's Oxford*, *Binsey Poplars*, *Henry Purcell*, and *Peace*; and the dejected Irish year of 1885, of which the bitter, strong, and wonderful consequences were *Carrion Comfort*, *No worst, there is none*, and probably the sonnet in which he says that he wakes and feels 'the fell of dark, not day', in which he says

> *I am gall, I am heartburn.   God's most deep decree*
> *Bitter would have me taste: my taste was me.*

Added to the poems, these few details of his life help to answer the debate about the effects of religious discipline on Hopkins as a poet.   Did it make him a poet?   Did it reduce the range, the strength, the quantity of his art?   Unprofitable questions either way.   As a strong poet in spite of himself, self-ripened, he wrote for some thirteen years, joining in that time the English company of Herbert and Donne.   His nature, one would affirm, ordained his development, his choice of calling, his submission to religious rules.   His religious meditation on the meanings, causes, and principles of things then conferred — whatever misgivings he retained, whatever restrictions he imposed — the highest sanction on his pursuit and interests as a poet; and livened them with the greatest glint, fullness, and flush.

III

This will be more apparent if one looks for a moment at the poet in his earliest days, before Newman, and before he began to tread the hard discipline of the Jesuit Order, which would bring him, declared Newman, to heaven.   His earliest poems and diaries show two characteristics, the boy 'hanging around words and listening to what they say', and this boy so in love with words reacting with an already individual acuteness and consciousness to everything else around him.   In a diary of 1863 — Hopkins was nineteen — both characteristics are clear.   For example, he picks up words with gr- and cr- sounds and listens to them discriminately and as kin to each other:

Grind, gride, gird, grit, groat, grate, greet, κρούειν, crush, crash, κροτεῖν, etc.
Original meaning to *strike, rub*, particularly *together*.   That which is

produced by such means is the *grit*, the *groats* or crumbs, like *fragmentum* from *frangere*, *bit* from *bite*. *Crumb, crumble* perhaps akin. To *greet*, to strike the hands together (?). *Greet*, grief, wearing, *tribulation*. *Grief* possibly connected. *Gruff*, with a sound of two things rubbing together.

Then a page away he catches carefully at the active facts of water coming through a lock, or he particularizes the blue⁄green of wheat: it suggests silver, is the 'exact complement of carnation', and nearest of any green he knows to emerald, 'the real emerald *stone*'.

The year before, during the Christmas holidays of 1862, Hopkins had completed the poem he called *A Vision of the Mermaids*. As Robert Bridges remarked, it was Keatsian, but it also involved fashionable interests and extroversions of the time which Hopkins liked. Sunsets — these were an interest which was to last him all his life. Already he tries to grasp their forms and colours:

> *Plum⁄purple was the west; but spikes of light*
> *Spear'd open lustrous gashes, crimson⁄white . . .*
> *And thro' their parting lids there came and went*
> *Keen glimpses of the inner firmament.*

In the fifties able naturalists had discovered and popularized by their books an aesthetic of sea pools and sea margins, of the delicate shapes and the fungal gemmy brilliance of their creatures. Hopkins had stared into the pools, he had examined, so one would think, books by the high (or low) priest of the mania, P. H. Gosse. His brothers followed the pursuit and kept marine aquariums. So Hopkins decorated the Keatsian mermaids of his poem with marine⁄biological adornments, *Nautilus, Strombus, Glaucus, Eolis* —

> metal⁄lustred
> *With growths of myriad feelers, crystalline*
> *To shew the crimson streams that inward shine,*[1]
> *Which, lightening o'er the body rosy⁄pale,*
> *Like shiver'd rubies dance or sheen of sapphire hail—*

[1] 'The most lovely species was the exquisite *Eolis coronata*, with tentacles sur⁄rounded by membranous coronets, and with crowded clusters of papillae, of crimson and blue that reflect the most gem⁄like radiance.' — P. H. Gosse, 1853.

— and with sea-anemones, which he names 'flesh-flowers of the rock'.

He tells a story reminding one a little of Keats covering his tongue and throat with cayenne-pepper (according to Haydon) so as to appreciate the coldness and glory of claret. One mermaid in the *Vision* had been diadem'd with the anemones. 'I thought it would look strikingly graceful, etc.', Hopkins said soon afterwards, in a letter in which he referred to the poem, 'to wear sea-anemones round my forehead. . . . So I put a large one on in the middle, and it fixed itself correctly. Now one has heard of their stinging, but I had handled them so often unharmed, and who could have imagined a creature stinging with its — base, you call it in sea-anemones? But it did, loudly, and when the pain had ceased a mark remained, which is now a large scar.'

'I have particular periods of admiration', he wrote in this same letter of 1863, 'for particular things in Nature; for a certain time I am astonished at the beauty of a tree, shape, effect, etc., then when the passion, so to speak, has subsided, it is consigned to my treasury of explored beauty, while something new takes its place in my enthusiasm. The present fury is the ash, and perhaps barley and two shapes of growth in leaves and one in tree boughs and also a conformation of fine-weather cloud.'

IV

Such was the exploration Hopkins began as a child and continued, though cautiously, after he had become a Jesuit and indeed for all his life. One must consider also his exploration of himself, a self individual, strong, originating, in some sense sceptical as well as proud. The young Hopkins had intellectual and sensual pride, yet little blindness, little deafness or dumbness. All must be examined afresh, nature, language, poetry and poetics, and religion. Dustiness must be blown off to reveal the solid. All that is too easily, too lazily accepted must be scrutinized and tested for truth. Accepted Tennyson, then the emperor of poetry, he examined and 'began to doubt', as he confided in 1864 to his friend of the story of the sea-anemones, discovering that Tennyson himself was Tennysonian, that he wrote chiefly in the average or lower poetic language which Hopkins (always liking to mint his own critical concepts and terms) named 'Parnassian'.

Accepted religion he examined, as if that as well were too 'Parnassian'. And accepted self: that also must be cleared and sifted. Rapidly, one may conclude, the young Hopkins came on guard against his own intellectual impatience, his own elastic steeliness, his own sensuality. As a boy at school, seeming slight and gentle, he withstood a headmaster 'whose logic was comprised in the birch'. There was no fight in him, another of the boys recalled, 'unless he was unjustly used or attacked, and in that he was godlike, for it sprang from his love of justice or truth'.

Here there were dangers. More than twenty years later the musician Sir Robert Stewart, who loved him as a priest and a man and attempted to instruct him in music, wrote to his 'darling padre' that he was impatient of correction when he had made up his mind on any point — 'I saw, ere we had conversed ten minutes on our first meeting, that you are one of those special pleaders who never believe yourself wrong in any respect. You always excuse yourself for anything I object to in your writing or music so I think it a pity to disturb you in your happy dreams of perfectibility — nearly everything in your music was wrong — but you will not admit that to be the case.' He could not always forgo the artist's self-certainty. Yet in his long correspondence with Robert Bridges (who destroyed his side of the exchange), love and self-examination had to fight an intellectual impatience with Bridges' shortcomings, which in another man would have become intellectual contempt.

Most of all it was the danger of a sensualism out of hand, the danger of the attractions of 'mortal beauty', even when checked and tasted and observed strictly, and of mortal beauty in part in his personal relationships, that Hopkins finely understood. 'To what serves mortal beauty — dangerous?' If he came to an answer which satisfied him, that lay in the future. When at twenty-four he chose his hard vocation, his discipline for life, one may suspect that he already feared this danger and other dangerous elements in the self that he now denied. They could be dedicated, nevertheless; they could be refined. It might be argued that his choice, as well as his superior intellect and finer nature, saved him from a collapse analogous to the poetic and actual collapse of Swinburne (whom Hopkins detested as a poet); also that his vocation did in fact preserve, test, refine, and concentrate the power which eventually broke out in his exultant and his despondent poems.

v

Nature, 'excluding nature's most interesting productions, the works of man', according to Samuel Butler's remark, and in the usage of the time taken 'to mean mountains, rivers, clouds and undomesticated animals and plants', ringed the mid-Victorian sensibility in all its forms. In a new way elementary details from the sciences of nature did not repel either poets or painters. A poet (Tennyson's brother) might observe in his sonnets how 'passive jellies wait the turn of tide' or explain how a child (she had, of course, been gathering shells) took the homeward path which led

> *Beneath yon dark-blue ridge, when, sad to tell,*
> *On her fair head the gloomy Lias fell.*

This concern with nature could be indulgent, adding up simply or luxuriously to nothing, like Humpty Dumpty's recitation:

> *In spring when woods are getting green*
> *I'll try to tell you what I mean —*

or like Edward Lear's pie of pale purple amblonguses, to which a small pigeon, two slices of beef, four cauliflowers and any number of oysters were added before it was served up in a clean dish and then thrown out of the window as fast as possible; or else it could be justified, the justification for naturalist-before-Darwin or poet-before-Darwin being in one form or another a simple resort to the Christian god: everything was this god's handiwork. 'Do not study matter for its own sake, but as the countenance of God', Charles Kingsley advised in the 1840s. 'Study the forms and colours of leaves and flowers, and the growth and habits of plants; not to classify them, but to admire them and to adore God. Study the sky! Study water! Study trees! Study the sounds and scents of nature!'

That might have been a programme entirely congenial to the young Hopkins twenty years later, had it not been for Kingsley's conclusion: that these beautiful things were to be studied 'in order to recombine the elements of beauty', were to be studied next 'as allegories and examples from whence moral reflections may be drawn', and last 'as types of certain tones of feeling'. Natural objects were thus, a little smugly, spiritual utilities. For Hopkins

they were, if sources of possible danger, also divine concrete realities; and
to such middle-protestant morality Hopkins the Catholic would much have
preferred Philip Gosse the Plymouth Brother and fundamentalist, lamely
and sincerely ejaculating over his marine animals: 'Yes, O Lord! the
lovely tribes that tenant these dark pools are, like the heavens themselves,
"the work of thy fingers", and do as truly as those glowing orbs above us
"declare thy glory".'

Indeed, it was simply the case for nature as a declaration of his god's
glory, an ultimately comprehensive nature centring upon man and the works
of man (i.e. including language, poem, poetic structures), that Hopkins
elaborated with subtlety and dignity; and it was this elaboration which
allowed him to break at last into the exultancy of the poems of 1877. He
had, one may believe, discovered what were the limits of self-abnegation,
he had learned to recognize the irreducible solid minimum of self which
could not be altered, whittled, or kept down. His particularizing science
originated in his own being, in that self now so straitly and willingly disciplined; if by that self it was developed intellectually, it was also justifiable
by religion and religious philosophy: it was indeed, as he came to see it,
a part of his religion, which worked upon it and flushed it with its own
increase and extra enthusiasm.

Hopkins was clear on that eventually; he was clear on the world 'charged
with the grandeur of God', he was explicit, in season, that the world of
nature is a leasehold let out by God, paying God for rent, he says, praise,
reverence, service and God's own glory. 'Passionate science' is justified also
as a description of his own activity, since Hopkins endeavours to be a re-
formed kind of poet, endeavours not to project *his* emotions into the objects
of his enthusiastic attention, the world not being charged with any grandeur
of his, of his own subjective devising. Endeavouring to let each object
exist *per se* in his apprehension of it, in the most sheer language entirely
and accurately correspondent to the sum of the qualities of the object, he
would hardly have agreed with Newman, of an older generation, in setting
science against poetry, in declaring that it was the 'aim of science to get
a hold of things, to grasp them', while poetry's business was to delight
only in the indefinite, having 'the vague, the uncertain, the irregular'
among its attributes. Hopkins knew that it was poetry, then more than

ever, which needed to hold and to grasp at least with the firmness, if not
with all the other characteristics, of science.   The school of Wordsworth,
which expired, he thought, in Newman as a poet, was not his school,
and was to be criticized as one of 'faithful but not rich observers of nature',
not concrete observers.   Crabbe, always underestimated by adherents of
the indefinitude of poetry, was the poet Hopkins praised for 'a strong and
modern realistic eye'.

VI

It is in the sermon which he based on the opening of the Spiritual Exercises
of St Ignatius, that Hopkins has left the most precise explanation of the
way in which creation, according to his belief, gives tongue to the glory
of God:

> The sun and the stars shining glorify God.   They stand where he
> placed them, they move where he bid them.   'The heavens declare the
> glory of God.'   They glorify God, *but they do not know it.*

That is the point.   'The birds sing to him', Hopkins goes on,

> the thunder speaks of his terror, the lion is like his strength, the sea is
> like his greatness, the honey like his sweetness; they are something
> like him, they make him known, they tell of him, they give him glory —

But they do not know that they give him glory, they do not know God, they
are brute things thinking only of food or of nothing, giving by themselves,
says Hopkins, 'poor praise, faint reverence, slight service', giving no more,
a fine phrase, than 'dull glory',

Yet amidst them all is man, created like the rest to praise, reverence, and
serve this one God, to give him glory: but man is different — 'but man can
know God, *can mean to give him glory.*   This then was why he was made, to
give God glory and to mean to give it.'   Hopkins sees glory given not only
in prayer but in the common avocations of man:

> Smiting an anvil, sawing a beam, driving horses, scouring, every-
> thing gives God some glory if being in his grace you do it as your duty.
> To go to communion worthily gives God great glory, but to take food
> in thankfulness and temperance gives him glory too.   To lift up the

hands in prayer gives God glory, but a man with a dungfork in his
hand, a woman with a sloppail, give him glory too. He is so great
that all things give him glory if you mean they should. So then, my
brethren, live.

In other words, man alone of creatures on earth transforms dull glory into
lively glory: if a man is a poet (Hopkins remarks in the sermon that poets,
their minds and all, flower and fruit as well as tree, are creatures of God),
in his poems he can transform the dull glory of the unintentional praise of
God-created objects into the bright glory of the intended praise of man:

> *And what is Earth's eye, tongue, or heart else, where*
> *Else, but in dear and dogged man?*

For glory, objects and beholder have only to meet, Hopkins declared in
that enthusiastic poem conceived as he walked home across the autumnal
evening Vale of Clwyd on 1 September 1877:

> *Summer ends now; now, barbarous in beauty, the stooks rise*
> *Around; up above, what wind-walks! what lovely behaviour*
> *Of silk-sack clouds! has wilder, wilful-wavier*
> *Meal-drift moulded ever and melted across skies?*
>
> *I walk, I lift up, I lift up heart, eyes,*
> *Down all that glory in the heavens to glean our Saviour;*
> *And, éyes, heárt, what looks, what lips yet gave you a*
> *Rapturous love's greeting of realer, of rounder replies?*
>
> *And the azurous hung hills are his world-wielding shoulder*
> *Majestic — as a stallion stalwart, very-violet-sweet! —*
> *These things, these things were here and but the beholder*
> *Wanting; which two when they once meet,*
> *The heart rears wings bold and bolder*
> *And hurls for him, O half hurls earth for him off under his feet.*

Hurrahing, praising, glorying, and exclamation — these explain Hopkins
as a poet. 'No single sentence', Humphrey House declared in a note to the
sermon I have just quoted, 'better explains the motive and direction of Hopkins' life than *Man was created to praise*', and he maintained that the sentence
should be remembered always when the critic regrets anything or grieves for

rard Hopkins, reflected in a lake
g. 14.

Gerard Manley Hopkins, drawn by himself, aged 20

William Barnes in old age

anything in that full life of Hopkins which was more than poetry — 'To remember it is not to share or advocate the belief; but it is essential to an intelligent reading of his work.'

VII

Nature and glory in nature must be grasped by reaching to nature's qualities and selfhoods. The god of Gerard Hopkins is not inside nature — 'he is under the world's splendour and wonder' — but one thing he does: through the nature he has made he passes the voltage of the current of his love, his grandeur. That current, in the words of one of the comments of Hopkins on the Ignatian Exercises, is 'the Holy Ghost sent to us through creatures'. So one penetrates to the full meaning of his sonnet on *God's Grandeur*:

> *The world is charged with the grandeur of God.*
>   *It will flame out, like shining from shook foil;*
>   *It gathers to a greatness, like the ooze of oil*
> *Crushed. Why do men then now not reck his rod?*
> *Generations have trod, have trod, have trod;*
>   *And all is seared with trade; bleared, smeared with toil;*
>   *And wears man's smudge and shares man's smell: the soil*
> *Is bare now, nor can foot feel, being shod.*
>
> *And for all this, nature is never spent;*
>   *There lives the dearest freshness deep down things;*
> *And though the last lights off the black West went*
>   *Oh, morning, at the brown brink eastward, springs —*
> *Because the Holy Ghost over the bent*
>   *World broods with warm breast and with ah! bright wings.*

And so his parallel statement that all things 'are charged with love, are charged with God and if we know how to touch them give off sparks and take fire, yield drops and flow, ring and tell of him'. This current runs through Hopkins as creature, through the stooks barbarous in beauty, through skies, clouds, stars; and he hoped, if he was a true poet, that the great voltage of love and grandeur would run through the best of his poems in their hammer-forged equivalence of words, objects, and purpose, in their

K

close structure, in the roll, the rise, the carol, the creation of *The Starlight Night*, for example:

> *Look, look: a May-mess, like on orchard boughs!*
>   *Look! March-bloom, like on mealed-with-yellow sallows!*
> *These are indeed the barn; withindoors house*
> *The shocks.   This piece-bright paling shuts the spouse*
>   *Christ home.   Christ and his mother and all his hallows.*

Deeply involved and involving all, is a concept it is necessary to understand, so far as it can be coldly analysed — that 'inscape' as he called it, which Hopkins had worked out in his twenties and which he employed all through his life. Well examined by Father W. A. M. Peters in his study of Hopkins, it includes more than pattern and design: inscape includes the distinctiveness of objects, the 'outward reflection of the *inner* nature of a thing', indeed all the 'set of its individuating characteristics'. Hopkins used it first, so far as we know, in some notes on Parmenides, on Being and Not-being, in the 1860s. Spanning the years, he spoke in 1886 of 'the essential and only lasting thing' which was lacking in certain poetry — 'what I call *inscape* — that is species or individually-distinctive beauty'. So inscape is akin to the 'self' Hopkins writes of, the totality of the animate or inanimate individual; and both inscape and self were reinforced by the *haecceitas*, or 'this-ness' of the philosophy of his admired Duns Scotus (see again the *Gerard Manley Hopkins* of Father Peters). 'Self', 'selving', is strongest of all in human nature, 'more highly pitched, selved, and distinctive than anything in the world'. Searching nature, says Hopkins, 'I taste self but at one tankard, that of my own being'. But in all beings, everywhere, selfbeing and inscape can be recognized, must indeed be recognized:

> *As kingfishers catch fire, dragonflies draw flames;*
>   *As tumbled over rim in roundy wells*
>   *Stones ring; like each tucked string tells, each hung bell's*
> *Bow swung finds tongue to fling out broad its name;*
> *Each mortal thing does one thing and the same:*
>   *Deals out that being indoors each one dwells;*
>   *Selves — goes itself; myself it speaks and spells;*
> *Crying What I do is me: for that I came . . .*

Thus in his passionate, god-praising science Hopkins is for ever grasping at what is elusive, yet not vague; at what is essence, yet solid, permeating quality, yet totality. Poetry itself he describes as 'speech only employed to carry the inscape of speech for the inscape's sake'. He grasps at the inscapes of Gothic tracery, the horse, Edinburgh Castle rock, bluebells, a man, a sonnet, a tree (in his journal, in 1874, he talks of a 'delicate flying shafted ash' having 'single sonnet-like inscape'), a sunset, the Milky Way, a view, a complicated swirl of water, a kestrel hanging, as he describes it, at the hover. So inscapes, no less than the things which have them, are of his god's glory.

VIII

Sunsets and water. Let us take these two, for a while. The observed complexity of either one exemplifies the passionate science of Hopkins, which is, after all, the science of inscaping. He hangs over runs of water, breakings of water, spreading of water, he stares at them, he describes them, he draws them as well in pencil with that kind of sureness and capture one sees in the notebooks of Leonardo. In 1872 he wrote in his journal of being unsatisfied with his observation of waves after they break, of how difficult it is 'to law out the shapes and the sequence of the running' — the running of milky surf up the beach. The natural complexities of individual sunsets he had been lawing out with a fantastic intensity from childhood, or the time of his early poems, as we have seen. Added to the sunsets in his verse, another fifteen at least are individuated by Hopkins in his journal. For the *materia* of all these sunsets his objects and substances include flowers — roses, yellow lilies, the pink to mauve flowers of the wild mallow, for example — plums and damsons, yellow and red candle wax, crimson ice, quilted crimson silk, oil, steel, gold, brass, bronze. As a climax to his sunset inscaping he was able to write letters to *Nature* at the time of the exceptional Krakatao sunsets in 1883 (after Krakatao in the Dutch Indies had stupendously erupted and ejected into the upper atmosphere dust which travelled round the world), in which he sets out the exact chromatic differences he was able to discern: he could do so because he held exactly in his knowledge, in that 'treasury of explored beauty', the inscapes of so many a sunset not interfered with by this volcanic dust from the other hemisphere.

He individuates the complex, he individuates the apparently simple — a species of tree, for instance, in its proper adjective: 'silk-beech, scrolled ash, packed sycamore, wild wychelm, hornbeam fretty . . .,' in which only 'wild' proffers an unusual vagueness;[1] and it is clear that editors of Hopkins and commentators should really familiarize themselves rather more than they do with his inscapes, with the natural objects, in their activity, which may carry a weight of implication inside his poems — with metals, jewels, flowers, fruits, birds, and the rest. Again and again in the collected poems, in the books and the many essays about him, missing notes or understandings are required, sensual and scientific. A key plant may ask for a note — for instance, the 'fretty chervil' which leaves and laces the banks and brakes in one of the greatest of his sonnets, in contrast to Hopkins himself who was then the eunuch of time with no water at his roots:

> *See, banks and brakes*
> *Now, leavèd how thick! lacèd they are again*
> *With fretty chervil, look, and fresh wind shakes*
>
> *Them; birds build — but not I build; no, but strain,*
> *Time's eunuch, and not breed one work that wakes.*
> *Mine, O thou lord of life, send my roots rain.*

That 'fretty chervil' at least requires to be known for the plant it is, *Anthriscus sylvestris*; not any species, but that one which so whitely and lacily is part of the juice and joy of the dangerous vegetative month along every road and every lane of Hopkins's elmy England.

In the *May Magnificat* Hopkins wrote of the thrush, 'star-eyed strawberry-breasted', above her 'Cluster of bugle blue eggs thin'. 'Bugle blue', goes the comment of the editor of Hopkins's poems, 'query, like blue beads'; which is dictionary scholarship. There does exist a kind of glass bead known as a 'bugle', though bugles are long tubular glass beads sewn on dresses as ornaments, usually black, not blue. Bugle blue — bugle, or *Ajuga reptans*, is a common plant blossoming in May, the month of the poem, a plant which shines like the surface of eggs, which is juicy, lush, and in its

---

[1] Yet the wych-elm does display a flexible wildness of structure in contrast to the dark-pencilled masses of the common elm.

flowers intensely blue, which grows conspicuously in the damp hedgeside grass of meadows, an element of the 'greenworld':

> *Flesh and fleece, fur and feather,*
> *Grass and greenworld all together;*
> *Star-eyed strawberry-breasted*
> *Throstle above her nested*
>
> *Cluster of bugle blue eggs thin*
> *Forms and warms the life within;*
> *And bird and blossom swell*
> *In sod or sheath or shell.*

The plant meaning is the primary one; a hint of glass and thinness may be included as well.

Or consider again the superbly scintillating analogues for the stars, the fire-folk in *Starlight Night*, including white doves, orchard blossom, sallow catkins, leaves of abele or white poplar — and whitebeam:

> *Wind-beat whitebeam! airy abeles set on a flare!*

Father Peters, generally one of the best critics of Hopkins, rashly thinks that *wind-beat whitebeam* has to do with white or silver beams of moonlight, though this night over Wales, which is giving Hopkins his ecstasy, is a starlight night in which the stars are sharp and fierce, not drowned or paled by a moon; and though the parallelism demands a tree. He does not believe that 'whitebeam' can be the tree *Sorbus aria*, which has that name, and which he and other commentators, one following another, only think of as a small tree which happens to have delicate white underleaves.

But what does this small tree do with the leaves? Hopkins knew: those who are expert on Hopkins but not upon inscapes, do not know.

With an exact appropriateness to the poem, to the starlight night, this whitebeam, in darker scrub or woodland, or among black yews, magnificently tosses its leaves back to front, the wind beats the whole tree magnificently white.

IX

These are small examples of neglecting the passionate science, and so the
meaning of Hopkins. A big example of imperfect attention, by which
Hopkins gives only half that he has to give, is in all the conflicting comments
upon *The Windhover*, that poem of 1877 once more, which Hopkins looked
upon as his best:

> *I caught this morning morning's minion, king-*
>   *dom of daylight's dauphin, dapple-dawn-drawn Falcon, in his riding*
>   *Of the rolling level underneath him steady air, and striding*
> *High there, how he rung upon the rein of a wimpling wing*
> *In his ecstasy! then off, off forth on swing,*
>   *As a skate's heel sweeps smooth on a bow-bend: the hurl and*
>   *gliding*
>   *Rebuffed the big wind.   My heart in hiding*
> *Stirred for a bird, — the achieve of, the mastery of the thing!*
>
> *Brute beauty and valour act, oh, air, pride, plume, here*
>   *Buckle!* AND *the fire that breaks from thee then, a billion*
>   *Times told lovelier, more dangerous, O my chevalier!*
>
>   *No wonder of it: shéer plód makes plough down sillion*
> *Shine, and blue-bleak embers, ah my dear,*
>   *Fall, gall themselves, and gash gold-vermilion.*

The discussions about this sonnet were opened in 1926 by the distinguished
critic I. A. Richards, yet in no interpretation down to the most recent ones
in England and America, does any commentator ever seem to have studied,
as a watcher of the bird, the one exciting activity on which the fullness of
the poem must hang. No commentator seems to have studied the wing-
beating, hovering, gliding, swooping and recovering of the kestrel or windhover, the way the bird forces itself into equilibrium against the wind, a
study which cannot be conducted inside a dictionary, a Cambridge college,
or a religious seminary.

There is no great trouble about the activity at least of the first lines. The
kestrel, favourite of the morning, drawn forward into prominence by the
dappled dawn, rides the air, a knight upon its horse, it hovers into and on
the wind; then strides to a new position:

and striding
High there, how he rung upon the rein of a wimpling wing.

He rings ecstatically on the rein of a wimpling wing. This ringing upon
the rein — it may not be easy altogether, yet what ingenious technical explanations for it have been advanced! To 'ring upon the rein', as of horses
reined to the trainer in the riding school — that suggestion was made first
of all by I. A. Richards. It doesn't do. It would be no credit to Hopkins,
who seldom stretches things so far. To 'ring' — it is a technical term of
falconry — to rise spirally in flight. Perhaps, but is that required? The
kestrel strides to its new position, it does not spiral. After the stride, it must
start hovering again, this hawk which is rider and not steed, it must ring
again upon the rein of its wing, to keep place in and on the wind, its steed
and its environment. But it is not only the rider, the dauphin of daylight's
kingdom, the favourite of the morning, it is a hung bell. That it rings on
the rein of its wing tells of the bird filling the sky with its own ringing fame
(a ringing rhyme runs through the first eight lines), its own report, its own
excellence, God's fame, God's excellence; tells also of the tense ringing
vibration of the kestrel's typical movement. '*Myself* it speaks and spells,'
as Hopkins affirmed of each mortal thing in the sonnet *As kingfishers catch
fire*. And recall Hopkins declaring that all things are charged with God:
all things *give off sparks and take fire* ('the fire that breaks from thee then'),
yield drops and flow, ring and tell of him.

The hung bell is clinched by that Kingfisher or selving sonnet, which
Hopkins wrote some years later; he returned there to the kestrel, its ringing
and its swing on the bow bend:

> *As tumbled over rim in roundy wells*
> *Stones ring; like each tucked string tells, each hung bell's*
> *Bow swung finds tongue to fling out broad its name.*

There, too, internally, he uses the same ringing rhyme. But on the rein?
It is complex. The wimpling wing, however, is a rein from the bird to
the air it rides and controls, and the bird, the rider, is also a bell ringing and
jingling upon that moving rein. 'Wimpling' is rippling, quick-beating.
Yet even this simple word has had its esoteric interpretation: that Hopkins
used it (as if he had watched the bird with powerful field-glasses) 'because

of the way the feathers appear in graceful folds when seen from below'. Wimpling is no more than the activity, not absolutely regular, but with a variation of speed and beat (the bird misses a beat sometimes), expressed already in the quick-acting words '. . . daylight's dauphin, dapple-dawn-drawn Falcon', in which the missing of a wing-beat — so close and material are the equivalencies between object and word, object and verse movement — is indicated in the pause one has to make after 'dawn': 'dapple-dawn-drawn Falcon'.

There is another crux of meaning later in the sonnet when Hopkins continues

> *Brute beauty and valour and act, oh, air, pride, plume, here*
> *Buckle!*

Much more ingenuity than is required has gone to unravelling, or smudging, the rest of the poem and its purpose — that from the conjunctive AND in the tenth line Christ begins to speak to the kestrel, or Hopkins begins to address his own heart; that his 'heart in hiding' is in hiding from the kestrel's natural world, lost in the dismality of his vocation. His heart for a while, in fact, was in hiding *from* his vocation, from his proper being, his God, as in a later fragment:

> *Once I turned from thee and hid,*
> *Bound on what thou hadst forbid;*
> *Sow the wind I would; I sinned:*
> *I repent of what I did.*

He was yielding for a while too much to the kestrel's dangerous mortal beauty:

> *To what serves mortal beauty — dangerous; does set danc-*
> *ing blood — the O-Seal-that-so feature, flung prouder form*
> *Then Purcell tune lets tread to? See: it does this: keeps warm*
> *Men's wits to the things that are; what good means — where a*
> *   glance*
> *Master more may than gaze . . .*
> *What do then? how meet beauty? Merely meet it; own,*
> *Home at heart, heaven's sweet gift; then leave, let that alone.*
> *Yes, wish that though, wish all, God's better beauty, grace.*

Nevertheless, the kestrel was a portion of that dull glory given to God, it was charged with God, giving off sparks and taking fire, ringing and telling of God; it was, though dangerous, heaven's sweet gift.

As for the last three lines, the fire broke from the kestrel, the windhover, the standgale (to recall another of its excellent English names), in the course of, and by dint of, its natural avocation; as in the sheer plod of ploughing, the steel mould-board or breast of the plough becomes shiny from the turned earth down the long strips of land (sillions),[1] and as embers which have become blue-bleak reveal, when their dull surface drops away, the heat and colour inside them. He thinks, addressing Christ in 'ah my dear', of the sheer plod of his own nine years, as it would soon be, of long preparation; of his own natural avocation since he had chosen to enter the Jesuit Order; of the asceticism of those years. The sheer plod puts a shine puon the plough which is himself; his at times bitter asceticism and exhaustion of mind reduces him to bleak embers which nevertheless gall and gash themselves to gold-vermilion — which are, in fact, the ashes of his other poem *Morning, Midday, and Evening Sacrifice*:

> *The vault and scope and schooling*
> *And mastery in the mind,*
> *In silk-ash kept from cooling,*
> *And ripest under rind.*

x

Of such a kind is the interweaving of subtleties, complexities, and force and fire which Hopkins can convey in the inscapes of his passionate science. His poetry can, of course, be read on different levels — for its delight in natural phenomena so ecstatically and so exactly caught in

---

[1] 'Ploughshare' is also intimated in 'sheer plod' ι. must, I think, be the plough that acquires shine, though the mould-board also imparts shine to the furrow. 'Plough down sillion' could be a composite noun. However the context asks for shine self-acquired by an *active* instrument, bird, plough, priest. Hopkins's editor, and this typifies the refusal to see as Hopkins saw, glosses 'sillion' as 'furrow', though sillions or selions, the long separate strips of each furlong in the Open Field, were still frequently to be seen when Hopkins wrote. There is a record, by the way of Hopkins, in Ireland, stopping the jaunting-car he was travelling in, and persuading a ploughman to let him have the feeling and experience of guiding the plough for a while as it cut through the soil.

language-structures of superb energy, which so refreshes one's response:

> *And a gray heaven does the hush'd earth house.*

We can love him for that 'touching of things', which is not small; or we can read him as well for the thought which, in his words, was fathered by such fine delight, for the religious poetry of a man beyond poetry, who could have said, as in his translation of the hymn *O Deus, ego amo te,*

> *O God, I love thee, I love thee —*
> *Not out of hope of heaven for me*
> *Nor fearing not to love and be*
> *In the everlasting burning.*

Hopkins wrote for no public, had no care for publication, and as a Jesuit did not entertain the thought of poetic fame. Only to eleven people had he shown any of his mature poems, to four members of his own society, his parents and his two sisters, and the three poets Dixon, Bridges, and Patmore.

The Foundation Exercise of St Ignatius begins not only that man was created to praise, reverence and serve God and by that means to save his soul —which was sufficient for Hopkins — but that all things else on earth were created to help man towards that end: man should use them just so far as they afford him that help and should 'withdraw himself from them just so far as they hinder him'. Composition could interfere, composition was then abandoned: upon his premises there was a pursuit for Hopkins utterly more compelling, but that pursuit was none the less the condition of the greatness and power of the verse — the best of it — which he did allow himself to write.

He considered that poetry was unprofessional. Yet among those letters to Bridges, Dixon, and Patmore, which themselves add up to one of the most direct, strict, piercing, and convincing bodies of criticism in the English language, he establishes a test which does not, and never can, defeat his own poetry — that 'a kind of touchstone of the highest or most living art is seriousness; not gravity but the being in earnest with your subject — reality'. By that being in earnest he lives.[1]

---

[1] I see that some of the annotations I suggested in this essay, which was first printed in 1953, have been adopted in the 4th edition of Hopkins's *Collected Poems,* 1967, though the point has not been completely understood every time.

TWELVE

William Barnes

RECOLLECTIONS we have of William Barnes are mainly of him as a middle-aged, old, or dying poet. Many of them are in the *Life* written by his daughter, Lucy Baxter — a book, so few were those who admired Barnes, which sold 267 copies. William Allingham, Coventry Patmore, Tennyson, and later on Edmund Gosse and Thomas Hardy, all knew him in this way as the patriarchal clergyman with the long beard.

Gosse and Hardy went to see Barnes not long before his death: 'We found him in bed in his study, his face turned to the window, where the light came streaming in through flowering plants, his brown books on all sides of him save one, the wall behind him being hung with old green tapestry. He had a scarlet bedgown on, a kind of soft biretta of dark red wool on his head, from which his long white hair escaped on to the pillow; his grey beard, grown very long, upon his breast; his complexion, which you recollect ["you" is Coventry Patmore] as richly bronzed, has become blanched by keeping indoors, and is now waxily white where it is not waxily pink; the blue eyes half shut, restless under languid lids ... I wish', Gosse went on, 'I could paint for you the strange effect of this old, old, man, lying in cardinal scarlet in his white bed ...' Palgrave also describes him a year before his death, his 'finely cut face', his 'hands fine like a girl's', adding, 'Titian or Tintoret had no nobler, no more highborn looking sitter among the doges of Venice'.

His death came on 7 October 1886. And on the 11th, when he was carried out, the sun flashed off his coffin to Thomas Hardy as, some fields away, he was walking across to the funeral — to the funeral of the man from whom he had learned the forms of poetry:

> *Thus with a farewell to me he signalled on his grave-way*
> *As with a wave of his hand.*

William Barnes was eighty-five or eighty-six when he died.   There is
some doubt whether the year of his birth had been 1800 (as Thomas Hardy
believed) or 1801, though certainly he was christened early in 1801.   Perhaps
because he was small and delicate there may have been some long interval
between birth and being taken off to the font.   'I, the son of John and
Grace Barnes', his own manuscript *Notes on the Life of William Barnes* begin,
'was born at Rush-hay, a farmling at Bagber in the Parish of Sturminster
Newton in the Vale of Blackmore' — and from there on, it is true, we know
at least the skeleton of his quiet and isolated life.   First there was a dame-
school, then a school at Sturminster, and then 'I was taken while yet a boy
into the office of Mr Dashwood, a learned lawyer of Sturminster, and after
a while I went into that of Mr Coombs at Dorchester, and was just then
eighteen years old, and very kind to me was Mr Coombs. . . .   I was not
unfaithful to my desk, but I daily spent a share of my spare time on the
study of those higher branches, Latin and Greek and others, which I had
not reached at school, but with my strong love of learning and art I felt that
I was not in my right, or most mind-fitting way of life.'   A chief event in
his childhood in the Vale of Blackmore had been the death of his mother,
a chief event in Dorchester his meeting with Julia Miles, whom he married
in 1827.   He had first seen her climbing down from the coach in High
Street, a child of sixteen with blue eyes, wearing a sky-blue spencer or
jacket.   She was the cause and the centre of his love poems in her life and
after her death; from his own boyhood, when he celebrated her 'bright,
azure eyes' in a poem in his first book printed at Dorchester in 1820, into
his old age.

When he married Julia Miles (whose father was in the excise at Dorchester), Barnes was running his own school, just outside his native county,
at Mere, in Wiltshire.   To his languages he was now adding Italian, French,
German, and Persian.   He practised wood-engraving — 'I had from a love
of Art, tried my graver on wood, quickened moreover by Bewick's works,
and it was a day-dream of my youth that I might follow Art as my way of

life' — wrote for the *Dorset County Chronicle* and the *Gentleman's Magazine*, concerned himself with etymology, with playing the flute, the violin and the piano, and singing and composing. He kept his diary in Italian; and was visiting Wales, and exploring Welsh poetry and prosody (long in advance of Hopkins). And at Mere he began for the first time to write poems in his native dialect. He had a liking for archaeology (he gave up the study of Russian, since it was 'wanting in old lore'). He had a turn for mechanical invention, instrument making, and mathematics. In fact, through all his pursuits, as through his poetry, goes a passion for form and reason. There is a good formality about his wood engravings, and throughout his life he felt the desire for visual order within a frame. At twenty-one he had gone so far in his wish to be a professional engraver and artist that approaches were made for him to a London art publisher, but the reply was discouraging. He remained an amateur, and later in his life became ardent in the collection of paintings and wood engravings.

Barnes left Mere in 1835 and went back to his own county to open a second school in Dorchester, where he was 'so lucky, as to have . . . a friend who was a good Oriental scholar, Col. Besant, theretofore of the native Bengal infantry, and author of the Persian and Urdu Letterwriter, with whom for some years I read a little Hindustani or Persian once almost every week'. In 1840 he lost the most intimate of his friends, Edward Fuller, who had shared his taste for art and letters. In 1844 Sheridan's grandson invited Barnes over to Frampton Court, to meet his beautiful sisters, the writers Lady Dufferin and Caroline Norton, who were taken by his dialect poems in the *Dorset Country Chronicle*. Barnes at first refused to go 'on the grounds that he was unaccustomed to society', but gave way to another letter, went, and enjoyed himself; and in Mrs Norton made a friend who was the first and for some years the last well-known writer to give him attention. He was ordained deacon by the Bishop of Salisbury when he was forty-seven, and priest when he was forty-eight; and when he was fifty he took his B.D. at Cambridge. But these steps led to no advancement; they were followed only by trouble and difficulties. Two years after taking his degree Barnes lost his wife, and his six children their mother. Julia Barnes, a woman who had been beautiful, lively, sensible, and full of laughter, but never robust, died on 21 June 1852, and for the days after Barnes wrote nothing in his Italian diary but

'June 22, 23, 24, 26, 27 — Giorni d'orrore'.   Nearly a year later his diary says:
'Heavy-hearted for my astounding loss'; and until his death he finished
his entries, night after night, with the word 'Giulia', written, as his biographer says, like a sigh at the end of each day.

   For the rest, his life was, on the whole, even.   When his school began to
fail (excellent schoolmaster as he was), his friends procured him a Civil
List pension of £70 a year; and ten months later, in 1862, he was presented
to the living of Winterborne Came, just outside Dorchester.   This meant
an end of anxiety.   It meant a comfortable and a peaceful old age in the
rectory through another twenty-four years.

                                    II

It was in these last years that Barnes became something of a celebrated poet
outside his own county.   Allingham had written to him in gratitude for
his poems as early as 1850.   Coventry Patmore had first cheered him with
praise by 1859, writing of the unmixed pleasure the poems gave him, and of
how he found in them a union, 'in a perfectly original way', of the spirit of
Burns and the spirit of Wordsworth.   Palgrave, Gosse, and others came
after.   Yet in all his early life — and it would not be easy to decide how much
of a handicap this really was — Barnes had had no friend or acquaintance,
so far as we can tell, of his own stature.   He knew and was helped by older
men with some scholarship and ability; but he was past middle age before
he had any contact at all with another considerable poet.   Most of his writing
had been done.

   He had not been aggressive; and beyond the approach to Ackermann
the art publisher, he never seems to have had a thought of moving nearer to
London than Mere, or of introducing himself to any other writer.   He liked
Wiltshire.   He liked Dorset still more.   He liked scything, he liked his wife,
his children, his pursuits.   'Mr Barnes,' his young wife would say to him,
'you are burying your talents in this poor out-of-the-way place.'   And indeed he had a 'marked shyness of demeanour, an awkwardness in his gait
and mien, and a certain indifference to his personal appearance'.   He was
'morbidly modest'; and 'so uniformly mild were his manners and language
that he was often suspected of being deficient in determination and spirit;

a suspicion which in reality had no very solid justification; but Barnes was such a decided advocate of peace at any price that he would never, except when driven by sheer necessity, enter any arena as a probable disputant'. He kept good discipline in his school, never used the cane, and always wore (in the class-room) 'a long light-blue rough-faced, flannel-textured dressing-gown'.

That was Barnes in his twenties and thirties — an odd scholar and schoolmaster, bald-headed before his time, and content with the peaceful obscurity of Mere or Dorchester. The pupil who recorded these recollections added that he was 'nearly isolated' socially, and was looked down upon in Mere, and in Dorchester as well. He had his few friends; but whether that 'nearly isolated' is an exaggeration or no, certainly all his richest years of creation were passed in a loneliness of spirit and intellect. Barnes, like his neighbours, was unaware of the comparative standing of his own ability, and the world was unaware of it until Coventry Patmore began to review him and praise him when he was nearly sixty. And then the world quickly returned to its old indifference. After his death, Tennyson, Browning, Arnold, Patmore, and others signed a memorial praying the First Lord of the Treasury to continue Barnes's Civil List pension to the daughter who had nursed him. They state that in the last years of his life Barnes's income from his poems was 'about £7 only'.

Patmore wrote of him: 'He is of no school but that of nature', which is true, so long as you do not interpret it to mean that he was a naive, or unlearned writer. 'Mr Barnes, in his poems, is nothing but a poet. He does not there protest against anything in religion, politics, or the arrange-ments of society;[1] nor has he the advantage of being able to demand the admiration of the sympathizing public on the score that he is a chimney-sweep or a rat-catcher, and has never learned to read.' But for all his meticu-lous, highly professional knowledge of writing, and his rare gift of sustain-ing his sensibility and skill through life, I doubt if Barnes ever quite looked upon himself as a 'poet' in our conscious European way. He was fulfilled. He was much more like a plant, which does not exist for its flowers; and such a lack of vanity and ambition coupled with so much expert skill may be unique. If he had moved among men of letters, he might have gained

[1] But see pages 168 and 169.

much; but he might equally have stained the clear run of his talent. Landor might have companioned him well, and invigorated him, but who
else? He was narrowed by Dorset; yet Dorset, for all its indifference, kept
him safe, as Clare was kept safe in his asylum.

III

His first book was *Poetical Pieces*, printed for him in Dorchester in 1820 —
ten poems in ordinary English. He was then twenty years old, and there is
nothing much to mark in these conventional album verses but their neatness,
and the fact that he began to write in the normal English, which he was to
use for many years. *Orra: A Lapland Tale*, Dorchester-printed in 1822, is
worth more. It stands to his later writing like *Gebir* to the rest of Landor,
or *Midnight* and *A Vision of the Mermaids* to the rest of Crabbe and Hopkins.
The subject is Orra's search for her lover, a night she spends in a rugged
cave, and the loss of her boat, so that the result (undescribed) must be Orra's
death; and it comes partly out of his reading of a book on Lapland published
twenty years before, partly from that recurrent vision in eighteenth-century
verse of a frozen sea. Barnes's unending love of clear, contrasting colour is
now put down for the first time:

> Her bosom seemed, beneath her long black hair,
> Like snowy hills beneath the clouds of night . . .

> As graceful as the silvery cloud
> That glides upon the summer air . . .

Twenty-two years went by before Barnes brought out another book of
poems — his *Poems of Rural Life in the Dorset Dialect* (1844) — though in
between he wrote much on languages and antiquarianism and published
several school books of a slender size. Yet first it will be as well, out of its
order, to look into the *Poems partly of Rural Life, in National English*, which
followed in 1846. It is a book almost as little known as *Orra*, in which the
sonnets, and probably several of the other poems, were written earlier —
the sonnets, or most of them, in 1830, when, swayed by Petrarch, he was
also writing sonnets in Italian. Barnes's poems never develop an emotional,
or rather a psychological subtlety. Simple elemental feelings are made to

pull upon' our hearts by an intricate subtlety of rhythm and pattern. That subtlety he had not made perfect by 1830, so that the simplicity of statement stands out a bit too much. Yet I do not see why so tranquil a poem as the sonnet on *Leaves* should stay obscured:

> *Whether ye wave above the early flow'rs*
> *In lively green; or whether, rustling sere,*
> *Ye fly on playful winds, around my feet,*
>
> *In dying autumn; lovely are your bow'rs,*
> *Ye early-dying children of the year;*
> *Holy the silence of your calm retreat.*

Other poems to be remarked in this book are *A Winter Night, The Lane, Burncombe Hollow,* and *Rustic Childhood.* Two stanzas from *Rustic Childhood* will show Barnes's eye for light and for objects. Many nineteenth-century poets observed exquisitely, not many could order this observation so well as Barnes, or space it out with such an infallible effect:

> *Or in the grassy drove by ranks*
> *Of white-stemm'd ashes, or by banks*
> *Of narrow lanes, in-winding round*
> *The hedgy sides of shelving ground;*
> *Where low-shot light struck in to end*
> *Again at some cool-shaded bend,*
> *Where we might see through darkleav'd boughs*
> *The evening light on green hill-brows.*
> > *I knew you young, and love you now,*
> > *O shining grass, and shady bough.*
>
> *Or on the hillock where I lay*
> *At rest on some bright holyday;*
> *When short noon-shadows lay below*
> *The thorn in blossom white as snow;*
> *And warm air bent the glist'ning tops*
> *Of bushes in the lowland copse,*
> *Before the blue hills swelling high*
> *And far against the southern sky.*
> > *I knew you young, and love you now,*
> > *O shining grass, and shady bough.*

L

The same qualities distinguish *The Lane*, one of the poems Barnes had written on the alliterative principles of Old English verse — again an anticipation by many years of Hopkins's concern with Old English. (Barnes had much else to import into the nineteenth century, out of the wide reaches of his scholarship and his curiosity.)

IV

Barnes's poems in normal English up to, and after this 1846 volume, are more numerous and more accomplished than is realized; but in the Dorset dialect, in the three dialect books of 1844 (*Poems of Rural Life in the Dorset Dialect*), 1858 (*Hwomely Rhymes*) and 1863 (*Poems in the Dorset Dialect, Third Collection*) he certainly came to the top of his classical perfection. Thomas Hardy had quoted from Barnes's statement that he wrote in dialect because he could not help it: 'To write in what to some may seem a fast out-wearing speech form, may seem as idle as writing one's name in the snow of a spring day. I cannot help it. It is my mother tongue, and is to my mind the only true speech of the life that I draw.' That always struck me as rather a puzzling statement. It is true that having spoken in dialect as a child, for some time he probably kept a Dorset accent (as Coleridge kept something of a Devonshire accent). As a man, he could no doubt slip from English into Dorset English; but his first promptings were to write poems in plain English, which he did until he was thirty-four, and continued to do, at intervals, all through his life. It was in plain English that he wrote a poem to Julia Barnes after her death in 1852; and after 1867, for his last nineteen years, he reverted to English and wrote, we are told, only one poem in dialect. In other words he could perfectly well help it, and often did. Had Barnes made a statement which was obviously untrue? In his fragment of his own life he wrote a little differently: 'As to my Dorset Poems and others, I wrote them so to say, as if I could not well help it, the writing of them was not work but like the playing of music, the refreshment of the mind from care or irksomeness.'

And others — that is to say, it was a general statement about all his poems, and perhaps a deliberate qualifying of his earlier statement that he could not help it — as if he felt that if nearly true, it was not quite true enough.

Writing in dialect began as a preference, a choice which Barnes made out of his philological delvings. His daughter Lucy confirms so much in her *Life* of William Barnes, and says 'when he began, it was as much the spirit of the philologist as the poet which moved him'. She quotes his statement that 'the Dorset dialect is a broad and bold shape of the English language, as the Doric was of the Greek. It is rich in humour, strong in raillery and hyperbole; and altogether as fit a vehicle of rustic feeling and thought, as the Doric is found in the *Idyllia* of Theocritus'; and in the *Gentleman's Magazine* in 1840, several years after his first Dorset poems were written, but several years before the first book of them came out, he affirmed that the Dorset dialect was 'purer and more regular than that which has been adopted as the national speech'. So, far from being a spontaneous act, this choice of dialect was a learned perversity, which he was able to carry through, since dialect had been his first speech, without the defects of being perverse. Once he began, he found he could do it by nature. Then, no doubt, he could not help continuing.

What I mean will be clarified by thinking of Doughty, who also set out to revitalize English, but by reviving, with an early dictionary always along- side his writing hand, the dead, unspoken language of the sixteenth century. Doughty is unreadable, Barnes is a delight. Barnes is genuine, Doughty a monster, and perverse with all the defects of perversity.

Gerard Hopkins recognized the truth about both of these poets. Doughty (whom Bridges admired) Hopkins dismissed. Barnes (whom Bridges des- pised, partly for his celebration of 'the supposed emotion of peasants') Hop- kins had already appreciated for a good many years when Coventry Patmore sent him the three dialect volumes in 1855. He had some sharp words with Bridges: 'I hold your contemptuous opinion an unhappy mistake: he is a perfect artist and of a most spontaneous inspiration; it is as if Dorset life and Dorset landscape had taken flesh and tongue in the man'; and writing earlier to Bridges, he makes a comparison, the rightness of which I will not argue about, between Barnes and Robert Burns. Burns, he says, does not translate: take away the Scotchness and something ordinary remains, but Barnes does translate, and without a great loss. That at least is true. Indeed, a lack of knowledge of the euphony of Dorset dialect does not, to my ear, make it impossible to enjoy Barnes's poems clearly and intensely. There are two lines I keep among the furniture of memory, and keep in this form:

> *The cuckoo over white-waved seas*
> *Do come to sing in thy green trees.*

Barnes wrote:

> *The gookoo over white-weäv'd seas*
> *Do come to zing in thy green tees.*

The translation I make, more or less without meaning to, is nearer Barnes's writing than, shall I say, Barnes's, or anyone else's reading of the Idylls of Theocritus was ever near to the original sound of Theocritus; and though I have no suspicion that Barnes ever wrote any of his Dorset poems first in ordinary English — in the English he habitually used in his reading, in his letters, and, I suppose, in his thoughts — the English versions he did make of some of the Dorset poems are lively and authentic. The English version of *The Mother's Dream*, for instance, is not less good than the Dorset original.

V

There is a remark in Llewellyn Powys's letters that Barnes never writes about the sea. That is nearly, if not quite, true. He had no taste for the sea, one of many facts which mark him off from other poets and painters and writers of his time — Darley, Tennyson, Swinburne, Patmore, Courbet, Melville, Emily Brontë, for example. And there is a deeper explanation for it than a land-locked childhood, and Barnes's intense cultivation of his inland, rural imagery. He had no use for the swell and turbulence and endless width of the sea — for its lack of form. He is not a poet for expansive mystery, for crossing the bar, for the infinite in any way. Tennyson has to cross the bar. Tennyson in death has to put out to sea. That was typical of the anxieties of the nineteenth century, whereas the attitude of the eighteenth century had been to sail calmly along to death or to put in from life's sea to death's harbour.

Barnes, on the whole, does not feel lost, or overwhelmed, or bound to fight against a universal ocean. He accepts, and does not interrogate, the universe. His form matches that feeling. However narrow Barnes may have been, the form and its variation in his verse is one of its qualities by which we may profit. He was not a fragmentary poet, or a Samuel Palmer

with only eight or nine years of lyrical vision and explosion. *White an' Blue*
and other lyrics with such airy vitality and youthfulness were written when
Barnes was nearly seventy years old. And often it is not easy, so much are
his poems conceived or carried out as a unit, to isolate a stanza, a line, or a
phrase for admiration. Coventry Patmore well remarked that 'often there
is not a single line worth remembering in what is, nevertheless, upon the
whole a very memorable poem'. The poems are rhythmically united with
the most delicate skill, and then tied together still more tightly by refrains
which, while they may be identical, yet sometimes advance the sense as in
My Love's Guardian Angel, where the refrain is worked up to the wonderful
emotional weight of its last use. The guardian angel of the girl he is in love
with (the poem is an example of Barnes's ability to put fresh emotional life
into a worn concept) tells him in the last stanza

> *Zee how the clear win's, brisk in the bough,*
> > *— in the night,*
> *While they do pass, don't smite on her brow,*
> > *— in the night;*
> *Zee how the cloud-sheädes, naïseless do zweep*
> *Over the house-top where she's asleep.*
> *You, too, goo on, though times mid be near,*
> *When you, wi' me, mid speäk to her ear*
> > *— in the night.*

Judging from the one volume in the Museum at Dorchester, Barnes in
his Italian journal seldom put down any more detail about the poems he
was engaged on than a laconic 'scrivendo versi' or 'versi scritti'. It would
not be easy to date their exact evolution or to follow in date and in detail
all his complicated experiments in form, which he worked out mainly in
the dialect. Yet through all his books, from *Orra* to the *Poems of Rural Life
in Common English* of 1868 and the small *Selection from Unpublished Poems*
produced by Winterborne Monkton School in 1870, with what remarkable
persistence does he keep up his sheer skill! Hardy maintained that 'on
some occasions he would allow art to overpower spontaneity, and to cripple
inspiration'; but he allows that rarely enough, if at all; and his art is so
fine and certain that he seldom seems monotonous through mannered repetition, or overworking, of successful effects. In this it is worth setting Clare

and Barnes side by side. What they have in common is an ability to express in language uncontaminated by literature, pure and cool (yet not liquid) after the warm syrup of Keats and his Victorian succession. What they teach us in common is this perfect sparing use of our language, which they may have owed in part to their isolation. With this uncommonest of skills Barnes does not achieve Clare's absolute hits: he is not a seer, he is less completely in nature. But it is form which saves him from Clare's dribble of absolute misses.

Form to him was fitness: he wrote several things about it, and he explored as well the origin and simplest nature of poetry. 'Matters most interesting to me are those belonging to man, in his life of body, mind and soul, so in his speech, manners, laws and works.' As for man 'the natural man is unfallen man, as he was finished by the hand of God, when He saw all that He had made to be very good'. And whatever fallen man may be, 'the beautiful in nature is the unmarred result of God's first creative or form-ing will . . . the beautiful in art is the result of an unmistaken working in man in accordance with the beautiful in nature'. He maintained 'there is no high aim but the beautiful. Follow nature: work to her truth.' But 'the beautiful is also the good by reason of a fitness or harmony which it possesses'. He admired 'the beauty and truth of colour and action in the Dutch school; and' — since he is anything but Dutch — 'the harmony, tone, and effect of colour, even with bad drawing, and, in some cases, it may be with want of depth, in a work of Turner'. In all the beautiful things of a landscape, he discovered fitness — 'fitness of water to irrigate growth, and to run for all lips to the sea; fitness of land to take and send onward the stream; fitness of strength to weight, as of the stem to the head of a tree; fitness of elasticity to force, as that of the poplar, and the bough whose very name is bending, and the bulrush and grass to the wind; fitness of protection to life, as in the armed holly and thorn, and the bush, or ditch-guarded epilobium; and a harmony of the whole with the good of man'.

Harmony was a favourite word, and harmonic proportion a favourite topic, with Barnes. He wanted harmonic proportion in churches — 'that too little understood and wonderfully neglected principle of harmony in form as well as in sound' ought to be applied, so he maintained, to the relative heights of the tower, the nave and the chancel. He framed his pictures and bound his books in harmonic proportion. He held that poetry must keep in with the fitness of nature and must conform to the nature of speech and the natural cause of poetry among men. 'Speech was shapen of the breath-sound of speakers, for the ear of hearers, and not from speech-tokens (letters) in books'; and discovering what he could about the origins of poetry from books of travel and philology and his own study of European and Oriental literature, he believed that poetry did not spring from cultiva-tion or refinement, but from elemental necessity; 'there has never been a full-shaped tongue that has sounded from the lips of generations of any tribe without the voice of song; and . . . to a bookless and unwriting people verse is rather a need than a joy'. It is curious to find him in his Dorset isolation writing that 'the measures of song . . . may themselves be measured, not only by the steps of the dramatic dance, but by the steps of a march, or by the strokes of oars, as in the Tonga songs of the kind called Towàlo or paddle songs, which Mariner says are never accompanied with instrumental music, but which are short songs sung in canoes while paddling, the strokes of the paddles being coincident with the cadence of the tune'.

In English poetry, his own practice was based on the Enlightenment; and no doubt he owed that salutary basis, in part, to being out of the swim, to being brought up in a countryside where the eighteenth century was still alive in the nineteenth; and to associating early with old-fashioned men for whom the Augustans were more important, still, than Wordsworth, or Keats, or Shelley. Such is the viable advantage of not always being modern, or up to date. He was little touched with an Elizabethan or a Miltonic romanticism, much as he studied the structure and prosody of Milton and the Elizabethans. Spontaneity, singing because you must, 'like the playing of music, the refreshment of the mind from care or irksomeness' — yes. But he read Dryden and Pope, and he quoted Mrs Cooper on Waller's poetry, that Waller 'rode the Pegasus of wit with the curb of good manners': it would be interesting to know when he first read and absorbed the Earl of Mulgrave's *Essay Upon Poetry*, with its emphatic praise of Homer and its emphasis on 'exact *Propriety* of Words and Thought' in the writing of songs:

> *Expression* easie, and the *Fancy* high,
> Yet *that* not seem to *creep*, nor *this* to *fly*;

No Words transpir'd, but in such *order* all,
As, tho' by Care, may seem by Chance to *fall*.

Mulgrave, said Barnes, 'writes to fancy or genius

I am fain
To check thy course, and use the needful rein.'

'Without *judgement*, fancy is but mad', he quoted, and he went on, 'A Welsh bardic canon says: the three qualifications of poetry are endowment of *genius, judgement* from experience, and *happiness of mind*'. Paraphrasing Mulgrave, he liked lines which are written 'with a skill that conceals skill', that 'keep all the strait rules of verse, yet flow as freely as if they were wholly untied'. Then, 'we cannot but feel that kind of pleasure which is afforded by the easy doing of a high feat, besides that which is afforded by good writing'.

After all that, neither the complexity of his lyric dodges and formalities, nor his care (how different from much in Tennyson) to pick over his observation and select from it, and never or seldom to overcrowd, continue to be surprising, however rare they are in other men's poetry between 1830 and 1870.

To analyse Barnes's skill exactly, one would need some degree of his own knowledge of Italian, of Persian (Petrarch and Sa'di were his favourites) and of Welsh, and other languages as well. On his eighteenth-century basis of 'exact propriety of word and thought' he heightened his verse by setting himself tasks of every kind. There are clues to this heightening, and to Barnes's mind, in the elaborate exemplification of rhyme in his *Philological Grammar* (1854), a book which he 'formed from a comparison of more than sixty languages'. He sympathizes with all rhyming tasks which can be alloyed into the structure of a poem. 'A poet may impose upon himself any task — as that he will introduce some forechosen word into every distich or line, or exclude it from his poem; or that every line shall end with a noun; or that his poem shall take a chosen form to the sight; or he may bind himself to work out any unusual fancy.' He mentions George Herbert's verse in the form of wings or an altar, and reproves Addison for calling Milton's matching of words of the same root 'poor and trifling', as in

That brought into this world a world of woe
Which tempted our attempt.

'However poor and trifling this figure might have seemed to Addison, it is sometimes very striking, as shown in the spontaneous language of mental emotion', and he gives other examples of this root⁄matching, 'called by the Persians . . . derivation', from Virgil, Sophocles, Crabbe, Tennyson, Cow⁄per, Coleridge, George Herbert, Shakespeare and other Elizabethans.   Other poets of his age had taken from the Elizabethans only an attitude, or fairy nothings (compare much of Darley or Hood), or insubstantial horrors. Barnes looked at the way they wrote, their word⁄repetitions, their collocation of two words alike in sound, unlike in meaning, their acrostics, their elaborate alliterations, and so on, which are paralleled by the elaborations and con⁄ventions of the Persian mediaeval poetry he so much enjoyed. The Persian poets and the Elizabethan lyric writers (and, for that matter the English poets of the Enlightenment whom Barnes learned from first of all) concerned themselves more with virtuosity of language than with originality of ideas. Beside the Augustan uniformity of common sense and a commonly held stock of knowledge, one could place the statement of the Arab historian, Ibn Khaldún, that 'the Art of Discourse, whether in verse or prose, lies only in words, not in ideas . . . ideas are common to all, and are at the dis⁄posal of every understanding, to employ as it will, needing no art'.[1]   That certainly was how Barnes thought of poetry, elaborate in art, simple in ideas, and straightforward in effect.   And he transfers much of the elaboration he discusses to his own verse — for example, from Eastern poetry the 'kind of word rhyming, or word⁄matching' called *adorning*, 'in which every word of a line is answered by another of the same measure and rhyme in the other line of the distich':

> *As trees be bright*
> *Wi' bees in flight.*

The Persians, he says, use an ornamental punning or 'full⁄matching', a full likeness in sound, of words which differ in meaning. He used it in *The Wold Wall*:

> *Ah! well⁄a⁄dae!   O wall adieu.*

He used the peculiar parallelism of Hebrew poetry — the principle of 'Tell it

[1] Quoted by E. G. Browne: *A Literary History of Persia*, II (1906) 85.

not in Gath, publish it not in the streets of Askalon' — in *Melhill Feast*, for
example:

> *The road she had come by then was soon*
> *The one of my paths that best I knew,*
> *By glittering gossamer and dew,*
> *Evening by evening, moon by moon —*

or in *Troubles of the Day*:

> *As there, along the elmy hedge, I go*
> *By banksides white with parsley — parsley bloom.*

Welsh and Irish poetry were sources for him. For instance, in Irish
poetry, 'there is a kind of under-rhyme called *union*, which is the under-
rhyming or rhyming of the last word or breath-sound in one line, with one
in the middle of the following one'. Here it is in *Times o' Year*:

> *Here did swäy the eltrot*[1] *flow'rs*
> *When the hours o' night wer vew,*
> *An' the zun, wi' eärly beams*
> *Brighten'd streams, an' dried the dew . . .*

But his most pronounced Celtic borrowing is the *cynghanedd*, the Welsh
repetition of consonantal sounds in the two parts of a line, divided by a
caesura, which is better known in English through its use by Gerard Hopkins. The familiar instance comes as a refrain in the poem so celebrated
through its musical setting, *My Orcha'd in Linden Lea*, in which the apple tree

> *Do leän down low in Linden Lea,*

where the *cynghanedd* consonants are DLNDNL/NLNDNL; but there are plenty
more, such as 'In our abode in Arby Wood', or 'An' love to roost, where
they can live at rest'.

Hopkins was made a bit uneasy about this particular borrowing. He
found his rhythms 'charming and characteristic', as they are, certainly. But
Barnes's use of *cynghanedd* he did not think successful. 'To tell the truth, I
think I could do that better', and he added that it was 'an artificial thing

[1] Cow-parsley.

and not much in his line'. I believe Hopkins was half-true, and half-wrong in not realizing how much Barnes's line was at once conscious and unconscious art — half-true, because although Barnes's most perfect poems are sometimes elaborate tasks, they are usually ones influenced by his borrowings from world prosody, but not embodying them pure and direct.

Barnes's soul was not lit by sulphur, he did not, like Melville, measure himself against fate or walk on the sea-bottom, 'left bare by faith's receding wave', or wrestle with God, or hang, as Hopkins hung, desperately, on the cliffs of the mind; he may, as Hopkins agreed with Bridges in saying, have 'lacked fire' (though that is not always so, in my judgement), but he *knew* and felt as much about the function in human life, the origins, nature, and adornment of lyrical poetry, and its form, as any poet who has written in English. To paraphrase a valuable remark by W. H. Auden (who is a devotee of Barnes), Barnes disciplined himself and proved the power of his creative impulses by accepting the limitations of form. He created a system of poetry for his own disposition.

VI

I have quoted Barnes's view of nature, though not completely: man has fallen, and nature as well is not unmarred, but 'the beautiful in nature' — that is 'the unmarred result of God's first creative or forming will' and 'the beautiful in art is the result of an unmistaken working of man' in accordance with this unmarred result, this natural beauty, which is good also by its fitness or harmony. The fallen working to the unfallen. 'Look for pleasure', Barnes wrote, 'at the line of beauty, and other curves of charming grace in the wind-blown stems of grass, and bowing barley or wheat; in the water-shaken bulrush, in the leaves of plants, and in the petals of flowers; in the outlines of birds, and even their feathers and eggs; in the flowing lines of the greyhound, the horse and cat, and other animals; in the shell of the mollusc, and in the wings and markings of insects; in the swell of the downy cheek, the rounded chin, the flowing bendings of the pole and back, and the outswelling and inwinding lines from the head to the leg of woman stepping onward in the pride of youthful grace; and tell us whether nature does not show us graceful curves enough to win us from ugliness, even in a porringer.' And 'fitness' made him an enemy of veneers and shams: 'does nature make you a handsome tree or flower near your town, and slight her work in the wold? or light up your water for a crowd-sought park, and not for the wanderers in the wilds? No. Nature and true art are faithful. . . . We have churches with a fine, high-wrought street end, and brick walls behind, out of man's sight (poor Pugin's eyesore) as if the builders worked not for good, but for man; and so a low aim has wrought a low work of art. Of such a sham some writer speaks somewhat in the following strain — for I quote from memory:

> They built the front, upon my word,
>   As fine as any abbey:
> But thinking they might cheat the Lord,
>   They made the back part shabby.[1]

Nature must therefore be sifted for the authentic, for the beautiful in nature; and the heavy grain of this sifting, its force, is concentrated into Barnes's epithets — 'green-treed':

> As evenèn äir, in green-treed spring,
> Do sheäke the new-sprung pa'sley bed —

or 'sweet-breath'd':

> An' sweet-breath'd childern's hangèn heads
> Be laid wi' kisses, on their beds —

or 'dim-roaded' night, or 'blue-hill'd' as an epithet for the world, or 'sky-back'd', for the flight of clouds, and many more — epithets which are impressed with the force of experience. He told Palgrave that 'he had taken Homer, and him only, as his model in aiming at the one proper epithet in describing'. This sifting gives his epithets a serenity and wide truth that one misses in the particular detail of much Pre-Raphaelite description, from Tennyson to the passionate observation of Hopkins. Read, or broadcast to an audience who have not the texts in front of them and do not know them, Tennyson's over-embroidered *Progress of Spring* (an early poem, it is true) and Dyer's eighteenth-century *Grongar Hill*: the one will be fuddling, the other will come to the listeners clear through the simplicity and sparingness

[1] 'Thoughts on Beauty and Art', in *Macmillan's Magazine*, IV (May–Oct. 1861).

of its effects. Barnes's poems are, for effects, half-way between the two; but riding his Pegasus on the rein, he would never go so far from the wide truth as Tennyson peering unfamiliarly into the inside of a horse-chestnut flower:

> *a but less vivid hue*
> *Than of that islet in the chestnut-bloom*
> *Flamed in his cheek —*

Barnes holds the rein at some such limit as 'where the black-spotted bean-bloom is out' or 'thatch-brow'd windows'.

He keeps in with this restraint in preferring the quickly taken truth of descriptions of states of light, states of air, and states of colour — sometimes all three in one. For instance, in *My Love's Guardian Angel*:

> *As in the cool-air'd road I come by,*
> *— in the night.*

Or

> *High over head the white-rimm'd clouds went on,*
> *Wi' woone a-comèn up, vor woone a-gone;*
> *An' feäir they floated in their sky-back'd flight,*
> *But still they never meäde a sound to me —*

or

> *I'm out when snow's a-lyèn white*
> *In keen-air'd vields that I do pass,*
> *An' moonbeams, vrom above, do smite*
> *On ice an' sleeper's window-glass —*

or in three stanzas from *In the Spring*:

> *O grey-leafy pinks o' the geärden,*
> *Now bear her sweet blossoms;*
> *Now deck wi' a rwose bud, O briar,*
> *Her head in the Spring.*

> *O light-rollèn wind, blow me hither*
> *The vaïce ov her talkèn,*
> *O bring vrom her veet the light doust*
> *She do tread in the Spring.*

> *O zun, meäke the gil' cups*[1] *all glitter*
> *In goold all around her,*
> *An' meäke o' the deäisys' white flowers*
> *A bed in the Spring . . .*

But Barnes's use of colour is often, as I have said, the setting of one colour sharp against another one, a visual antithesis, like two halves of a line in Pope balanced against each other. Long after he had begun this, he began to look deliberately for its counterpart and warrant in nature, making a list of 'the contacts of sundry pairs of colours on natural bodies', such as white and black in the bean blossom, or yellow and orange in toadflax or the brimstone butterfly. 'Nature is very sparing of showy contrasts of warm and cold colours. Red and blue are very rare, and of yellow and blue the cases are but few; and black and blue are found in lepidoptera more often than white and blue are seen in our Flora and Fauna.'

White and blue, all the same, was the coupling he most often repeated, though frequently he set yellow against black:

> *There near the wheatrick's yellow back,*
> *That shone like gold before the sky,*
> *Some rooks with wings of glossy black*
> *Came on down wheeling from on high*
> *And lightly pitched upon their feet*
> *Among the stubble of the wheat —*

white sometimes against red, elder flowers against red campion, or

> *Oh! the cherry-tree blossom'd all white*
> *And again with its cherries was red —*

or white against green, as in the cuckoo lines or *Zummer Thoughts in Winter Time*:

> *When white sleev'd mowers' whetted bleädes*
> *Rung sh'ill along the green-bough'd gleädes.*

But white and blue began with *Orra* (and even before that in a poem in his first book of 1820):

[1] Gilt cups, i.e. buttercups.

And softly now her snowy eyelids close,
  Weighed down by slumber, o'er her bright blue eyes,
As bound beneath the cold and wintry snows,
  The azure wave of ocean frozen lies —

and they were observed together again and again, in his wife, in skies, in butterflies, in flowers against sky or reflected sky. Examples are in *White an' Blue*, where the colours are the substance of the poem, in *The Water Crowfoot*:

  Thy beds o' snow⁄white buds do gleam
    So feäir upon the sky⁄blue stream.

— in *Zummer Stream*:

  There by the path, in grass knee⁄high,
  Wer buttervlees in giddy flight,
  All white above the deäisies white,
  Or blue below the deep blue sky.

— in *Not Sing at Night*:

  Or where below the clear blue sky
  The snow⁄white linen hung to dry.

And white and blue well express the mathematics, the clear, the serene, and the harmonious in Barnes's make. White and blue are the serenity of nature — the nature, said Barnes, which 'is the best school of art', adding 'and of schools of art among men those are best that are nature's best interpreters'.

VII

We have too much of a habit of reflecting our discontent with an author's political convictions, or his political indifference, or his inconsistency, back on to all of his work, as though the issues of the sadness of our time were immeasurably greater than ever before in human history. We forget that there are still for each of us what we must regard as constant transcending verities, that what appears to be 'reaction' may be much more vitalizing than the thirty⁄shilling suit of modernity or *avant⁄garde*, or immediate politics, that being a trimmer need not imply a lack of inward truth, whether the trimmers are Dryden, or Turgenev, or a good many modern European authors who have had touches of fascism about them. Barnes may, in a very good sense, be a minor poet; but not in the sense that his writing is a mess of words occasionally lit by a sparkle of pure intuition. And I may have suggested, wrongly, if you recall the quotation from Patmore, that Barnes was indifferent to the times, or separated from them entirely. As far as not being indifferent possesses value, that was not so. The anxious bewilderment between faith and science scarcely reached him, and scarcely ripples in his poetry. I can only recall one open reference to it, in his poem, *The Happy Days when I wer Young*:

> *Vrom where wer all this venom brought*
> *To kill our hope an' taïnt our thought?*
> *Clear brook! thy water coulden bring*
> *Such venom vrom thy rocky spring —*

— the venom being 'what's a-talk'd about By many now, — that to despise The laws o' God an' man is wise'; and he affirmed in another poem

> *My peace is rest, my faïth is hope*
> *An' freedom's my unbounded scope.*

'That is a subject connected with politics, not with poetry', he said to his son when he reminded him of a request that he should write a Dorset recruiting poem. 'I have never written any of my poems but one with a drift.[1] I write pictures which I see in my mind.' The one poem, the early Dorset Eclogue, *The Times*, with its fable of the pig and the crow, he had written against the Chartists. He felt that the Chartists would unsettle the Dorset labourer without remedying his condition; and, with his views of God, nature, man, harmony and fitness, what did disturb him, deeply, was the unfitness he saw in the social development of the nineteenth century, and in the consequent decay of freedom; the unfitness which caused him to write the curious amalgam of wisdom and simplicity he called *Views of Labour and Gold* (1859), in which, not unaffected by the Christian Socialist writing of the fifties, Barnes was concerned 'to show the possible effect of

[1] He should have said 'my published poems' — 'poems in my books', since there were others.

the increase of great working-capitals and monopolies on the labourer's freedom or welfare'. Two extracts will give its tenor:

> The kindness which is done by capital when it affords employment to people from whom, by a monopoly, it has taken their little business, is such as one might to do to a cock by adorning his head with a plume made of feathers pulled out of his own tail.

> It is more healthy to rack one's mind in effectual devices to win a skilful end, than to work as a machine without a free aim or thought: and so, as a Hindoo poet says, to be like a smith's bellows, breathing without life.

But Barnes's social views, simply consistent with his views of the world of life and art, are only a stroke in the drawing of a full portrait of Barnes. They are less important than the wavy, mazy, slow, river-like rhythm of his poem *The Clote* (clote is the yellow water-lily):

> O *zummer clote, when the brook's a-slidèn*
> *So slow an' smooth down his zedgy bed,*
> *Upon thy brode leaves so siafe a-ridèn*
> *The water's top wi' thy yoller head,*
> *By black-rin'd allers,*
> *An' weedy shallers,*
> *Thee then dost float, goolden zummer clote.*

— less important than the rhythm with which he patterned his life and his impulses to describe and sing. There are poems which are slightly embarrassing, in which Barnes tails — I hesitate to describe it so — into a provincialism of sentiment; but his tailings are more innocent and slighter than the monstrous, wallowing falls into the same weakness — not confined to Dorset — of some of Barnes's greatest coevals. And even his weakest poems are strengthened by their pattern and dexterity. In the narrow sense, there are not art-and-society reasons for urging that Barnes should be read, urging that he should have the status given to him ungrudgingly by Patmore, Hopkins, and Thomas Hardy, and other poets in England and America, from W. H. Auden to the late Robinson Jeffers. He may have given to English writing more than has been suggested or allowed. Hardy he very much influenced; and in turn Hardy's rhetoric and pattern seemed

M

the archetype of poetry to the young W. H. Auden: 'He was both my Keats and my Carl Sandburg', the archetype and also the expression oı the Contemporary Scene.　And how much effect did he have on Gerard Hopkins, who read Barnes when he was an undergraduate, complimented him by critical admiration, and put some of his poems to music?　Both Hopkins and Barnes were after a revitalized language for poetry.　Were Barnes's poems — to name only a little thing — the seeds of Hopkins's own concern for Welsh and for Anglo-Saxon?　Is it entirely a coincidence of period and a consequence of identical aims that 'or as a short-stand-night-watch quick foreflown' and 'which at early morn with blowing-green-blithe bloom' are not lines by Hopkins, but translations from Old Friesian[1] by Barnes?　Or that both invented their own critical terms rather than take them ready-made and devitalized from philologists and prosody?　Or was Barnes not the instigator of much which has come down through Hardy and through Hopkins as well?

Yet these questions are only, again, the more trivial baits to reading him — to reading one of the few ninteeenth-century poets who 'conceived of art, like life, as being a self-discipline rather than a self-expression', a poet of life in its happiness and the sad recollection or reliving of happiness or sweetness for their own sake — I think of such poems as *White an' Blue, In the Spring, Heedless o' my love, The Broken Jug, The Wind at the Door,* and *Woak Hill.*　Barnes, if he were more read, could become one of the healthy, if lesser, counterpoises to a sick indulgency, to that reviewers' poetry, English and American, which finds its own lack of style and shape, its own slack awkwardness of diction.　He is not a rustic aberration; but just as Barnes kept in Dorset during his life, so he has been kept in Dorset ever since. The point is to deliver him — to extract him from his rather snobbishly affixed integument of clay; to exhibit his imagination's cool-aired quality.

[1] *Early England and the Saxon English* (1869).

THIRTEEN

Down a Rushy Glen

To explore William Allingham in his poems will never be the most rewarding of expeditions into literature. Before the explorer starts on his expedition he will know *The Fairies* — 'Up the airy mountain, down the rushy glen' — which Allingham's friend Coventry Patmore printed in a children's anthology for the first time more than a hundred years ago. He may come back with an early lyric from Allingham's *Day and Night Songs*, and he may wonder why Allingham's long fictional poem *Laurence Bloomfield in Ireland* has been forgotten.

Turgenev admired *Laurence Bloomfield*, and with justice. It gives an honest, saddening taste of land troubles and evictions and the destruction of cabins. Its directness and carrying power make it better — not admittedly the highest of claims — than most novel-poems of the century. But it never caught on, which is precisely what could be said of Allingham himself, as he rose with painful slowness from bank clerk and then Customs Officer to a fixed place in the floating world of literary business.

He lives most in his diary, lately reprinted; and though the diary is of capital interest for its records of Tennyson, I would recommend it also to anyone who wryly observes the writing life of his own day, the painful transit from periphery to centre, and the way in which grandiose success puts up with faithful unsuccess. To say that the diary records a man who was in himself exceptionally interesting, would be to exaggerate. If Allingham was intrusive — having his own yearning for a grain of immortality — he was not aggressive; he was fairly content, in spite of periods of depression and loneliness (he made a poor Victorian's late marriage), to be about, to listen, and not himself, though he became editor of *Frazer's Magazine*, to innovate, direct or dictate. His type and his role are familiar inside the 'literary world' of any period.

First of all, though, one needs to be aware of the keepings of this minor poet. Allingham's aboriginal darkness — no Oxford, no Cambridge, not even the pampas grass of a rectory intervening, — was Co. Donegal, where his father was a merchant in a small way, at the port of Ballyshannon, which is graced (recall *Up the airy mountain*) by a far sight of the blue ridge of Slieve League. Here Allingham was born in 1824, here he grew up feeling, from his own account, more than usually or geographically isolated, since he had little in common with his younger brother and sisters, and was divorced emotionally from his undemonstrative parents by the invalidism of his mother (she died when he was nine, and was succeeded by a stepmother) and by the short temper of his father. Dreams were his satisfaction, and place or places rather than people the object of his emotions. Combining dream and place he dreamt of an Elsewhere, as in that lyric from *Day and Night Songs*, which is relevant enough and little enough known to be worth including here in full:

> *The Boy from his bedroom-window*
> *Look'd over the little town,*
> *And away to the bleak black upland*
> *Under a clouded moon.*
>
> *The moon came forth from her cavern,*
> *He saw the sudden gleam*
> *Of a tarn in the swarthy moorland;*
> *Or perhaps the whole was a dream.*
>
> *For I never could find that water*
> *In all my walks and rides:*
> *Far off, in the Land of Memory*
> *That midnight pool abides.*
>
> *Many fine things had I a glimpse of,*
> *And said, 'I shall find them one day.'*
> *Whether within or without me*
> *They were, I cannot say.*

He wrote in prose as well as verse about his attachment to places, rather than people; his attachment especially and naturally to that little town of Bally-shannon; he wrote about the Erne, and the boats which tied up to the quays of the Erne, about the tight glitter of its salmon, about yellow gorse and about the blue distances (such as that distance of Slieve League), which were always edging from actuality into dream. But without weight or convincingness as a rule. Also he was Protestant middle class, and of Plantation descent. It was too early for such a young man to be at all powered by his Irishness. Ireland, he declared in his prosier sixties, and he no doubt felt it in his twenties, 'presents an ungrateful soil for the cultivation of the higher *belles lettres*'. London — not Dublin — was his capital, his desirable and distant place, in which great and plangent poems were written magically, by Poets — deities rather than persons — whom he longed to meet. And in the lyric sky of London the Evening and Morning Star was Alfred Tennyson.

He read Tennyson in his Customs offices, in Ireland, he said Tennyson over to himself as he measured ships and inspected their lading. It was after a dose of Tennyson (and of a book on Norway) that he composed *The Fairies* one winter day in the single street town of Killybegs, in Co. Donegal, when he was twentyfive (8 January 1849).

Allingham now had the nerve to write round to faroff poets, the nerve to introduce himself in person whenever he took his literary furloughs, of course in London. He began with Leigh Hunt, radical hero of a literary generation older than Tennyson's, dedicating his first book to him. But by age and inclination he fitted into the PreRaphaelite circle, Coventry Patmore two years younger than himself, Rossetti three years older. He came to know these two in particular (as well as Carlyle and Browning). But it was Tennyson, as soon as they met (through Patmore, at the time a young official in the British Museum Library), who was inevitably raised to the throne in Allingham's diary, which runs more or less from the death of Wordsworth in 1850 (27 April. 'Home and find Wordsworth is gone! Rode back to Stonewold, chanting an improvised psalm to the departed spirit. Do not tell of the death: nobody to care. Sunset beautiful') to the High Victorian era of Tennyson in old age as poetry's peerless peer of the realm.

Again and again there is more than a hint of patronizing — or suffering — this large, longnosed, darkhaired, not so very well educated 'Englishman' from outer Ireland, who always found himself, as he recorded, 'tootoo lacking in *savoir faire*'. Friends more or less of his own age, such as

Patmore, who once thought of him as 'a nearly tip-top man', or Rossetti, grow away. He is apt to be mentioned like a piece of the furniture of youth in their later memoirs, from which he is rapidly dismissed ('It was at about this time that William Allingham, the poet, became well known in our Circle' — Holman Hunt in his *Pre-Raphaelitism*. Enough, and no more).

The year when he had at last met his Poet of Poets, fifteen years older than himself, was 1851. Allingham was then twenty-seven, Tennyson was forty-two, living at Twickenham in the first year of his own poverty-post-poned marriage. Allingham felt that a major desire of his life had been fulfilled; and his deity welcomed him — and snubbed him. Mr Alling-ham from Ireland, on this first occasion, upset the wine. 'I spilt some port on the cloth, and T.' — always T., not Alfred, even in the seclusion of his diary — 'with his usual imperturbability spread salt on it, remarking as he did so "I believe it never comes out".'

So it went on, year in, year out, Tennyson treating Allingham with a condescension he records without complaint. Tennyson corrects his pro-nunciation, the way he pronounces 'dew': 'There's no *Jew* on the grass!' The poor man forwardly remarks that a large tangled fig-tree in the garden at Farringford resembles a breaking wave. '"Not in the least", says he'. And at once Allingham continues in his diary 'Such contradictions, *from him*, are no way disagreeable.' Tennyson writes to Gladstone about the possibility of increasing Allingham's Civil List pension of £60 a year (it had come to him not long after the publication of *Laurence Bloomfield in Ireland*, lines from which Gladstone had quoted, for his politics, not for Allingham's poetry, in a Commons debate): the maximum of Tennyson's unexcessive praise is to claim that 'the man has a true spirit of song in him'. He has known him for years, 'he is very industrious, and in his life sober and moral'.

A sign of irritation under the surface of the presence and the exchanges is so often to be detected. Mr Allingham is coming up the drive. Mr Allingham is in the house. I suppose we must ask Mr Allingham to dinner, or to stop the night. And they do. Yet Allingham has his doubts about Allingham, not Tennyson. He hangs around Farringford, does not go in, and says afterwards to his diary: 'I have lost the faith I used to have in people's wishing to see me.' But he is soon there again, soon snubbed again, soon happy again to be recording Tennyson's acts, tastes, sensations, and opinions; never defeated, and if at times sentimental, if frequently sad, always, one feels, inoffensive and honest, and loyal, and humbly obedient to his biographical principle, 'admit your limitations, attend to what interests you and try always to be sincere'. The result was that so often immediate and fresh report, spanning almost half a century of Victorian life and showing that Allingham, as well, could be expert in the Victorian art of the brief, telling sketch in words, whether pencil-words or water-colour-words. For pencil-words I would pick Spurgeon the preacher observed in three strokes: 'I walked behind him; he has a big body, short legs, flat feet.' For a colour-note, sentimental as it may be, personal rather than Tennysonian, I would choose a sad entry put down four days later on a Sunday, in the same June of 1863, a summer of dejection when he was newly transferred to the Customs at Lymington in Hampshire, thirty-nine, conscious of his failure, still unrelieved by his first small Civil List pension. (His editorship of *Frazer's Magazine*, and his consequent marriage, coming so late, to Helen Paterson the illustrator, were still eleven years away):

In the evening walked sadly along the shore of the Solent eastwards by Pylewell — returning, brought home a glow-worm and put it in a white lily, through which it shone.

By 1881 he could afford to move with his wife — and children — to art-commuter's country at Witley in Surrey. Towards the end as in the beginning: from Witley he was soon to write to the poet William Barnes: 'We have been living here four years in a beautiful region of woods, hills and commons. Tennyson's hill, Blackdown, is opposite our windows, 6 miles off, and we often see him, tho it is farther than we could wish.'

It is as if Tennyson was not a person, as if he was always the Desired Deity in the Desired Place, half real, half dream: as if Tennyson was that 'tarn in the swarthy moorland' — 'opposite our windows'. Allingham was still drawn to that gleam which had beckoned him from rough Donegal to their first meeting so long ago in Montpelier Road, Twickenham; where for the first time, but not the last, not the last, Mrs Tennyson had so politely, as he rose to leave, remarked, 'Won't you stay for dinner?'

In fact Tennyson outlived him. Allingham died, obscurely, in Hamp-
stead in 1889, three years before Tennyson was carried with national pomp
into Westminster Abbey. His widow saw to it that Allingham — or his
ashes inside an urn — went back to Ballyshannon, but this was the first
time for more than twenty years that Allingham had revisited that Ireland
of soil so poor for the higher *belles lettres*, in which he had been nurtured.

FOURTEEN

The Great Drum

I

A GREAT drum sounds, sways and sounds deeper in an enormous space, a continental one, far from empty, a space containing not only grass, ants, rivers, mountains, stars, but men and cities, mortuaries and beds of maternity; and then the enormous space is edged by an infinite, yet extremely palpable sea, the Atlantic stretching away to Europe, the Pacific stretching out from California to China and Russia.

The great drum, great and grand if sometimes monotonous in its pounding rhythms, of course is Walt Whitman; and let me agree at once that great drummers in poetry or painting, essaying always grandeur, are creatures to suspect, often easy to dismiss. Also it is difficult to be grand all the time; and tempting, if you find the great man occasionally small, ordinary or even ridiculous, to dismiss his genuine grandeurs. Whitman, man with poet, orchestrator with attitudinizer, is very mixed. It does not, I believe, do a great deal of good — unless you can digest rusty iron like the fabled ostrich — to know much of Whitman's in some way little and ordinary life, to know of him as a compositor, a journalist, an editor of newspapers, a writer who could turn out a temperance tract, a man who could lie and cheat. Yet it may help to have visited Whitman's country, changed as it may be; first, to have crossed the Atlantic the slow way by liner, in order to discover what the vastness and endlessness and heave and shift of an ocean really is; then to have felt the scale, natural and human, of a country which is not a small European state. One learns a little about the circumstances which bred Whitman by observing in America the rawness of an excavation for a road or bridge, by allowing oneself to be caught without ear-pads by a blizzard in an American city, or by looking at a weather map in a daily paper and seeing how the trails of weather causation stretch away across a thousand or two thousand miles of land, by observing the Atlantic one has crossed pushing at the low glaciated edge of New England, or by experiencing in a cross-continental journey the endless repetition of natural features — and then if in the cities one also observes the human reply to this scale, this power, this enormity. Buildings no less enormous; and I mean not so much the steel towers either of New York, looking out over the vast ferry paths which gave Whitman such cosmic delight, or of Dallas, looking out over limitless prairie. I mean rather such an 'old' building as the Metropolitan Museum, in New York, that piece of pseudo-Renaissance raised, broadened and swollen to what seems, as one first stands under it, and before one enters, in search perhaps of Sassetta's *Journey of the Magi*, altogether monstrous. In the fall, clouds in a blue sky round the top edges of the Metropolitan turn pink towards evening; one stands below, the height of masonry leans back into the pink and blue, and one recognizes vast, vulgar, — yes, but heavenly cornices out of Tintoretto or Tiepolo.

Standing in front of Walt Whitman is not a dissimilar experience. One's European temper, one's training, one's habituation to a smaller scale, one's neater conception of the arts — all this inclines the investigator to see only vastness and brag, only vulgarity and the imitation of grandeur; and a first remedy is to discover or remember straightaway as if *de novo* some of the great openings of Whitman's poetry — how he began his *Memories of President Lincoln*:

> *When lilacs last in the dooryard bloom'd,*
> *And the great star early droop'd in the western sky in the night,*
> *I mourn'd, and yet shall mourn with ever returning spring . . .*

— how he began poems in *Sea-Drift*:

> *On the beach at night,*
> *Stands a child with her father,*
> *Watching the east, the autumn sky.*

> *Up through the darkness,*
> *While ravening clouds, the burial clouds, in black masses spreading,*
> *Lower sullen and fast athwart and down the sky,*
> *Amid a transparent clear belt of ether yet left in the east,*

Ascends large and calm the lord-star Jupiter,
And nigh at hand, only a very little above,
Swim the delicate sisters the Pleiades.

From the beach the child holding the hand of her father,
Those burial clouds that lower victorious soon to devour all,
Watching, silently weeps.

Weep not, child . . .

— to remember 'As I ebb'd with the ocean of life' or

Out of the cradle endlessly rocking,
Out of the mocking bird's throat, the musical shuttle . . .

II

You see what happens to someone infatuated by Walt Whitman. He starts making rhetorical repetitions and becoming ecstatical. But why not? The tenderness and the grandeur, the inclusiveness and the cosmicality, are not false, in the best of Whitman. Desert the fringes of the great building, walk inside, and in Whitman's depth you will find delights, you will find your Sassetta's *Journey of the Magi*, the pink houses, the flighting geese, the land-scape of the corner and of the world, the hawk on the wrist, the men in pink and blue and brown and letter-box red, the naked trees, the grasses, the rock, the finch and the star; you will find perpetual elements; in American terms, if you like, but they are none the less perpetual and universal.

Belinsky, a contemporary almost of Whitman's in Russia, called art 'the immediate contemplation of truth, or a thinking in images'; it was, he said, a blend of two contraries, philosophy and poetry, to which the common view has also ascribed 'a similar striving towards a single aim — to the heavens'. He saw — and it is well to quote a Russian about an American — he saw in nature 'a kind of mode by which the spirit becomes reality and perceives and recognizes itself'.

That was, in a big way, seen also by Whitman. When *Leaves of Grass*, which he had published in 1855, became known, it upset all well-bred ideas of art, art fixed to an ideal end, but a false one instead of such a viable ideal as his own, art on the end of a lead like a well-bred lap-dog. Before ten years were up, Whitman lost two jobs, two government jobs (and don't think he would not have lost them in England as well) for authorship 'of an indecent book'. After the poetry of good breeding and never-going-too-far by Arnold or Tennyson or, when all is said, by Browning, discreet in language on the whole, and within the bounds of the poetical, the body clothed, the real sweetly iced, the energy subdued, that huge catalogue of man and nature which Whitman called *Song of Myself*, and so scandalously included in *Leaves of Grass*, is overwhelming:

> *The pure contralto sings in the organloft . . .*
>
> *What is removed drops horribly in a pail . . .*

Art by social pressure always tends to acceptable social standards, to the maidenhair only in the pot, to the platform, to the board-room of an Arts Council. Whitman drove it back to itself by an 'immediate contemplation of truth', which was also a 'thinking in images'; and we should hold in mind, bogged as we may be at times on the way to it, the end of that enormous poem, Whitman being Whitman, being his embracing enormous self for ourselves:

> *The spotted hawk swoops by and accuses me . . . he complains*
> *of my gab and my loitering.*
>
> *I too am not a bit tamed. . . . I too am untranslatable,*
> *I sound my barbaric yawp over the roofs of the world.*
>
> *The last scud of day holds back for me,*
> *It flings my likeness after the rest and true as any on the shadowed*
> *wilds,*
> *It coaxes me to the vapor and the dusk.*
>
> *I depart as air. . . I shake my white locks at the runaway sun,*
> *I effuse my flesh in eddies, and drift it in lacy jags.*
>
> *I bequeath myself to the dirt to grow from the grass I love,*
> *If you want me again look for me under your bootsoles.*
>
> *You will hardly know who I am or what I mean,*
> *But I shall be good health to you nevertheless,*
> *And filter and fibre your blood.*
>
> *Failing to fetch me at first keep encouraged,*
> *Missing me one place search another,*
> *I stop some where waiting for you.*

There was with him a lucky conjunction of an Old Testament prophet with ideas not at all suited to the Old Testament, who could take the world and life into his splendidly incautious vision. His continent provided him also with war, terror, pity, full moons over slaughter, and grandeur in the savagery of the swaying contest between North and South. In making poems of the war, as he felt it, grand rhetoric would have been out of being. He was able, this rhetorician, to reduce it to short, extraordinarily sparse, and so vivid and immediate pictures of an event, a thing seen, a set of circumstances experienced:

A line in long array where they wind betwixt green islands,
They take a serpentine course, their arms flash in the sun — hark to the musical
clank,
Behold the silvery river, in it the splashing horses loitering stop to drink,
Behold the brown-faced men, each group, each person a picture, the negligent rest
on the saddles,
Some emerge on the opposite bank, others are just entering the ford — while,
Scarlet and blue and snowy white,
The guidon flags flutter gayly in the wind.

It is like a pause in a Western — the first of all Westerns. It might change into a poem by Tu Fu. No occasion to swell, to brag, to be expansive. Absolutely what was given to him. Yet one may see how in poems such as this one or *A march in the Ranks Hard-prest and the Road Unknown* or in *Song of Myself*, Whitman does not simply report. Though he does not always underline the obvious by an extra statement or explanation, though he does not always *delineate* the imaginary garden, he performs what another American poet has called the function of poetry: a literalist of the imagination, above insolence or triviality, he presents for inspection "imaginary gardens with real toads in them." But not always toads.

III

Whitman was envied, I think, by more than one English poet in the nineteenth century: he was free, not in the sense of a Carl Sandburg, but free of brilliant silk embroidery, like Tennyson's, free of the literary and rhythmical echoes and clichés which form the language of Rossetti or Francis Thompson (or Thomson's latter day disciple Dylan Thomas); he wrote in a language of a fresh clarity which wears well after a century. To me there is no more fascinating, more illuminating comment on Whitman than that one made by Gerard Manley Hopkins. In his heart, he said, he always knew 'Walt Whitman's mind to be more like my own than any other man's living.' He need not have been so worried. Both poets immensely grasped and embraced the natural world —

> *Delightfully the bright wind boisterous ropes, wrestles, beats earth bare . . .*

> *I turn the bridegroom out of bed and stay with the bride myself,*
> *And tighten her all night to my thighs and lips . . .*

Both took nature in its own right and as a 'mode by which the spirit becomes reality'. Hopkins's end was his deity. Whitman's deity ('Why should I wish to see God better than this day?') was the universal kinship of men.

Our job is to erect no absolute for what is or is not art; it is to find in each mode its rule, to ask honestly, in the case of Whitman, whether he moves us or not; and if he moves us, not to complain that his form is not the tighter form of Hopkins, not to lie to ourselves about what has moved us because such breaking, or bursting into speech, does not, after all, fit our conception of how the speech of poems ought to be shaped and ordered. If we do so lie to ourselves, if we are superstitious towards art and artists and think that the great artist must be great all through, as consistent as God, we are answered by Whitman himself:

> *Do I contradict myself?*
> *Very well then I contradict myself.*
> *I am large, I contain multitudes.*

And isn't Whitman's subject-matter, a song of others through himself, the most durable and the one held most deservedly to be grand? I am at any rate certain that Whitman is not read enough, that when he is read he is not read honestly enough, and that the elevation which may come of reading him lasts inside the reader.

FIFTEEN

The Sprig of Lilac

IT subsists, Walt Whitman's great carol which begins the *Memories of President Lincoln*, not in history, but in the sprig of lilac:

> *Here, coffin that slowly passes,*
> *I give you my sprig of lilac,*

in the meeting of April and death. Familiar with the poem, a reader and user of English from birth who is not American may require to remind himself that its occasion was the death of Abraham Lincoln, in the April of 1865. And it is arguable that only such a reader can see this poem clear and clean. He can read it without historical or national emotion. The history of it is someone else's history. Whitman wrote: 'Dear to the Muse — thrice dear to Nationality — to the whole human race — precious to this Union — precious to Democracy — unspeakably and for ever precious — their first great Martyr Chief.' He exaggerated. The victory, 'the million dead, too, summ'd up', belong to America, but not to those other readers. If they know the scraggy form and features, the beard, the smile, the Adam's apple from the photographs, the shock and the scene, when the body fell in Ford's theatre, and Booth called out '*Sic semper tyrannis*' and the soldiers of the President's guard (says Whitman) burst in, 'literally charging the audience with fix'd bayonets, muskets and pistols, shouting Clear out! clear out! You sons of — ' (presumably bitches) — all these affect them only as an *Et tu, Brute*. Not being their grand death, or their 'most important inheritance⁄value', the historical death drops from the poem; leaving behind something altogether first⁄hand and immediate, as poetry; which is its measure as a masterpiece.

The lilac usurps the poem. Lincoln is not named except in the title. Whitman smelt the lilac on the day of the assassination. Early herbage, early flowers were out: 'I remember where I was stopping at the time, the season being advanced, there were many lilacs in full bloom. By one of those caprices that enter and give tinge to events without being at all a part of them, I find myself always reminded of the great tragedy of that day by the sight and odour of these blossoms.' Lilac is named; Lincoln, through the poem, is the unnamed corpse of the loved man, in the coffin, who is made — but without the anaemia of an idea arising from generalization — into all death, straightaway. First the lilac, in its particular place, 'when lilacs last in the dooryard bloom'd', then the Evening Star in the west after day, then mourning, then the cause of mourning, the 'thought of him I love'. If black murk obtrudes in the second section and hides the Evening Star, the song of the withdrawn hermit thrush quickly comes into the growing night, in the fourth section; and twelve sections follow which are a sequence of variations on lilac, star, and death and the bird's song.

Senses are quickly engaged, sight, scent, hearing. The poem proceeds in a great movement of contraction which demands expansion, expansion which counter-demands the necessary strength of the single image. After the thrush of the fourth section, in the fifth and sixth sections a universe of the spring season and a billion of mourners, and flambeaux, and dirges and bells and shuddering organs attend the one coffin, which is given the one sprig of lilac; and this coffin in the next section — section seven — multiplies to all coffins and all death; this sprig of lilac multiplies to blossoms and branches and roses and early lilies, and lilac now broken off and loading the arms:

> With loaded arms I come, pouring for you,
> For you and the coffins all of you O death.

Star-night — all stars. Thrush — and songs of eastern and western sea winds meeting on the prairies; and song or sound combining with perfume. The interplay goes on of single, or few, with multitude. Pictures for the room of death become all country and city that can be pictured, all sun over an infinity of the particularized; then narrow again to the song of the gray-brown bird singing, 'limitless out of the dusk, out of the cedars and pines', and to the setting star, and to the lilac with mastering odour; and to Whitman — but Whitman who sat in the close of the day

> In the large unconscious scenery of my land with its lakes and forests,

and saw himself and everything enveloped in death; but in death as, after all, rest, which embraced the armies of the dead, the white skeletons, 'the debris and debris' of the killed.

So a resolution. After this great review or parade, Whitman, involved in comradeship (one recalls D. H. Lawrence, in *Studies in Classical American Literature*, celebrating in this poet 'the love of comrades: a recognition of souls, and a gladder worship of great and greater souls, because they are the only riches'), returns from all death to the one death: since he makes his poem end on its beginning. 'For the sweetest, wisest soul of all my days and lands', for the sake of the one dead, 'lilac and star and bird twined with the chant of my soul'.

A poet, or his poem, is sometimes definable in a central phrase from another poet of the same nature. Gerard Manley Hopkins, so upset because he saw in Whitman his closest affinity, Whitman being a sensualist like himself but without his canonical discipline, named in one sonnet the characteristics he wanted, but then lacked, in his own verse: *The roll, the rise, the carol, the creation.* These four are superabundant in *When lilacs last in the dooryard bloom'd*, the result in this poem of receiving a reality — the death of Abraham Lincoln — and the realities of lilac, star and hermit thrush into dream or vision.

Notice, incidentally, one not insignificant item in Whitman's creation: that nowhere in his poem is the recurrent blossom of the dooryard lilac given its colour. Its scent only. Otherwise the force of it is left in the word, in the name.

N

SIXTEEN

The Poet in D. H. Lawrence

A N 'egghead' has been defined as someone who insisted on calling Marilyn Monroe Mrs Arthur Miller. It is not a bad definition. But I could think of one which is most exact if less witty. For many years an egghead has been the man in our midst who has admired D. H. Lawrence, *as an artist*, for the wrong reasons, not for the art in him, not for the words in him or out of him, not for the poet in him, if you like, but for his particular attitudes to sex; but not only to sex: his particular attitude to sensuality, sensual experience, feeling 'with the blood', or whatever else Lawrence may call it. The egghead is the man who confuses the attitude with the art. And I have observed that he is often a dry man or woman peculiarly lacking by nature in such sensualities, and aware of such a lack, though he may not confess it to himself; or at least to others. Lawrence too was not above such a confusion of his attitudes, or his convictions, or his hortatory impulses, with *art*.

I should add that I was never fortunate enough to know Lawrence. I came near to meeting him: I saw his back but never his red beard and blue eye. I can claim (I was then a journalist on the *Yorkshire Post*) to have written the only leading article on his death to appear in any newspaper. I remember that I told the editor that his father had been a coalminer; which was no doubt why the leader was permitted. For the most part my editor read other newspapers and Ruff's *Guide to the Turf*; and was luckily unaware that Lawrence was also, on various grounds, an occasion of scandal to the righteous. Let me also add that *The Times*, when Lawrence died, dismissed him in an obituary less than half a column in length.

I was young at the time of Lawrence's death; and I remember, after that leader had gone up the wire from Fleet Street to Leeds, walking home across Lincoln's Inn Fields in a degree of — shall I call it cosmic sorrow as well as personal sorrow over the snuffing out of such a vitality. I knew a number of Lawrence's friends (several of them, I must admit in passing, suffered from that egghead's debility which I have mentioned), I had read *Lady Chatterley's Lover*, decidedly unexpurgated, with the extra delight of being a clergyman's son delivering himself from the last relics of a sense of sin over carnal enjoyments. The flowers at any rate seemed right and wonderful. I was particularly fond of a few poems by Lawrence, even if I found many of his novels turgid. I was delighted, too, by a fine contemptuous assault he had delivered not long before upon all the values of Galsworthy and *The Forsyte Saga*, the respectable master and the respectable masterpiece of the twenties or early thirties. Since then the fact is that Lawrence has never been quite out of my system. I have found myself in places known to Lawrence — for instance, Sturzing or Vitipeno below the Alps, where he stayed with Frieda Weekley, when he ran away with her, and Lago di Garda, where he lived with Frieda Weekley in the first months of combined ecstasy and dismay. I have even found myself in New Mexico, staring at a bust of Lorenzo in a bookshop window at Santa Fé, and contemplating at Taos the thumbed manuscript notebooks of *Lady Chatterley's Lover*, which as another writer has expressed it, 'fall open, with a dreadful submissiveness, in the expected places'.

In other words, for all my life as a writer Lawrence has been a familiar presence, influencing me willy-nilly; and I think I can claim neither to have turned excessively to him nor to have turned excessively from him. In what I say about Lawrence, or against Lawrence, there may be detected, I hope, not prejudice, not a judgement before, but a judgement afterwards.

Lawrence now stands, and will appear in the future to stand, upon several shaky legs; partly because he is the imperfect artist, the more than usually imperfect artist, who can be taken in so many roles, the insight man, the feeler, the bleeder, the blood-diviner, the rebel, the envelope of one of the many *zeitgeists* of our time, the preacher, the Adventist and Gospeller, the new century's Thomas Hardy, as well as the novelist, the short-story writer and — last of all, as well as first of all, the poet. And he is shaky because he does not stand level on these legs; he spills the teacup or the wine glass, because there is scarcely a role in which he is altogether satisfying.

For dogmatic and emotionally anaemic and shrivelled pedantry (my egg-heads) Lawrence is a crumb of God's bread, beyond any but surface criticism. For T. S. Eliot he was a heretic of insights insufficiently grounded, improperly educated. For many readers, since of course the remarkableness of Lawrence is never in question, he is a man in his many standings exhilar-ating at times, a man at times with his finger on life, a poseur not at all in-frequently, with his finger on something else altogether, or in gentler terms, he is frequently a victim of his own nonsense deserted by his own consider-able sense. And too often, as a result, he is bad at writing, he is deserted by style, he appears only to offer long lumps of tedium and, in terms of art, improbability.

I shall just mention, for the confusion in Lawrence of artist and life-force preacher, the opening chapters of *The Rainbow*. Can you accept the dark currents of relationship between the Man and Woman? I cannot. And I believe they can be mistaken for the real thing, the deduction artistically, from the authentic observation, only by two classes of reader: the young (who have still to experience a man and woman relationship); and those, the stunted or the starved, who have scarcely the power to experience such a relationship, and so lack a personal means of recognizing it. By either of those two classes it is accepted that Lawrence *knows*, and with a valid interpretation or transmutation, presents, what they do not know. On the whole, I think (and I take *The Rainbow* since those who are fanatic for Lawrence consider it his greatest work), Lawrence's figures are impossible as fictional men and women. Emotional 'meeting' just is not so; and these men and women are also unconvincing symbolically. While the Lawrentian tides of attraction and repulsion swirl, retreat, return, and exasperate the reader, it is as well to remember the peculiarity of Lawrence's own major experience. Himself emerging from a milieu given to crude, curt, and largely covered attitudes about the intercourse of the merest bodies, in his own deep struggles of attraction and repulsion he engaged with a woman, Frieda Weekley, Frieda von Richthofen, from that oddest of the psychic communities of Europe, the German educated class, already an expatriate, already married, and tortured with guilt over her deserted children. No, it became Lawrence's habit to turn idea into feeling and feeling into idea, at times falsifying both as a consequence. A special case he could elevate into a universal. With lyrical senses this man could borrow actuality;

which he then betrayed or smeared with his own peculiar ectoplasm; and if I say that Lawrence was too obsessed after all with 'sex', what I mean (though not as the ghost of his enemy Gosse, or Galsworthy, and not as the vicar's critical churchwarden) is that he involved himself too much in the abstraction, without resting enough in the real thing, on actual man-and-woman, for instance. He involved himself too much in a concept, for which (it does no hurt to remember) there was until recently no word, *sex* being a modern transference from descriptive biology.

Then what of the poet in Lawrence, the solid in the marsh? In his poetry (and the three volumes he has left are much for a committed novelist and theorist to have written) let me say first that he was from early on too involved in a theory which his own deeper feeling very strikingly contradicted.

Possessive inescapable emotion in the artist, the emotion of love for whatever object, or in whatever form, positively or negatively (negative love explains satire), does beget, or can beget, with hard work, that formal rhythmical release, or ritual and rhythmical satisfaction and celebration, which is a work of art, which is a poem, self-evident and true like a syllogism, or a snake biting its own tail.

Lawrence, though, began writing, early in this century, when particular forms and particular rhythms were shiny with automatic usage and acceptance. Freedom to feel in his own way seemed to him to demand freedom, not merely from that usage and that acceptance, but from all dictates of form; and Walt Whitman (even though enough of feeling had swirled Whitman to roll, rise, carol and creation, in eloquent bursts of form) — Walt Whitman seemed his guarantee. Flecker of the *Golden Journey* irritated Lawrence in 1913, in contrast to Whitman, as a norm of detestable formalism. Now Lawrence's sustenance as a poet began romantically: it began with nightingale and skylark, in a traditional romanticism, with Keats and with Shelley. More indeed with Shelley. Lawrence wrote at this time: 'I think Shelley a million thousand times more beautiful than Milton.' His sustenance began also with early Yeats; before shifting on to Whitman — and himself. 'I have always tried to get an emotion out in its own course, without altering it', he tells Edward Marsh in 1913. 'It needs the finest instinct imaginable, much finer than the skill of the craftsman . . . Remember skilled verse is dead in fifty years.' Nonsense, in an exaggeration of sense. 'A free, essential verse, that cuts to the centre of things', he proclaims three years later. Free verse, he is still proclaiming in 1924, is all that matters, 'direct utterance from the instant, whole man' — which 'toes no melodic line', obeys no drill sergeant, says Lawrence, and contains no rhythm returning on itself, 'no serpent of eternity with its tail in its own mouth' — 'none of that finality which we find so satisfying because we are so frightened'.

Certainly this is a last drip of the romantic eighteenth-century formula of the supreme value of the first impression — with its virtue, and with an added virtue or two; but also with the later substitution of a vague *instinct* for skill. Lawrence, all the same, was driven to his better poems in spite of his ideas about poetry, and in spite of his sustainers.

Consider the groups he called *Nettles*, *Pansies* and *More Pansies* (O that transference, forethought or afterthought, of the French *pensées* into the English pansies! That blowsy element in Lawrence!). With few exceptions these satirical or exclamatory or ejaculatory versicles are simply things which a poet of a more controlled vehemence would have preserved as prose notes in a notebook. *How beastly the bourgeois is!* and so on. Some posthumous day such prose notes, even if not cut up into lines, might have been published, as Coleridge's notebooks are at last being published. But I think the interest of these Lawrentian snippets, good tempered or bad tempered, is badly served by presenting them as poems: the thought that they are *not* poems may always obscure the fact that some of them are worth attending to for what they state, and may also throw doubt on Lawrence's ability as a poet in his better work.

Next consider the group he calls *Birds, Beasts and Flowers*; I suspect the most popular poems he wrote, partly because they make no very great claim on the readers' poetic response. In these an actuality of felt life, of felt being, is offered in a trance of concentration, and is seldom travestied or betrayed. Thus he shapes, rather than describes the bull, in *St Luke*:

> *A living forehead with its slow whorl of hair*
> *And a bull's large, sombre, glancing eye*
> *And glistening adhesive muzzle,*
> *With cavernous nostrils where the winds run hot*
> *Snorting defiance*
> *Or greedily snuffling behind the cows.*

He offers an actuality of turkey, fish, bat, snake, she-goat, of aspen, sage and piñon tree, in his poem *Autumn at Taos*. He offers in these poems, too, an *actuality* of language.

Yet I find I go back to these more or less 'free' poems without eagerness. Why? Because vividness of perception, unless submitted to pressure, is a poor diet, after all. If I go back to the rest of the poems which Lawrence divided into *Unrhyming Poems* (his division, by the way, is not a strict one) and *Rhymed Poems*, I rediscover with relief that formal element which contradicted him: the stronger the emotion of the poem, the more definite its structure.

In the early derivative wallow of the *Rhymed Poems*, which are nearer Shelley or early Yeats than Whitman, Lawrence in his own phrase does at times tear away his hand from his mouth — suddenly, for example, in *Wedding Morn, Guards, Scent of Irises, Kisses in the Train*, and supremely in a poem altogether divorced from wallow, in his least impeded speech of the *Ballad of Another Ophelia*, that 'good poem' which, said Lawrence, he couldn't do again to save his life. He goes with Frieda Weekley (the break, the splendid drive) to Bavaria, the Tyrol, and Lago di Garda in the autumn of 1912. Union, feud, repulsion, union again. He *knows* — whatever he may do to the knowing later on. Actuality and feeling (he was twenty-seven) push aside both personal theory and traces of accepted manner. Structure, rhyme, rhythm, ritual, assert themselves, in *Giorno dei Morti*, in *Green* —

> *She opened her eyes, and green*
> *They shone, clear like flowers undone*
> *For the first time, now for the first time seen* —

in *Gloire de Dijon* —

> *She stoops to the sponge, and her swung breasts*
> *Sway like full-blown yellow*
> *Gloire de Dijon roses.*

Out of *Pansies* a few poems emerge. One of them is the fine *Leda*. In his *Last Poems*, new ecstasies and concentrations of an extra clear statement, *The Man of Tyre, Maximus, Whales Weep Not*, insist upon attention; and then a few poems related, in his more feminine way, to Whitman, though they deny Lawrence's old betraying theory in as much as they trail, a little loosely like smoke, from the grand elegiac trigger lines. *Bavarian Gentians* is one of the last few,

> *Not every man has gentians in his house*
> *In soft September, at slow, sad Michaelmas.*

Lucifer is another one, 'Angels are bright still, though the brightest fell'; and the best — 'Now it is autumn and the falling fruit' — is *The Ship of Death*, of his own death.

The fuller strength and excitement of Lawrence's shaping sensuality swept him, of course, into his fiction; poems are an overplus, which do, with theory's aid, decline to notes preserving, more or less, only a poetic *look*. So this case is the opposite of the case of Hardy, who influenced Lawrence and with whom Lawrence shares a provinciality. Lawrence expected to live in his novels (only novelists, he said in *Phoenix*, are masters of the whole of man alive), Hardy in his poems. The poet Lawrence is inside the novelist, who is inside the prophet; and his potentiality was to have been a more considerable poet (though he never thought enough about the nature of poems) than his fiction — or his prophetic activity — allowed him to be. Yet, like Hardy, I rather think it is by his better poems that Lawrence in the end may keep hold of his readers. Whether that would be the future he deserves is another matter, though by his better poems I do mean the ones unadulterated by much of what is so outside of art in Lawrence's writing. Poems, particularly short ones, leave less room for transposing their occasions into pseudo-philosophy.

SEVENTEEN

Poet of Over-Poetry

DYLAN THOMAS'S *Selected Letters*[1] explain much of him as a poet, and much of him — the two meet and diverge — as the person who existed hidden away inside the posthumously woven cocoon. '*In the Bath.* The water is lapping upon my abdominal shore.' There you have the person one remembers with regret, no more than nineteen, writing one of his long, long letters to Miss Pamela Hansford Johnson, whom he had still to meet, who was also young, and who contributed poems, like himself, but of a very different kind, to the Poets' Corner in the *Sunday Referee*. Chipping out of the suburbanism in which writers begin, he is already the joker at his own expense, ironically observing himself, his abdominal shore, with an amused fatalism, as if his own reflection in a bathroom mirror was commenting on the original. The reflection cocks an eye, birdlike, and sees himself from an odd angle of entertainment. This was his charm, sober or drunk, anxious or momentarily forgetful of his anxiety, fearful or fundamentally, yet momentarily confident, for the twenty years he had to spend. 'I smell quite nice, I look about fourteen, and I have a large round nose; nature gave it to me, but fate, and a weak banister, broke it.'

At the same age, in these letters from Swansea to the young girl in Battersea, he was also able to stand outside his early poems, cock a bird's eye at them, and say how he hoped his poems would develop. Am I 'a little freak of nature, whose madness runs into print rather than into ravings and illusions'? (a question he never seems to have settled). Is it an illusion — 'the illusion of myself as some misunderstood poet of talent' — that keeps me writing? But then he will be remarkably objective (which does not mean entirely clearsighted) about poems, as well as his own poems. He told Pamela Johnson how his poems — at this time — were made through

[1] *Selected Letters of Dylan Thomas*, ed. Constantine Fitzgibbon (1966).

193

the only thing he knew intimately, which was embodied self. 'The des'
cription of a thought or action — however abstruse it may be — can be
beaten home by bringing it onto a physical level. Every idea, intuitive or
intellectual, can be imaged and translated in terms of the body, its flesh,
skin, blood, sinews, veins, glands, organs, cells, or senses. Through my
small, bonebound islands [he had been reading Donne's *Devotions*, or pass'
ages from them] I have learnt all I know, experienced all, sensed all. All
I write is inseperable [*sic*] from the island. As much as possible, therefore,
I employ the scenery of the island to describe the scenery of my thoughts.'
He told Miss Johnson — whom he soon regarded as his 'only friend', the
only person he could be open with, at a distance — that he had been writing
since he was a very small boy, that he had 'always been struggling with the
same things, with the idea of poetry as a thing entirely removed from such
accomplishments as 'word'painting', and the setting down of delicate but
usual emotions in a few well'chosen words' (which sounds like a crib).

'There must be no compromise; there is always the one right word: use
it,' he orders Miss Johnson, 'despite its foul or merely ludicrous associations;
I use "double'crossed" because it was what I meant. It is part of a poet's
job to take a debauched and prostituted word, like the beautiful word
"blond", and to smooth away the lines of its dissipation, and to put it on
the market again, fresh and virgin.' (He warned Miss Johnson not to
call herself, as writer, Pamela Hansford Johnson. 'If you do I shall call
myself Dylan Marlais Thomas.')

Turning his practice and problems round and round, this intelligent boy
quickly realized that it would be better, if he could, to reverse; to emerge
from his first island world of blood, sinews, veins, glands, organs, and cells.
He had instructed Miss Johnson, his submissive whetstone in these early
letters, that she must 'leave the lambkins alone, or never at least use them
unless you can take them literally'; advice — this taking of things as they
are — he repeated and expanded frequently through his twenties. 'I think
in cells; one day I may think in rains.'

Quite early he wrote of having believed, and wanting passionately to
believe again 'in the staggering, bloody, starry wonder of the sky I can see
above and the sky I can think of below'; and to one of the Swansea friends
of his adolescence he was to write from Glen Lough, a nowhere valley of

beauty and drama in Co. Donegal, where he had been staying with the present writer, of the way his own eyes would insist upon squinting inwards. 'When, and if, I look at the exterior world, I see nothing or me; I should like very much to say that I see *everything* through the inner eye, but all I see is darkness and not very nice.' The letters show a determination, if he could, to take the lambkins literally, to compel symbol and reality to agree, or to make reality impart its force to symbol. The crux is whether he succeeded, whether an eventual 'thinking in rains', was simply, in spite of himself, a change of symbols equally symbolic. In *Fern Hill*, in *Poem on his Birthday* or *Over Sir John's Hill*, his soberer admirers would argue his success, in the end. (Perhaps one day, if they are still at all busy with his poems, American academics will set a question, asking their students to compare *Poem on his Birthday* or *Poem in October* with something else written at Laugharne, a hundred and fifty years before, which might have fascinated the Thomas of the late poems — Coleridge's not so long published notes on the village, its hills, tides, birds, cottages, and inhabitants — 'shrivelled Shrimps of cold and hunger' — its gravestones and their inscriptions which Coleridge copied into his notebook, and the flourishing weeds on the sad winter graves in the Laugharne churchyard, where Thomas is buried. 'While I took the copy, the groundsel showered its white beard on me. Groundsel and fern on the grave, and the thorns growing that had been bound over it.' Which is effective with the realness, the clearness, the strength of active symbol, the poems, or the notes? But the comparison is unfair.)

So far one can follow in these letters a track of intellectual growth and living good sense; but one can also follow a trail of curious insensitivity — literary insensitivity, to leave an insensitive egocentricity (he was young, after all) on one side. For all his talk of renewing the word, in fact he renewed images (as well as renewing, or freshening up, clichés, a weak process). Words, and the rhythmical and formal matrices in which his words were held, he did not renew. This was the failure he was unable to recognize, and it goes unrecognized by his allornothing panegyrists, from ignorance, or from delusion. It is fascinating, in this respect, to read him answering a cricitism which Stephen Spender made of his earlier poems. Stephen Spender wrote of them as tap poetry: 'just poetic stuff with no beginning or end', which could be turned on, turned off. Thomas indignantly but confusedly rejoined that his poems were 'watertight compartments': 'The last thing they do is flow; they are much rather hewn' — though if they were 'watertight com, partments', they were presumably filled with arrested flow; and there is little point in hewing a flow, or a liquid. Also, off guard, when there was no critic to be answered, he could discourse happily enough, as we have seen, about the veins and the flow and the flesh of his verse. 'Nearly all of my images, coming as they do, from my solid and fluid world of flesh and blood', etc. In fact, confusing word and image, squinting inwards and into litera, ture, Thomas used words which he derived from the amalgamated practices of nineteenth,century romanticism, early, middle and late, the 'accepted language' of poetry, the Keats,Poe,Arnold pattern in most of us, which was equally the source of his rhythm and movement.

> *It was late*
> *For his strange kind of poet*

Louis MacNeice (a poet of the opposite kind) had to admit in his valedic, tion to Thomas. It was certainly late; and years have gone by since it was first argued that the poems of Dylan Thomas owe their popularity to the romantic stereotype of their movement, sonority, and language. Much other 'unmodern,modern' art, including painting and sculpture, wins an un, critical public by its mixture of old modes and modern discontinuity.

Some of the explanations advanced for the too poetic nature of his poems are snubbed in these letters by Thomas himself. How many times are we re, minded that he was Welsh, he was Celtic, he was bardic, he was *capel*! How often in his letters he repudiates Wales and all Welshness — 'dirty Wales', 'my natural hatred of Wales', 'the eternal ugliness of the Welsh people'.

> The more I see of Wales the more I think it's a land completely peopled
> by perverts. I don't exclude myself, who obtain a high and soulful
> pleasure from telling women old enough to be my mother why they
> dream of two,headed warthogs in a field of semen.

And directly of his writing:

> The Welshness of my poetry: this is often being mentioned in reviews
> and criticisms, and I've never understood it; I mean I've never under,
> stood this racial talk, 'his Irish talent', 'undoubtedly Scotch inspiration',
> apart from whiskey.

By literary descent and relationship, it is evident from these letters — but then it was evident before — that he was 'English', in a literary sense. English was the language he wrote in. English — and incidentally with no marked Anglo-Welsh or Swansea intonation — was the language he spoke. (One objector to his Englishness asked if it could seriously be main-tained that Thomas would have been as good a poet, if he had been reared in Swanage and not Swansea ? It could be so maintained: with that origin he might have been a better poet, and less provincial.)

For some of his English peculiarities, how often, too, is an explicative Hopkins banged — by professors and assistant professors — like a drum in an echoing Saturday procession in downtown New York! Hopkins, 'the poet whom Thomas most resembled stylistically', according to Professor Moynihan of the University of Connecticut, in his *Art and Craft of Dylan Thomas* (hardly a book which earns a high mark or even a pass for literacy) is surely the poet Thomas least resembled in style, intention or performance (one need emphasize no more than Hopkins's naked and sharply indicative words, joined into a movement of new emphasis and effect, of new toughness, suppleness, and articulation). The identification stems from the first callow book on Dylan Thomas, by the late Henry Treece. Treece warned him o a Hopkins chapter. Thomas replied that he would be interested to read the chapter 'because I have read him only in the most lackadaisical way'. The chapter came. Thomas havered. 'I never realised the influence he must have had on me.' But still he could not, and would not, agree. He looked over his earliest poems — 'There was and still is, to me, not a sign of Hopkins anywhere.' 'I see no Hopkins.' 'As I told you before, I have read him only slightly. I have read' — and the curtain, or one curtain, is aside for the moment — 'far more Francis Thompson.'

Long ago I suggested that Francis Thompson and his *Ode to the Setting Sun* were the source of Thomas's softly agglutinated images. But that over-poetic poet (who was like Thomas in so many ways) lacks the academic or critical respectability of Hopkins as a source or a comparison; and it has been left to Thomas himself to point now to the influence which the aca-demics have refused to see or refused to discuss. (Earlier, writing in 1933 to a Swansea friend, Thomas approves of 'the dark-eyed company' of Poe and Thompson, and tells his friend 'to be a Thompson in prose'.) It matters. Dark-eyed Francis Thompson, yes: clear-eyed Hokpins, no (or clear-eyed Wordsworth, whom Thomas disliked): Hopkins was in no doubt of the immediacy of the divine, charging the world with the electricity of divine glory; Francis Thompson searched for the divine, groped for it, to make sense of himself. So, in his way, did Dylan Thomas. (A nice hypothetical point — how would Thomas have reacted to a Francis Thomp-son chapter in that early book ? But his eulogists have been spared.)

The editor says that he has included — apart from Thomas's letters to Mr Vernon Watkins, which have already been published — nearly every letter bearing directly on 'his methods of composing poems, on his views concerning poetry in general and on his own poetic ambition'; which is sound. He also intends that these letters 'should give so far as possible the flavour of the man, of his complex, enchanting, maddening and ultimately tragic personality'; which is less sound, but may be inevitable in the mor-bidity of our lust for entire biography. An editor who was not a novelist by profession might attend less to making a novel of the letters or the poet than to heeding some recently translated words by George Seferis, — that 'there are two ways in which we examine the personal life of an artist: one is by means of anecdotes, surprises, jokes, medical reports; the other is by humbly trying to see how the poet incorporates his perishable life in his work'. Mr Seferis was writing of Cavafy. He called Cavafy 'the most anti-poetic (or a-poetic)' of poets, declaring him of no great interest apart from his poems. In contrast Thomas may be called the most pro-poetic or over-poetic of poets; and his myth (especially in America, where we are told by Mrs Louise Murdy, in her *Sound and Sense in Dylan Thomas's Poetry*, they have bought more than 400,000 records of Thomas reading himself, and where they have lately published a concordance to his poems, so that he joins Shakespeare and the Bible) may be explained as a projection of this over-poetry on to another personality of no very remarkable or at any rate of no adult interest, when coolly examined. Accept the over-poetry, and a personality which became sentimental, sterile, squalid and repellent, must be splendid: and Dylan Thomas can then be seen as the hero-poet at war with convention. Accept this hero-poet, and the poems of the hero must be splendid; and opinions, too, which were unremarkable, and some-times nonsense reached *ex post facto* in justification of his practice, need not be criticized. It was said of a political general of the First World War that he erected at the sight of a politician. There are those who erect at the myth-mention of a Poet who dies with the right opportunism. It would be better if they performed the act in private, without their cries of 'Genius!'.

Yet the perishable life of this child in the light and in the dark, and in his reading and in Swansea, in the Gower, Llanstephan and Laugharne and the estuaries, which he did his best to incorporate in his poems, had its resistant core. The letters, particularly after 1937, his twenty-third year, show other growths more and more encircling that core, constricting it, and tending to its dissipation and dismay. Fear punished him. 'I'm not half as brave, dogmatic and collected in the company of Literary persons as I might have led you to believe,' he confessed to his Miss Johnson in 1934, after a first incursion into London. 'Thank God it's dark. Now I can't see the people outside.' And after a while he seems deliberately to increase the area of comforting dark. If he moves into a supporting company of unraffish poets of his own literary generation, more or less, he rapidly moves out of that company into a literary sub-world, he rapidly finds less exacting friends — and correspondents — among the lie-abouts of writing, among elderly, faded or tarnished Bohemians, needing Brasso and short of brass, supported only by beer and bar and the idea that poems are carried around by storks, as if afraid of those intellectually and imaginatively more insistent contemporaries on whom he might have stropped and strengthened his abilities. Letters to such are missing because they were never written.

Yet in this company the undeluded person was — with less and less protest, unfortunately — Thomas himself. He was the Actor, he was the Reader — how ham the acting, how tiresomely over-poetic the reading on all those discs, in all those broadcasts; yet it was Thomas himself, his un-seen, unexhibitionized self, castaway as he may have been from an earlier mode, who knew the facts. The enthusiasts may have fastened on to the over-poetry of the act, on to Genius (that expendable word and concept) lecherous, drunken, outspoken and at bay against the respectable, they may have glued their ears to the recorded and taped over-poetry of the reading, that gusher of words coated in warm maple-syrup, to which Mrs Murdy's book is a useful guide, yet it was Thomas who still kept his real search for kinship precariously inside him (to Henry Treece, who had exclaimed with

satisfaction that Thomas did not 'lean over gates, seeking kinship with
daffodils and sheep', he had replied that in fact 'seeking kinship' 'with
everything, daffodils, sheep, shoehorns, saints, bees, and uncles is exactly
what I *do* do, I think, with all due lack of respect'), it was Thomas who
described his reading in the funniest and most devastating way, substituting
marble, which may be neither sticky nor warm enough, for the maple syrup,
in a letter to his American publisher headed more fatefully than he could
have realized 'October 13th. 1949 (Thomas-hunting begins)':

> I've been asked by John Malcolm Brinnin — what's he like? — to
> read, grandly and solemnly, like a man with the Elgin Marbles in his
> mouth, poems to the Y.M. and Y.W.H.A. at New York . . .

Many of the letters after 1937 are starred with such sparklers, such brief
judgements translated into image, very entertainingly, 'Empson leaning over
his teeth to stare down an ice-cold throat at the mathematical mystery of his
doom-treading boots', and so on.   But many of them, too many of them,
exhibits what happens, terribly (tediously as well), when a man weak and
arrested in his curriculum takes to the heroin habit of being a parasite, and
is excused in it and encouraged and sustained in it by worship of the over-
poetry of 'genius'.   Surviving friends, who were more sceptical, will read
without surprise but with a renewed regret letters of sycophancy, letters which
crawl, and letters in which he betrays, for immediate (if eventually desperate)
interest, principles and convictions which he shared with them — or so they
believed, not allowing for that late Victorian humus, that Swansea humus,
in which he was potted (and which he shared, for example, judging from
the flowers, with that other Swansea poet, Vernon Watkins); they will see
paraded again the deterioration which so distressed them and ran parallel
with the staggering transformation of the 'thin curly little person' they knew,
'curled up in an old copy of the *Funeral Gazette*, sneering at the worm', into
the fat, death-filled uncherub with projecting eyes, who looked like a composite image or allegory of Drink by Arcimboldi (see Arcimboldi's *Il
Cuoco*, though he is made of pans and not barrels and mugs, for a startling
likeness of the ultimate Dylan, to set against the romanticized cherub by
Augustus John or the more realistic cherub or changeling by his friend
Alfred Janes, which are reproduced side by side in another of the recent

items of hagiolatry, *A Garland for Dylan Thomas*, in which are collected many sorrowful, but predominantly insipid poems on Thomas's death). These old friends, of an earlier vintage than the editor, may question how much the numerous letters of the kind belong to that perishable life which indeed was incorporated in his poems. Too many, they may think, are irrelevancies.

His editors and exegetes seem always to fare badly with Dylan Thomas, who so often — and one cannot blame him — seems to rise and hit them (it's me again, poor Dylan) with a numbing sandbag or a large chunk of the Gower limestone.

EIGHTEEN

A Man of the Thirties

THE year of my birth was 1905, so I do not feel old yet. But I observe already that a label has been stitched to the uniform I am now sup-posed to wear, saying that I am — which again I do not feel myself to be — a Man of the Thirties; and perhaps there are only particular seats and car-riages which a man with this large Three-O on his back should be allowed to occupy. All the same, a Man of the Thirties may perhaps be permitted a retrospective examination.

Ironically, he observes the political warfare of letters repeating itself. As a very young man he may have had no use for what he called the hedgerow poetry of Mr Edmund Blunden. He rejected the pastoral episode of the Georgians. He remembers Imagism and those who expounded it, and wonders what happened in the end to H. D. or F. S. Flint (the historians are now telling him). He recalls now that Herbert Read, as the lieutenant of T. S. Eliot, was sceptical about the new poetic style and formalism of the Thirties, made his reservations about W. H. Auden, and believed that a triumph of free verse was then betrayed. He may recall Swift telling Stella about the emergence of a new young poet named Diaper — 'Pox on him, I must do something for him, and get him out of the way. I hate to have any new wits rise, but when they do rise I would encourage them; but they tread on our heels and thrust us off the stage.' (Luckily — for he had considerable talent — Diaper died young.)

An old story, told in a new way; since our time — if so inclusive a term can be allowed — has been unusually divided up into these short tribal times or periods, each with its temporal label, Twenties, Thirties, Forties, Fifties, each with its distinctive heroes, loyalties, and rejections. Yet if you examine them, the boundaries are not really so distinct. Up to a point these boundaries are drawn and these labels affixed as conveniences, by

literary journalism.   Up to a point — though the shifting of loyalties is a
symptom of the disease, or at any rate the process of muddle around revolution.   Two mountain ranges stand up, the first and the second wars, with
the Twenties and the Thirties lying in the rough valley between them, and
there are of course passes over mountains.

When a young commentator on this side of the second range refers
opprobriously to the Thirties, the demoded hero he has in mind is W. H.
Auden, as though Auden had been fossilized into stone and left down in
the valley, the demoded poetry he has in mind is 'political' poetry with a
Left bias, though in fact the amount of such poetry was small and the best
of it was political only on the surface, or in a sense deeper than 'political'
at all indicates.   The commentator of the Forties or Fifties or Sixties has,
in fact, taken over another of the shallow categorizations of hostile journalism.   If you look at the years between 1930 and 1939 there were in England
several 'Thirties' and not a single one.   There were, for example, Oxford
Thirties and Cambridge Thirties.   The Oxford Thirties were fertile (I
should say) and the Cambridge Thirties were dry.   The Oxford Thirties
poured out poems, the Cambridge Thirties devised criticism and on the
whole disliked the poems, the prodigality, the fertility, the healthy mixture of
energy and, if you like, vulgarity.   On the one side W. H. Auden and
Louis MacNeice and if he had not died, alas, Clere Parsons, on the other
William Empson and F. R. Leavis; on the one side *New Verse*[1] on the
other *Scrutiny*, both of them children, with a decided difference of temperament and character, of T. S. Eliot's *Criterion*.   So far as *New Verse*[1] is to
the point, I can at least speak of it with authority, since I invented this
periodical and was its editor up to the last number in 1939.   And if with
the recollection of *New Verse* in your minds, I say that the Oxford Thirties
were distinguished by generosity, the Cambridge Thirties by a closed system
of dogmas, you may be inclined to laugh and say that the editor of *New Verse*
has forgotten what that paper contained, the cuts with the billhook, the
reviews with such headings as 'Flip-flap-flop, or a Wet Whiting', or ' A
Little Pig's Tale' (for a book of forgotten poems named *Straight or Curly*),
or even 'The Stuffed Goldfinch' for Wallace Stevens's *Ideas of Order*.   The
savagery of *New Verse* was defence by offence, defence of that space in which

[1] Reprinted in one volume, by the Kraus Reprint Corporation (New York, 1966)

there were poems. If you were to turn to *New Verse* for June 1935 you would
see in a report headed 'Literature Speaks Out' the contemptuous assault
to which every poet from Eliot to Auden was liable, J. B. Priestley declaring
'It would have been better for contemporary English literature if Eliot had
stayed in Louisville, or wherever he came from', Edmund Blunden wondering why Eliot had 'to feel so badly about things' — 'There is no reason
why he should have to write in that "I cannot be gay" manner: He did
not have to go through the war', Humbert Wolfe announcing that Auden
was no poet and Eliot a poet who cannot write poetry. That isolation of
the new — the real — poetry in the Thirties is now forgotten; and though a
savager return in kind may not have been a wise policy, it can, I think on
a backward glance, be understood, even excused. Politically, moreover, *New
Verse* was so little a journal of the extreme Left as to earn a cutting reproof
from Moscow in 1936 for what Prince Mirsky called Catholic propaganda
about Gerard Hopkins, entering into a bloc with the French surrealists,
and 'hounding Day Lewis' for 'an excess of Communist loyalty'; to which
the editor replied that *New Verse* was never Left wing or Right wing — if
anything its bias was left — and was not founded as a wing journal.

So far as generosity went, *New Verse* came to feel more and more that the
central and only viable attitude, the attitude to be defended if necessary by
the sharpest cuts at those who condemned it, was Auden's 'We must love
one another or die', and, goodness knows, nothing which has happened
since has made that imperative any the less central (there are critics who
have ridiculed the alternative, ignorant that Auden was restating William
Morris's 'fellowship is life, lack of fellowship is death', from *A Dream of
John Ball*, or St John's 'He that loveth not his brother abideth in death').

The Oxford Thirties felt in their Cambridge counterparts not only an
aridity but a jealousy, such as you may see in William Empson's poem
'Just a Smack at Auden'. Eliot appealed to them both, but to the Oxford
Thirties it seemed that the Cambridge critics isolated certain critical pro-
nouncements by Eliot and elevated them into ungenerous and exclusive
dogmas. Eliot had come down from the mountain with the tables of the
law, which must then be applied with the exclusive rigidity of a Communist
clique. I have just been reading again William Empson's *Seven Types of
Ambiguity*, which it would perhaps be fair to describe as derived from Eliot

(and Robert Graves) by way of I. A. Richards. It appeared — how disturbing to reflect — thirty-four years ago, and though it is by far the best *written* bible of Cambridge criticism, though from beginning to end it offers many clear and rewarding perceptions of the nature of English poetry, I felt once more that old revulsion towards a style of writing, and of criticism, which is dry and bloodless or can easily be made so by its imitators. The analysis, for example, of *The Windhover* by Gerard Manley Hopkins still seems to me ingeniously misdirected by the intellect and uninformed by a reading of the senses. Such a reading of the senses would never have attributed to the poem ambiguities which cannot have been in the mind of Hopkins. Hopkins wrote of the hovering and plunging kestrel

> *Brute beauty and valour and act, oh air, pride, plume, here*
> *Buckle! . . .*

The question of ambiguity, wrote William Empson (I shall decline to call the poet of earlier years *Professor* Empson), was whether 'buckle' meant that these things — the bird's beauty, valour, act, pride and plume and air — buckled tensely together like the buckling of a belt, or whether buckle implied uselessness and distortion, like the buckling of a bicycle wheel. It did not occur to William Empson that a poet writing in 1877 was not likely to have much experience of the buckling of bicycle wheels. It did not occur to him also that familiarity with the thing, if you like the hedgerow thing, Hopkins was writing about, the kestrel, the small brown predator, hovering, hurling, and gliding, rebuffing the wind and hovering again, would at once do away with an ambiguity in the word 'buckle'.

I do not mean to poke fun at Mr Empson's book by isolating and ridiculing a single example of his method, but it was not a method which appealed to the other party. Also the exclusive dogmatism of Cambridge delivered by writers far less skilful than Mr Empson in a stiff, cliché-ridden prose again made no appeal to those who were spawning poems in the Thirties. This dogmatism — which is continued, at sixth-form level by middle-aged pedants who have not yet recovered from brain-washing — drew up canons of poetry or canons of fiction. If you agreed with the canon, salvation was yours, if you disagreed, damnation, excommunication. The Cambridge Thirties pronounced that there could be no poetry without an audience, the

Oxford Thirties believed that there could be no poetry without poems, which without caution and prodigally the Oxford poets proceeded to supply. The Cambridge Thirties deified T. S. Eliot, the Oxford Thirties respected him — they were even heard to murmur 'he is the best we have, but what a pity he is the best' — and opened their senses to all that seemed to them alive. The difference was lucidly put by Wyndham Lewis in his *Men Without Art*, in 1934. Eliot, wrote Lewis, had instilled a '*fear of speech* — a terror of the *word*'. But Eliot's spell had been broken by the volubility of W. H. Auden, for whom words had no terror, though Lewis prophesied that it would take some time 'for the emancipatory effect of Mr Auden's volubility to get things flowing easily again'. The Oxford Thirties took risks, the Cambridge Thirties tried to reduce risk to the meanness of a restricted, costive, academic certainty — a certainty of not being wrong. T. S. Eliot could not be said to be in love with such writers as Lawrence or William Blake or Herman Melville. These new poets could risk a love for Henry James and Blake, for Dryden and Herman Melville, which was the advantage of having no closed system and of preferring the dangers both of volubility and a fundamental generosity. Volubility and generosity, indeed, were conditions of growth. Among their elders these poets could accept, with some reservations, shall I say Eliot, Wyndham Lewis, and E. M. Forster — Eliot for astringency and for being-in-earnest, Lewis for energy and art being a conscious and formative process, Forster for a gentle yet un-relenting humanism, a triple parentage by no means unhealthy.

If the Thirties exist poetically, they exist above all in the poems of W. H. Auden, who, making nonsense of these temporal tribal divisions, still exists, still writes, still grows. Much could shortly be learnt of the Thirties by reading those poems which Auden has written to writers who have moved him or helped him — to E. M. Forster who promises still, though bombs are real and dangerous, that 'the inner life shall pay', who recalls us from denying reason and ignoring love, trips us as we run gladly down the slope of hate, and interrupts us when we are closeted with madness; to Yeats:

> *In the deserts of the heart*
> *Let the healing fountain start.*
> *In the prison of his days*
> *Teach the free man how to praise*

— to Henry James:

> *Master of nuance and scruple,*
> *Pray for me and for all writers living and dead;*
> *Because there are many whose works*
> *Are in better taste than their lives; because there is no end*
> *To the vanity of our calling: make intercession*
> *For the treason of all clerks.*

— to Freud, rejected by 'the ancient cultures of conceit' because he would make impossible the generalized life, break the monolith of State and prevent the co-operation of avengers, Freud the healer who went his way

> *Down among the Lost People like Dante, down*
> *To the stinking fosse where the injured*
> *Lead the ugly life of the rejected.*
>
> *And showed us what evil is; not as we thought*
> *Deeds that must be punished, but our lack of faith,*
> *Our dishonest mood of denial,*
> *The concupiscence of the oppressor.*

And in that poem to Yeats hadn't he also spoken — rare mention in present times — of poetry as an *art*:

> *Time that is intolerant*
> *Of the brave and innocent,*
> *And indifferent in a week*
> *To a beautiful physique,*
>
> *Worships language and forgives*
> *Everyone by whom it lives;*
> *Pardons cowardice, conceit,*
> *Lays its honours at their feet.*
>
> *Time that with this strange excuse*
> *Pardoned Kipling and his views,*
> *And will pardon Paul Claudel,*
> *Pardons him for writing well.*

On 1 January 1940 Auden at the end of the Thirties dates his *New Year Letter* —

> *Tonight a scrambling decade ends,*
> *And strangers, enemies and friends*
> *Stand once more puzzled underneath*
> *The signpost on the barren heath*
> *Where the rough mountain track divides*
> *To silent valleys on all sides,*
> *Endeavouring to decipher what*
> *Is written on it but cannot,*
> *Nor guess in what direction lies*
> *The overhanging precipice.*
> *Through the pitch-darkness can be heard*
> *Occasionally a muttered word,*
> *And intense in the mountain frost*
> *The heavy breathing of the lost;*
> *Far down below them whence they came*
> *Still flickers feebly a red flame,*
> *A tiny glow in the great void*
> *Where an existence was destroyed;*
> *And now and then a nature turns*
> *To look where her whole system burns*
> *And with a last defiant groan*
> *Shudders her future into stone.*

As at the end of the Thirties, so in the Forties of hatred and destruction, so in the Fifties of doubt, so now in the Sixties of the twisted mouths and snot-like surfaces of Francis Bacon, or the awkward mumble from the confessional box where Robert Lowell kneels behind his curtain.   But later in that same poem Auden wrote that

> *will is free not to negate*
> *Itself in Hell.*

Our job is to continue climbing up the mountain through Purgatory —

> *Our faith well balanced by our doubt,*
> *Admitting every step we make*
> *Will certainly be a mistake,*

but still believing that we can climb higher — we are not boy scouts or scoutmasters — and still ascending the penitential way 'That forces our wills to be free'.

There was more to the Thirties than the sheer song and the eloquent teachings and faith of Auden, only they happen to be its best and most distinctive act and contrivance. A scrambling decade, yes, but a breathing space of possibility, in which there was a chance to absorb the earnestness, the acuteness, the revolutionary re-establishment of tradition achieved in a somewhat thin, brittle and patchy way by that great generation of writers — Eliot is one of them — whom we label modernist; but it was possible also to join up the patches, to infuse blood and freedom and fullness into what was thin and brittle, to devise, at any rate for W. H. Auden to devise, a poetry the best of which is a full expression of our time, which does enhance the ways and means of living well. So as far as I feel myself a Man of the Thirties — the more vital Thirties — I wear the Three-O on my back with pleasure as I might have worn the badge of some connection with the time in which Milton then Dryden, then Wordsworth were the formative champions. It so happens that the vital Thirties are demarcated at one end by the emergence of a new poetry, at the other, accidentally, by the barrier of war. They are demarcated also at the latter end by Mr Auden's transference from England to America, turning him, so far as our day-to-day literary affairs go, into a figure out of sight, a figure of legend if not of the past. But if indeed there is an eclipse to be observed here, eclipses are always no more than transitory; and from legend and America he has since, this light in a darkness, made many welcome returns.